AT HOME RECOVERY HANDBOOK

KEITH ANGELIN, LAADC, CNMI

KEITH ANGELIN, LAADC, CNMI
Keith4Counseling@gmail.com · (949) 939-9222 · www.InterventionRx.com

Copyright © 2014 by Keith Angelin. All rights reserved.

AT HOME RECOVERY HANDBOOK is protected by copyright. Unless a statement on the page grants permission to duplicate or permission has been obtained from the author, duplicating all or part of this work by any means is an illegal act that violates the rights of the author.

Printed in the United States of America

ISBN: 0692236589
ISBN-13: 978-0692236581

DEDICATION

AT HOME RECOVERY HANDBOOK is dedicated to all of us who are the life of the party but don't usually remember the party. To the high-octane personalities who refuse to accept 'No' for an answer, don't like to lose and are never satisfied. To the chronic risk-takers that have an exceedingly high tolerance for physical and psychological pain. To the master manipulators too smart for their own good. To the emotionally raw, deep thinkers who keep a running scorecard of hurts and resentments. To everyone willing to trample their own boundaries yet still believes they are in control of their life. To those who are smart enough to deal in metric weights and measures yet too sick to see the dismal reality of everyday life. To all of us who are dying inside and out. Remember that the qualities which made you great at being an addict or alcoholic will *also* make you great at whatever else you choose to do in life.

To Mom and Dad, for loving me *no matter what.* To my grandparents who continue to live in my heart. To Kyle, Kara, Kory, their spouses and families who I disrespected with my shameful behaviors. Whether you forgive me or not, I am sorry. To my special friends Joe and Cheri, Gene and Nancy, Robin and Joe and our entire dog park clan. Thank you for your love and support. To Dave and Scott for not abandoning me. To Dr. Elaine Yee, Dr. Jeffrey Bloom and Dr. Jerry Synold: thank you for looking over and after me, and inspiring me. To Max, Rhonda and Steve for being my first. To Buster and Tiger, who have brought more joy to my life than I can express in words. To God, for never making it easy, and always meeting me exactly where I am.

KEITH ANGELIN, LAADC, CNMI

FORWARD

Recovery requires action. This program was written for those people who are drowning in the quicksand of their addiction, who have accepted that they cannot break free by themselves, and are willing to grab a lifeline and hold on *no matter what*. **At Home Recovery Handbook** is that lifeline. It does not matter what drugs you used, how much you used or for how long. Nor does it matter how far you have fallen or how much time and money you have lost. Follow this step-by-step treatment plan *no matter what*, and I guarantee you will learn how to thrive in life without chemicals.

I am passionate about At Home Recovery Handbook. It is a comprehensive plan for recovery on par with the best inpatient or outpatient rehab program. It is affordable to everyone and can be worked at home without abandoning your other responsibilities.

As a licensed therapist and interventionist, I treat people on the front lines of this battle every day. It was not always so. There was a time when I was nearly a permanent casualty of a severe addiction. My story is one of countless stories of people who have been to the gutter and back. It is no more or less insane than anyone else's. Hopefully you will have the good fortune to hear many such stories. Of course you will never hear from all those who lost their battle and died through overdose, accident or suicide. Soon you will write down your own story of addiction, such as it is at this moment; that is to say, the ugly and desperate part. You have not experienced the miracle yet. You will.

Writing your story will help you take ownership of the wreckage you have caused. To this you might be saying: "There is no way you or anyone can imagine the shameful things I've done in the name of my addiction. I don't want to rehash all that." I will not be asking you to do anything which I have not already done. As you are about to see, my own experience includes details one would not normally want to share with a stranger. But you are not a stranger. Every person who compulsively abuses drugs or alcohol is part of the same great family. We are not bad people trying to be good. We are sick people trying to get better. Never forget that.

So by describing my own personal experience with substance use disorder, here, I hope to demonstrate that you are not alone. I was once where you are right now. Despite impossible odds, I recovered and have remained sober since October 21, 2008. So, when I tell you that this battle can be won, it is with absolute certainty. You can succeed, too.

As you read about my downfall, look for similarities with your own experience. From my recovery take the strength and hope which is abundantly available to you through this book, if you are willing to hold on *no matter what*.

****

I'VE BEEN BANGING ON THE FRONT DOOR long enough to make me feel uncomfortable. If I keep it up much longer I'm afraid I will draw the unwanted attention of neighbors. Just in case this visit turns out to be something other than the life and death crisis I'm pretty sure it is, I cease the racket. Drawing a deep breath, I grasp the handle and twist. Overhead is a brilliant Southern California sky, though precious little sunlight snakes its way through the thick blinds barring each window from prying eyes. This is an established and upscale neighborhood full of recent vintage automobiles and front lawns all the same hue and height. However, there is an aura about this particular house that is all too familiar. It is the sour milk of spoiled opportunities and unrealized potential. The demon lives here. I can always recognize my old friend. For years I relied on him for everything. Then he killed me. But I am getting ahead of myself...

I *do not* have fond memories of my adolescence. I'm not blaming my addiction on it. I'm just saying... My parents were good people and providers. My mother was a teacher. My father commuted ninety minutes each way every day to a corporate finance job in Manhattan. There was absolutely no history of alcohol or drug abuse in our family history. Unfortunately I had Attention Deficit Hyperactivity Disorder (ADHD) before anyone knew what that was, and my parents just did not have the skills to handle me. So I was labeled a "problem child". I learned to fear my dad's leather belt and my mom's wooden spoon. As a result we never established a bond build on unconditional love, which is so important. In my mind I believed I was a bad kid, and often wondered why some kids were born" bad" and others good, and why God had made me bad. The best I could hope for was to be "less bad".

For many years I had no real friends, was the last one picked for games, and was beaten by a number of neighborhood bullies on a regular basis for absolutely no reason. My anxiety was so bad I carried rosary beads in my pocket and happily walked far out of my way just to avoid certain kid's houses. I grew up afraid of my parents, other kids, dogs, the dark... I was just plain afraid, period. I escaped into books during the summer reading program at the local library, and through advertisements in the back of *Boys Life Magazine* for x-ray eyeglasses and Charles Atlas muscle-building secrets. I fantasized about being anyone other than who I was.

By the time I entered high school I had been shuffled around to six different schools. Then things began to change when I saw the opportunity to make friends with cool kids who participated in sports and music. Like a good addict-in-training, I overcompensated for low self-esteem by immersing myself in those programs. I participated in three sports plus I played in the band. Off-season I lifted weights like a madman. During the homecoming football game I actually played football and marched in the band all at the same game. High School is when I first experimented with alcohol and marijuana. Although I didn't particularly care for either, I was impressed by how much more comfortable I was at parties when I had a drink in my hand. High School marked the first time I felt I belonged somewhere, but the old insecurities were never far from the surface.

My first alcoholic blackout certainly foreshadowed the trouble that was to befall me years later. It happened my first week of college. I was nine long hours away from home and my high school sweetheart. That was before email and texting, when nine hours could feel like nine centuries. The day my parents waved goodbye to me I was so traumatized that my nose bled spontaneously. That's a fact. I felt completely out of place and ill-equipped to make my own way. One night I joined my new roommates at a local bar where I proceeded to match them beer-for-beer and shot-for-shot of sambuca. Next morning I awoke half dressed and laying in vomit with the room spinning. But alcohol helped me break the ice and make friends. Thankfully I wasn't fond of nasty hangovers, and spent all my money on telephone calls to my girlfriend.

I spent the decade after college working corporate jobs and hiding behind a superficial lifestyle based on my looks, car, job and girlfriends. I continued my obsession with bodybuilding and dieting. I bought my first Corvette. Sometimes I moonlighted as a bouncer at a Manhattan nightclub owned by one of the actors in *Goodfellas*. He liked to sit outside talking with us while chomping a cigar. Girls came and went. As soon as a relationship started to get serious, I found an excuse to end it. In my mind I was still a bad kid who fooled everyone into thinking he was good.

At thirty-five years old I landed the job of my dreams in Southern California. It brought money and a bit of notoriety in fitness magazines and on television. Additionally I was fortunate to work with professional athletes, celebrities and models. That's when I first met Arnold Schwarzenegger, Clint Eastwood and the Dallas Cowboys players. That's also when I met the demon.

My chronic abuse of alcohol and drugs came later in life. Some of us are like that. Unfortunately the move to California only magnified my insecurities. The pressure to fit in was greater than ever. So I continued the lifestyle I knew, gravitating towards big personalities at the gym and at work. We worked, trained, ate and travelled together. And, when they partied, so did I. Nobody ever twisted my arm to use drugs. I loved being high. I thought "Finally! The way I feel on the inside matches the way I *look* on the outside." When you first meet the demon, he wears a big, toothy smile.

Methamphetamine was my first drug of choice. My tolerance grew fast. Initially I would snort a few lines on weekend nights before going out. Pretty soon I was using alone in the bathroom at the end of each workday so I could train at the gym. After that it was first thing when I got to work and then in my car during lunch, too. I'd quickly progressed from *experimentation* through *recreation* to *habituation*.

Other drugs followed. Cocaine, ecstasy, opiates, benzos, GHB, ketamine... I combined different drugs together and drank when I used. Like a garbage receptacle, I would consume anything, even if I knew nothing about the chemical. The first time I tried GHB was in my hotel room before a business meeting. It hit me so hard in the elevator on the way down that I nearly fell on my face before reaching the lobby. I just barely made it back up to bed where I passed-out for hours. Something else was happening, too. I was having trouble controlling the amount I was using. In fact, I had no 'off switch' at all. Just like my first blackout at college, I plowed through whatever there was until there was no more.

My sick mind glamorized the lifestyle. We served ecstasy pills to each other on dinner plates. Drugs were my god. The gleaming stainless steel of the public bathroom stall was my altar. But no matter how I rationalized it, drugs were nothing more than a desperate attempt to feel comfortable in my own skin. Without chemicals in my body, I felt like that college freshman waving goodbye to his parents with one hand while wiping the blood from his nostrils with the other.

Eventually I went into business for myself, got married and bought a house. We became active in the local church. The business became quite successful due to an association with superstar actor Sylvester Stallone. Despite the outward signs of success, I still felt like a phony and, thus, never really happy. Gradually I abandoned weightlifting, relationships, faith and fun activities because they could not make match the freedom I experienced from chemicals. I became a drug *abuser*; abusing over and over, despite negative consequences. For example, I snorted so much powder that I required sinus surgery. Yet as soon as the snake of blood-crusted gauze was unpacked from my nose I was at it again, snorting more cocaine *plus* abusing the opiate pain medication prescribed after the operation. One time I was pulled over on the freeway while carrying cocaine. As the patrolman approached my window, my best thinking was to swallow it all. Turns out I had been stopped for an expired registration sticker. By the time the patrolman drove off I was shaking uncontrollably. For the next few minutes I tried making myself vomit, without success. I raced to the hospital scared to death. Later the doctor said that I would have died had my tolerance not been so sky high. I swore that I would stop. But if you have the disease of addiction, willpower alone is never enough. Days later I was at it again.

As long as the business was making money and the bills were being paid, I felt I could make up for my indiscretions. That was all about to change because of something I never saw coming.

Turns out that celebrities are often sued under false pretenses in order pressure them to settle quickly, quietly and out of court. These lawsuits are referred to as "meritless", "malicious", "nuisance" and "frivolous" lawsuits, and are an abuse of the legal system. Yet celebrities opt to settle these lawsuits out of court anyway so as to not jeopardize their reputations.

Sure enough, it didn't take long before we were targeted with a frivolous lawsuit which I insisted we fight. That lawsuit hijacked the next four years of my life. During that period I would be bullied by attorneys and the legal system worse than I ever was as a child. After the first two years of litigation, the business could no longer afford inventory because all our revenue were going to pay legal expenses. Likewise, all my time was being spent working with attorneys, stalling bill collectors and dealing with whatever new legal horror arrived in the mail that day.

I became *dependent* on chemicals to numb the anxiety and quiet the voices in my head. Buying drugs, using drugs, hiding drugs and recovering from drugs became my daily routine. I would keep using until nothing was left. If it was one o'clock in the morning and I wanted to go to sleep but still had cocaine left, I had no choice but to use it all up, including scraping the baggie clean. My tolerance was so high that I could consume a month's worth of painkillers in a day. If I was binging on alcohol, I would drink all the booze in the house including the mouthwash. Where was the fun now?

I continued even when the chemicals stopped working. Instead of making me high, they bathed me in unrelenting paranoia. I lived in constant terror that someone was "out to get me". I saw and heard things that weren't really there. I would search the house top to bottom... under the beds, in the closets, jiggling the window and door locks... over and over each day. An irrational fear would come over me suddenly while I was driving. It was so bad that I would have to pull to the shoulder and search the entire car, even if I was on the freeway. I couldn't fall asleep unless I was actually grasping the remote 'panic' button for our home alarm system. Later, after my wife moved out, I would drag a large dresser in front of the bedroom door, pile a television on top and prop a chair against the dresser. I moved that dresser so many times, the leg snapped off.

Unfortunately I could never escape my imagination, so things just got worse and worse. Incredible as it sounds; my best thinking was to use more chemicals. On three separate occasions I was defibrillated in the hospital emergency room. No one was able to get through to me. Countless times I resolved to quit, told my dealer I was done and flushed whatever I was holding down the toilet; only to have him laugh in my face the very next day I showed up to buy more. My dealer was always ready to take my money! Like the demon, he wore a big, toothy smile.

Eventually that meritless lawsuit found its way into the courtroom. The trial lasted five days. We presented a mountain of evidence, renowned scientists and legal specialists. The opposing side didn't call a single expert nor cite a single legal precedent. Instead they portrayed themselves as the poor victim of a rich celebrity. The jury bought their story and ruled against us. Two years later the Court of Appeals overturned the decision and ruled in our favor. People like to remind me that justice always prevails. That's crap. I was robbed of my livelihood, savings and sanity – not to mention the jobs people lost and the creditors that went unpaid – in what turned out to be an utterly meaningless legal battle. The fact that I was *legitimately* wronged was of no consequence. Lots of addicts claim to be "victims" of one thing or another. I hear heartbreaking stories from clients all the time. Sometimes the feelings are legit, other times they are imagined. In the end, the result is always the same. We use resentment as one more excuse to escape reality. That's exactly what I did.

I tried quitting cold-turkey a couple of times. Withdrawal from opiates and benzos are tough when you're doing it on your own. I suffered panic attacks for twenty straight nights. When I agreed to rehab, it had to be on my terms, which meant on an outpatient basis. Despite a half-hearted commitment, I found it an eye-opening experience. I learned that addiction is a brain disease which convinces you that *you don't have a disease.* I learned that addiction has nothing to do with willpower. I learned that I was still a good person. I learned that many other people had stories similar to mine. I found my first sober friend. We both stayed sober about six months before he relapsed, drank himself into multiple organ failure and dropped dead in his living room. After the funeral I fell back into old thinking and behaviors and found myself worse off than ever. I tried outpatient treatment for a second time, but couldn't make it more than a few weeks.

I had reached a state of *incomprehensible demoralization.* One afternoon, while in deep despair, I stripped off my clothes, piled them on the backyard patio and lit them on fire. My wife tried to have me involuntarily committed. The demon really had his claws in me, whispering half-truths that kept me feeling hopeless, worthless, hateful and disconnected.

Along with our pastor, my wife tried to intervene. They gave me two choices: either I agree to inpatient treatment or I agree to leave the house. Boy was I ever angry at being ambushed! Addicts often become enraged to protect their addiction. But it is not really anger that drives us. It is panic at the thought of losing the one thing that has become as important to us as air and water. Consumed by emotion, I could not see what a gift I had been handed. Instead I felt like someone was trying to disconnect me from life support and I had to fight back. I became defiant, choosing to remain exactly where I was. So my wife packed her stuff instead and left our marriage that very day.

As a therapist, I find that families have a difficult time comprehending the insanity at the heart of addiction. They are constantly trying to persuade us with reason and logic. They don't get it. Here I was, unemployed and unemployable, broke, grungy and sweaty and in paranoid psychosis; and my *best* thinking was to refuse a thirty-day "vacation" to a nice, clean place with good food, Netflix, exercise equipment, hiking trails, no pressure, no daily grind of a drug habit... All that was required of me was to talk about myself and learn more about a subject I was already interested in. Looking back on it now, of course I can see why people can't wrap their heads around the thinking of an addict.

Things went downhill quickly. Drugs were the only thing I could think of. I craved them at the expense of everything and everyone. I supported my habit by selling all my possessions. Many things had special meaning, but it didn't matter. I accepted whatever price somebody was willing to pay. I manipulated my estranged wife. I scammed doctors. I stole drugs from family and friends. I picked through dumpsters. I hardly ate or showered. My time was spent isolated, bug-eyed and paranoid.

The saying goes; "You don't know God is all you need until God is all you have." My last day as a drug addict and alcoholic was October 21, 2008. That's the exact day God intervened in my life. After all, you don't often come face to face with three 9MM handguns and live to tell the tale.

Unbeknownst to anyone, my idiot dealer's little enterprise had been under surveillance by law enforcement for six months. And I, with all my education and business experience and street smarts didn't have a clue. Cops had observed many customers coming and going during that period, but when it came time to spring their trap, they selected the exact moment that *I* showed up, broke, broken and begging my dealer for a few lines to satisfy the merciless cravings. Don't think the same thing can't happen to you, too. It can and will if you do not turn your life around. I truly believe that the events of that day were no accident. I believe God did for me what I could not do for myself. I was more afraid of going to jail then I was of dying or of being homeless or, most importantly, of getting sober. *Finally, I hit a bottom that mattered.*

What I felt more than anything else was overwhelming *relief*. For a moment the demon was silenced and I could see things as they actually were. It was as if the microscope lens was adjusted *just right* so my life suddenly burst into focus. At last I truly understood the one thing I'd heard over and over but needed to learn for myself. It was the truth about addiction that the demon works so hard to hide from us. The truth is that regardless of how smart, dumb, rich, poor, privileged, motivated, cunning, desperate or cautious we are; *every* addict and alcoholic eventually ends up in jail, the hospital or dead. I had experienced my first miracle of the day.

As I sat there handcuffed and waiting to be questioned, I surrendered my pride. I was out of control and needed help if I wanted to change. Silently I begged God for help. I did not plead to be released or escape the consequences of my behavior. I simply wanted to *stop being a slave to chemicals*. Nothing else mattered. Without consciously realizing it, I had adopted the first three steps of Alcoholics Anonymous in a way I had not previously.

The first thing I did was *thank* the detectives for saving my life. We talked about my experience over the past ten years; how I came to live a life of incomprehensible demoralization and just wanted to die. They listened intently and asked me questions. When I was done talking, I felt at peace. They walked a short distance away and conferred with one another. I accepted my fate... jail and a criminal record. Then I experienced my second miracle of the day.

A detective returned and helped me to my feet. He told me that given the small quantity of drugs I had in my possession; it was at his discretion whether or not to arrest me. Coupled with the frankness with which I spoke with them and the earnestness of my feelings, they decided to give me a second chance. *After years of daily trips to that very same address where I purchased hundreds of dollars worth of drugs at a time, I was stopped on the one and only day I had no money and was carrying next to nothing.* Within minutes I was behind the steering wheel and driving home.

Though God had removed the obsession to use, I was just beginning to deal with the severe chemical imbalance in my brain caused by a decade of compulsive substance use. My brain would heal, I knew, but it could take years. In the meantime it was imperative that I adopt healthy coping skills to manage the triggers, cravings and persistent anxiety and depression. And, I had to do it without the luxury of rehab, which I could no longer afford.

So, I turned to Alcoholics Anonymous and Narcotics Anonymous, which I had become familiar with during my earlier treatment. Twelve Step programs work, they are free, and there are always meetings around. Accepting the Twelve Step philosophy was no problem at all because I wanted my freedom *no matter what*. Honestly, if people were praying to their toasters and getting sober, I wouldn't have hesitated to do the same. I attended meetings every day. They weren't always my favorite thing to do. But what mattered was that I was going anyway, and I accepted that as a daily victory. It was proof that I could change. I digested all the recovery literature I could get my hands on, including the *Alcoholics Anonymous Big Book*, the *Twelve Steps and Twelve Traditions*, *Narcotics Anonymous*, *Cocaine Anonymous* (Volumes I and II) and *Marijuana Anonymous*. I never had a problem with marijuana, but recovery wisdom is universal, and I couldn't get enough of it. Never did I sit down to read a page without a highlighter in my hand. Never did I turn a page without having highlighted at least one word, sentence or paragraph. I was forty-eight years old, and oftentimes I would fall asleep with the Big Book in my hand like a baby's security blanket, which was fine by me.

I stepped way outside my comfort zone and found a sponsor. Why? Because that's what I was told to do. He in turn introduced me to other sober guys. Recovery looked *good* on them. These people were cool, funny, confident, generous, trustworthy and real. They were always willing to go out of their way for you; even on days you were a jerk. One Sunday I was feeling particularly sorry for myself. I called and told the guys I wanted to be left alone. Next thing I know, the whole group is at my door with a box of donuts. They loved me until I could love myself.

Gradually, new behaviors were formed. I started praying for faith instead of for stuff. I downloaded free study guides from the internet. I meditated, went for walks and thought up a gratitude list in my head every night while lying in bed. One habit which I continue to practice each day without fail is to spend one hour or more with my dogs. Typically we walk to the park, play for a while, then stretch out on the grassy hillside or lay together like lizards on a warm, stone picnic table, and I think about absolutely *nothing*. It's amazing how good that feels. I always leave my phone at home.

The most difficult thing for me was facing my feelings and the substantial wreckage I created, and doing it all sober. For example, I faced the shame of losing my home to foreclosure. When I moved out with the two dogs I faced the fear of being homeless. Yet I did not use. Likewise, when we first started going to the park, I was extremely uncomfortable around other dog owners. That was because I never addressed the feelings of inferiority I had as a child. So I kept my ball cap pulled down low and avoided eye contact. Recovery helped me hang in there and face that issue without drugs. Though I didn't have the communication skills, I learned them by studying how *others* communicated. I discovered that successful talkers would use a simple icebreaker. The one I liked best was: "Nice weather, huh?" Just three words. I forced myself to greet everyone that way. On the odd day it was cloudy, I would say: "Cloudy day, huh?" Still three words. Before I knew it I was engaged in actual conversations. Whereas for most of my life I felt different from everyone else, learning how to communicate with fellow dog owners – three words at a time – helped me to fit in everywhere. In A.A. they tell you to **Fake it till you make it,** which is exactly what I did.

My brain was beginning to heal, and at some point during early recovery I had an *epiphany*. The dictionary defines "epiphany" as: "A sudden realization or intuitive leap of understanding, especially through an ordinary but striking occurrence." It is a serious word. In my case, the *ordinary but striking occurrence* was my sanity returning after being absent for years. And the *sudden realization...* was that my purpose for living had been all wrong. Working a corporate job never truly satisfied me. A large paycheck didn't bring me joy, just relief followed by anxiety. In other words, I was relieved to be able to pay bills and such, but in no time I was worried about getting that next check. Without realizing it I had followed in my father's footsteps, and it was the absolute wrong path for me.

I began to wonder what it would be like to ditch my corporate career of twenty-four years and begin anew, this time helping others face the demon. The more I thought, the more passionate I became. What I was considering was more than a job. It was a purpose for living. Ironically, it was a decision that would never have been made had I not suffered through addiction first. That is the miracle of recovery... It turns our life upside down, only for us to realize that we started life that way and, now, for the very first time, it is right side up.

SO, HERE I AM, YEARS LATER, letting myself into this house, pretty certain of what I will find. Initially, I need both hands to force the door past the collection of supermarket circulars littering the entryway. Sunlight leaps past me. I step on something. It is a shotgun shell. Many more are scattered about. The television is on one of those twenty-four hour shopping channels. The floor is littered with garbage, cigarette butts, broken furniture, beer cans and plastic bottles of liquor.

I turn off the television and call out "Hey bud. You here?" Flies are crawling over open food containers in the kitchen. The refrigerator contains an empty carton of two-dozen beer cans.

I find my client sprawled on the bedroom floor. An open bottle rests on its side next to his limp hand. It holds a few swallows of amber liquid, but not enough to overtake the bottleneck and spill on the floor. Next to the bottle is a shotgun. The red button screams that the safety is off. Gingerly I lock the trigger and eject a single cartridge. The fact there is only one shell in the chamber is more distressing than had the weapon been fully loaded. I apply my fingers to his neck. He is cold and waxen. Shockingly I find a pulse. After a few moments of jostling and calling his name, his eyes flutter open. "Who are you?" he asks, in a fog.

"Don't you recognize me?" I reply evenly.

"Are you a cop? You gotta leave if I ask you too. I wasn't doing anythin' wrong." The words stumble over his tongue. Remarkable, I think to myself. Even in a blackout, he still knows his rights.

"No. I'm not a cop", I reassure him. After several minutes he seems to come around. "My God", I say, struggling against profound sadness. "What have you done to yourself?! It looks like you have two days left to live." Still flat on his back, he lifts his head off the floor, straining to look into my eyes. A genuine grin spreads from one ear to the other. "What in the world are you smiling for?", I ask.

"Because," he replies. "I thought I had only one day." – I know exactly what he means. I've been there myself.

****

Nothing about my own experience with substance use disorder makes me any different than you. We are gifted with intelligence, creativity and unrelenting drive. We don't take "No" for an answer. And, we will work around the clock if necessary to get what we want. When we are lured by the demon, those gifts make us frighteningly good substance abusers. But, when we put those same gifts to good use, then we can achieve what most people only dream about.

Prior to my recovery, every problem I ever faced could be traced back to my inability to cope with life in a healthy way. I am here to tell you that alcohol and drugs *never* made that any better. I didn't recover in time to save many important things in my life. But, I did recover. I continue to enjoy a reprieve from my addiction, every day that I work my program. You heard me right. I work my program every day. For example, I read recovery literature every night for about a half hour in bed. I have gone through the A.A. and N.A. books dozens of times. They are dog-eared and duct taped and marked with lots of different colored pens and highlighters, and they are priceless to me. When I turn off the light, I still think of my gratitude list and thank God that I am free bondage. I go to meetings occasionally, especially speaker meetings. I spend my hour with the dogs, hang with sober friends, try to listen twice as much as I speak, continue to step out of my comfort zone, push myself to find something positive in every negative situation, and perform volunteer work. No longer is it a "program". It is just my life. There are plenty of struggles, to be sure. But, as it says on page 144 of *Cocaine Anonymous, Volume II*, I have learned to "walk through the rough times with dignity and grace." If I can do it, so can you.

In the Sylvester Stallone movie: "Rocky Balboa," Rocky explains what it takes to get through life: "The world ain't all sunshine and rainbows. It's a very mean and nasty place... and I don't care how tough you are, it will beat you to your knees and keep you there permanently, if you let it. You, me or nobody, is gonna hit as hard as life. But it ain't about how hard you hit... It's about how hard you can get hit, and keep moving forward... how much you can take, and keep moving forward. That's how winning is done."

When you submit yourself to this recovery program, you enter into a contract which promises certain rewards. Every person I have ever counseled who has worked the program has received those rewards. That includes the client who thought he had just one day left to live. He got sober.

As you begin, I promise you two things. First, it is *never* too late. Second, I have been exactly where you are at this moment, and if I can do it, so can you. It's no accident that you have this book and are reading these words. What you have or have not done up to this moment doesn't matter. Your desire to keep moving forward is all that counts, because *that's how winning is done.* May you be blessed and guided every step of this marvelous journey.

> "You'll never know how good you are until you try. Dream the impossible and go out and make it happen. I walked on the moon. What can't you do?"

**Eugene A. Cernan, NASA Astronaut, Apollo 17 Commander.
The last man to walk on the moon.**

An old Cherokee is teaching his grandson about life...

"A fight is going on inside me," he said to the boy. "It is a terrible fight and it is between two wolves. One is evil – he is anger, envy, sorrow, regret, greed, arrogance, self-pity, guilt, resentment, inferiority, lies, false pride, superiority and ego." He continued, "The other is good – he is joy, peace, love, hope, serenity, humility, kindness, benevolence, empathy, generosity, truth, compassion, and faith. The same fight is going on inside you – and inside every other person, too."

The grandson thought about it for a minute and then asked his grandfather, "Which wolf will win?"

The old Cherokee replied, "The one you feed."

Table of Contents

1.	Getting Started	1
2.	How the Program Works	5
3.	Autobiography of Substance Abuse	17
4.	Substance Use Disorder and Brain Drain	21
5.	Delusional Thinking and Defense Mechanisms	31
6.	Sick and Tired of Being Sick and Tired!	37
7.	Health Danger(s) of Your Drug(s) of Choice	41
8.	Substance Use Disorder Kills	45
9.	Do Twelve Step Programs Work?	53
10.	Principles of Recovery	57
11.	Is My Life Really Out of Control?	61
12.	Why is Spirituality So Important to Recovery?	67
13.	The Serenity Prayer	73
14.	The Meaning of Recovery	79
15.	Finding and Working with a Twelve Step Sponsor	83
16.	Saying Goodbye	89
17.	Changing Old Behaviors	93
18.	Managing Stress	99
19.	Anger and Substance Use Disorder	107
20.	STOP to Communicate	113
21.	Guilt and Shame Are Not the Same	119
22.	Boosting Your Self-Esteem	125
23.	Triggers and Cravings	131
24.	Seemingly Irrelevant Decisions	135
25.	Dry Drunk	145
26.	Toxic Thinking	149
27.	Post Acute Withdrawal Syndrome (PAWS)	155
28.	Relapse Prevention Planning	157
29.	Bonus 1: Eating Your Way to Recovery	167
30.	Bonus 2: Finding Your Dream Job	181

Appendix

I.	Quiz: Do I Have a Substance Use Disorder?	195
II.	Alcoholics Anonymous Handy Reference	197
III.	Attendance Form for Support Group Meetings	199
IV.	Key Statistics on Alcohol and Drug Use	201
V.	The Big Book and The Good Book	205
VI.	For Family and Loved Ones Part 1 of 5: Signs and Symptoms of Substance Use Disorder	211
VII.	For Family and Loved Ones Part 2 of 5: Codependency and Enabling	217
VIII.	For Family and Loved Ones Part 3 of 5: Implementing Boundaries	223
IX.	For Family and Loved Ones Part 4 of 5: Intervention	225
X.	For Family and Loved Ones Part 5 of 5: Forcing Someone to Get Help	229
XI.	Crisis and Treatment Resources	231
XII.	Suggested Reading and More	233
XIII.	Reference Sources	235
XIV.	Notes	241

1. Getting Started

Congratulations! The decision to recover is one of the most important you will ever make. With courage and the program explained in this book, you will accomplish your goal.

AT HOME RECOVERY HANDBOOK is the perfect tool for recovering alcoholics and addicts, anyone without the time or finances for a top-notch treatment center, sponsors, professionals, students, anyone predisposed to addiction, and everyone who is *sick and tired of being sick and tired.* (If you still have any doubt that you have a substance abuse problem, I welcome you to take the quiz in the appendix of this book.)

In 2015 21.7 million people needed treatment for an alcohol or drug use disorder. Only 1 in 10 people received it. Why the shocking disparity? For one thing, treatment can cost many thousands of dollars and not everyone is fortunate enough to have insurance coverage. Second, not everyone has the time for treatment. Oftentimes, commitments to job and family cannot be put aside *no matter what.* Removing ourselves for 30... 60... 90 days is *unthinkable*. Finally, some people reject treatment because they are skeptical. They disagree with having to go *someplace*: even on an outpatient basis, and are uncertain as to how Twelve Step programs like Alcoholics or Narcotics Anonymous can help.

The good news is that regardless of your finances, free time or faith in your ability to change, AT HOME RECOVERY HANDBOOK was created for you. Is it worth your time? You bet! You are going to learn things that expensive rehabs charge big money to teach. More importantly, you will learn that recovery from alcoholism and addiction is possible without going away to a treatment center. In fact, people like us have been doing it for decades.

Realize that treatment centers are a relatively new phenomenon. In the old days, your only choice for recovery was the mental ward or the drunk-tank of the local jail. Neither offered much comfort for the violent withdrawal symptoms or delirium tremens that ensued. After convalescing for days or possibly months, you were then packed off home with a recommendation to follow-up with your psychiatrist (who sent you there in the first place), or with no recommendation at all.

With the advent of Alcoholics Anonymous came a new understanding of addicts and alcoholics, who learned they weren't "bad", "weak-minded" or "lazy". (LOL! If people only knew the monumental effort and ingenuity it took to keep our habit going every day!)

The Twelve Steps and Twelve Traditions, published by Alcoholics Anonymous, says this about willpower: **"The philosophy of self-sufficiency is not paying off. Plainly enough, it is a bone-crushing juggernaut whose final achievement is ruin" (page 37.)** Ouch! I love the imagery of *willpower* as "a bone-crushing juggernaut". It is a perfectly accurate metaphor for an out-of-control ego that won't stop, under any circumstances, until we are dead and gone.

In 1956, the American Medical Association recognized alcoholism as a physiological disease, formally acknowledging what we already knew: our compulsion to abuse mind-altering substances is symptomatic, primary, predictable, progressive, chronic and fatal if untreated... *but treatable.* No more hiding in the shadows. Patients were unstrapped from their hospital beds. They found the support they desperately needed from like-minded sufferers at free, local meetings. They became educated by reading the A.A. Big Book and other material. They benefited from a growing body of research on their disease. They listened to the wisdom of their fellows. *And, they recovered.*

Nowadays, treatment centers are common. They are even the subject of television programs which are interrupted by commercials advertising other treatment centers. The word "treatment" itself has, unfortunately, become synonymous with a *place* as much as a *process* of rehabilitation.

AT HOME RECOVERY HANDBOOK focuses on the *process* of recovery, not where it takes place. It is a **strengths-based, spiritually-centered, Twelve Step oriented** prescription you can follow when a treatment center is out of the question, and when the thought of showing up cold at an Alcoholics Anonymous or Narcotics Anonymous meeting bristles the hair on the back of your neck.

You can trust the material that follows, because it has been used with great success by hundreds of fellow addicts and alcoholics at expensive rehabs. The only difference between them and you, is they have the time and financial wherewithal to put life on hold. You do not. AT HOME RECOVERY HANDBOOK makes it possible for you to experience recovery on your terms, with assignments designed to help you uncover uncomfortable feelings and deal with them in new ways. Stick with it. You can do this. The same courage, perseverance and drive that made you a superb substance abuser, will make you great at whatever else you choose to do. Those qualities are part of who you are.

If you are the least bit motivated to change, then you can recover at home. You are holding the solution in your hands. Your life-changing journey has begun.

EXERCISES
1. **Starting today, there are no more secrets. Declare your willingness to change by signing the enclosed declaration. Then post it on the refrigerator or another place where those close to you can see your tangible commitment to recovery.**

2. **Clear the house, garage, car, office etc. of all alcohol, drugs and paraphernalia, as follows:**
   - **Marijuana can be flushed. Pills should be disposed of in a medication drop box located at your local police or sheriff's station. Don't hold onto anything "just in case."**

   - **For the time being, drugs which a physician has prescribed to you should be given to someone you trust for safe-keeping, and to dispense when required.**

   - **Ask others in the home to support you by securing their own pharmaceuticals.**

   - **If others in the house drink, then ask them to support you by agreeing to not drink around you, and keeping their alcohol locked away.**

   - **Collect and dispose of everything you can that reminds you of drinking or using, including: Air freshener, bongs, cotton, drink cozy's, foil, hand sanitizer, lighters, small mirrors, mouthwash, pill dispensers, pipes, razor blades, rigs, straws, special wine or cocktail glasses etc.**

3. **Delete all partying-related contacts from your phone and your life. These rats aren't your friends, and never were. The next time they call, tell them you have reason to believe you're under police surveillance. I guarantee they will never bother you again!**

DECLARATION

I am sick and tired of being sick and tired!

Starting on the date of _____, I commit to forgetting everything I think I know about my disease, because admitting that I do not have all the answers is not weakness or stupidity. It is strength.

For the next twenty-eight days, I commit to following the **AT HOME RECOVERY HANDBOOK** treatment plan exactly, even if I do not agree with the recommendations or understand the reasons, or I think I know better. I will not drink or use drugs *no matter what,* I will be *rigorously* honest in everything I do. I will complete the assignments on time and to the best of my ability. I will do the required reading. I will attend Twelve Step meetings daily, and obtain a sponsor.

I understand that nothing less than my life is at stake.

_____
Signed

_____
Witness

_____
Keith Angelin, LAADC, CNMI
Licensed Advanced Alcohol and Drug Counselor

2. How the Program Works

> **WARNING: DO NOT ATTEMPT TO DETOX AND/OR CEASE USING ALCOHOL OR OTHER CHEMICALS WITHOUT CONSULTING YOUR DOCTOR FIRST, AS IT CAN BE LIFE-THREATENING TO STOP SUDDENLY!**

This material represents the entire twenty-eight day curriculum which has been delivered by certified substance abuse counselors at licensed treatment facilities. To successfully graduate the course, you must adhere to the following guidelines:

1. **Before you go any further, you must get a standard physical examination including a blood test.** Tell your **physician(s)** what you are planning. They can assess your health and any risks in moving forward. Additionally, they can discuss **medications** that might reduce your cravings and/or ease the discomfort over the next few weeks or months, including: **Disulfiram (Antabuse), acamprosate (Campral), buprenorphine (Subutex), naltrexone (Revia, and Vivitrol once monthly extended-release injectable), and Suboxone (Subutex and naltrexone combination.)** Meeting with a **psychiatrist** is recommended because they are more experienced with **psychotropic medications.**

2. **Recovery begins with *total abstinence* from ALL mind-altering substances:** that means anything you swallow, snort, smoke or stick into your body that affects you from the neck up.

3. **Complete one assignment per day, six days a week. (No written assignments on Sundays.)** Each assignment will take between one to three hours.

4. **The topics covered over the next four weeks are separated into the following modules:**
    WEEK 1/MODULE I   Self Discovery
    WEEK 2/MODULE II   Recovery Essentials
    WEEK 3/MODULE III   Changing Behaviors
    WEEK 4/MODULE IV   Relapse Prevention
    OPTIONAL/MODULE V   Nutrition and Employment

5. **Complete the assignments in the order they are listed on the enclosed AT HOME RECOVERY Treatment Plan.** Topics are structured precisely to move you through each stage of your transformation in a way that is efficient and sensible. The only exceptions are the two **bonus topics**, which are explained below. (Quotes from Alcoholics Anonymous are always printed in a different style so they catch your attention.)

6. **Typically, each assignment includes a reading followed by thought-provoking, self-guided questions. Answer each question thoroughly.** Remember, no one is looking over your shoulder, so strive to be **rigorously honest** at all times. Honesty and recovery go hand in hand. You will learn that alcohol and drugs are not your problem. It's true! In fact, up to now they have been your solution. In other words, your compulsive abuse of chemicals has been the unhealthy way you have coped with problems like fear, anxiety, anger and depression. *Recovery is the process of self-discovery leading to*

changes in attitudes and behaviors. These are the changes you will be making over the next twenty-eight days. In Alcoholics Anonymous, the saying goes: **"Uncover, discover, and discard."**

7. **Attend one Twelve Step meeting a day, every day, beginning TODAY.** If you really want to be free of misery and hopelessness, then you must get plugged into a **supportive community.** Even expensive treatment facilities mandate you attend at least one Twelve Step meeting per day while in treatment. (Some facilities go further by advocating ninety meetings in ninety days, which is also what A.A./N.A. recommends.) *I'm just asking you go to one, one-hour meeting each day for the next twenty-eight days.* Twelve Step programs like **Alcoholics Anonymous, Narcotics Anonymous, Cocaine Anonymous, Heroin Anonymous and Marijuana Anonymous** offer free meetings in your town every day. Simply search for the schedule online. Start with **www.aa.org, www.na.org** (or any of the alternative support groups listed in the **Appendix**). Follow the links to find meetings in your hometown. Try different meeting times and locations until you find a favorite. Your favorite meeting becomes your **Home Group**, because it is the meeting you will attend most regularly. Never forget, addiction can be fatal. The more meetings you attend, the better your chances for lasting recovery. It helps to be accountable, so an optional **Attendance form** is included in the appendix as well.

8. **Beginning week two, you should connect with at least one person in your home group and ask him or her to serve as your Sponsor.** What does "connect" mean? It means you should listen for someone in the meeting with more sobriety than you, and with whom you have something in common (such as your drug of choice, circumstances, occupation, hobby etc.) That will make trusting them much easier. *They must also be of the same sex.* You are certainly not looking for a new best friend or a priest to hear your confession. Sponsors guide you through difficult periods, teach you the Twelve Steps and review your assignments. The Bible sums this up succinctly when it states; "As iron sharpens iron, so one person sharpens another" (Proverbs 27:17.) Your spouse, family, friends or hairstylist are not your sponsor. You will learn more about sponsors by working the assignments and reading the Big Book.

9. **Twelve Step programs aren't the only resource available.** If you are a person of faith, you might also benefit from resources offered by your worship center. For example, **Celebrate Recovery** is a Christian Step program. You can find meeting schedules for this and many other support groups, by using the contact information in the appendix. Of course, if your budget allows, you can always seek regular counseling from a **psychiatrist, psychologist, marriage & family therapist or addiction counselor.** They can also perform an **assessment** to screen for any other issues.

10. **It is mandatory that you purchase the Alcoholics Anonymous Big Book, and begin reading today.** All that's required is you read *four pages* each day. (Yes... that's all!) Purchase the book online, at a meeting or a bookstore. You can even find it free online at www.aa.org. The information is invaluable not just in your recovery from addiction, but in recovering your life. You do not have to accept the Twelve Steps. However, you do have to understand them. The principles are universal. Skeptics will be particularly interested in worksheet nine: *Do Twelve Step Programs Work?*

11. **A *urine analysis* test at the end of each week is highly recommended.** This is the policy at rehab programs. Testing has added importance when recovering at home, not only in keeping you accountable, but as a tangible sign of your progress. *Consistent results help rebuild trust with loved ones who want to believe that your efforts are genuine.* So, you are actually doing yourself a favor. Anyone can administer the test. Inexpensive test kits can be purchased at the drugstore. (Make sure

the kit you select, tests for your drug[s] of choice.) The **Treatment plan** indicates when each of the four tests should be administered, and a **Test log** is provided to record your results.

12. **Add to your Daily Gratitude List.** A log is included for you to record those things for which you are thankful *each day.* Get in the habit of making this effort every morning or every night.

13. **Included are additional Bonus Chapters**. AT HOME RECOVERY HANDBOOK addresses two issues which are prevalent among those of us in early recovery: physical health and financial freedom. You may work on either at any time during the first twenty-eight days or afterward.

    BONUS 1. What better time to recover your health then right now, as you strengthen your mind and spirit! The enclosed health and nutrition plan is *not* a one-size-fits-all program. It is a change in *lifestyle.* The macro-nutrient reapportioning and low-glycemic focus is tailored to your body and goals, while extremely easy to adopt.

    BONUS 2. The money we spend fueling our disease can be staggering. Often we are driven to utter financial ruin, suffer career setbacks or struggle beneath crushing debt. Whatever your situation, you deserve a career that provides purpose and produces fulfillment. It affects your state of mind, your self-esteem and your finances. Therefore, you should consider it a *crucial* part of recovery. It might surprise you to learn that it is common for a client at a rehab facility to receive a treatment plan that addresses career issues. The enclosed assignments help you identify where your interests and abilities intersect, how to develop an effective resume, and how to prepare and interview for a job. Give it a try. Amazing things can happen. During recovery, I discovered that a paycheck didn't satisfy me. Helping others did. So I stopped chasing a salary, left a business career of twenty-four years, and took up counseling. Turns out, switching careers was among the best decisions of my life.

14. **Find valuable information in the Appendix.** Find the latest statistics on drug and alcohol use, important websites and phone numbers, and other useful information.

15. People around you and close to you have been traumatized by your disease. They need recovery, too. For this reason the appendix includes a five-part series of readings designed to educate family and friends about your disease, including the role they may be playing in **enabling** the situation to continue. You would do well to insist they read these materials as well as attend meetings of **Al-Anon** or **CoDependents Anonymous**. There they can learn how to deal with emotional pain and control issues without involving you. Your chance of success will improve dramatically with their participation.

16. **San Diego County** is often thought of as the center of recovery for the country. If you are already in the San Diego area, or plan to recover here, you will find the expanded directory of County mental health resources in the appendix very useful. Many of these services are available at no charge. To locate State-funded treatment programs and related services in your particular State or County, search online for your local **Health and Human and Services Agency (HHSA)**.

"You miss one-hundred percent of the shots you don't take." (Wayne Gretzky)

AT HOME RECOVERY Test Log

Instructions: Administer using standard breathalyzer device (for alcohol), and/or urinalysis (UA) home drug test kit (for drugs), available for purchase at any pharmacy. Make sure you select a UA kit that tests for Amphetamines, Benzodiazepines, Cocaine, Marijuana, Methamphetamine and Opiates, such as Easy@Home™ 6-Panel Drug Test.

DATE	TIME	RESULT	COMMENT	TESTER INITIALS	CLIENT INITIALS

Your AT HOME RECOVERY Treatment Plan

My goal is total abstinence from all mind altering substances for life.

SUBJECT ☑ UA

MODULE I: SELF DISCOVERY
1. Getting Started ☐
2. How the Program Works ☐
3. Autobiography of Substance Abuse ☐ ☐
4. Substance Use Disorder and Brain Drain ☐
5. Delusional Thinking and Defense Mechanisms ☐
6. Sick and Tired of Being Sick and Tired! ☐
7. Health Dangers of Your Drug(s) of Choice ☐
8. Substance Use Disorder Kills ☐

MODULE II: RECOVERY ESSENTIALS
9. Do Twelve Step Programs Work? ☐ ☐
10. Principles of Recovery ☐
11. Is My Life Really Out of Control? ☐
12. Why is Spirituality So Important to Recovery? ☐
13. The Serenity Prayer ☐
14. The Meaning of Recovery ☐
15. Finding and Working with a Twelve Step Sponsor ☐

MODULE III: CHANGING BEHAVIORS
16. Saying Goodbye ☐ ☐
17. Changing Old Behaviors ☐
18. Managing Stress ☐
19. Anger and Substance Use Disorder ☐
20. STOP to Communicate ☐
21. Guilt and Shame Are Not the Same ☐
22. Boosting Your Self-Esteem ☐

MODULE IV: RELAPSE PREVENTION
23. Triggers and Cravings ☐ ☐
24. Seemingly Irrelevant Decisions ☐
25. Dry Drunk Syndrome ☐
26. Toxic Thinking ☐
27. Post Acute Withdrawal Syndrome (PAWS) ☐
28. Relapse Prevention Planning ☐ ☐

MODULE V: OPTIONAL
29. Bonus 1: Eating Your Way to Recovery ☐
30. Bonus 2: Finding Your Dream Job ☐

Daily Reminder
- ✓ Honesty.
- ✓ Humility.
- ✓ Total Abstinence.
- ✓ Complete one AT HOME assignment.
- ✓ Read at least four pages in the A.A. book.
- ✓ Support group meeting.
- ✓ Gratitude list.

Don't Forget...
- ✓ Home group and Sponsor after first week.
- ✓ Encourage loved ones to get support.
- ✓ Bonus chapters on finances and fitness

Daily Gratitude List: What Am I Thankful For TODAY?

Instructions: To be completed every morning when you arise, or evening before you retire.

The purpose of a gratitude list is to help you get unstuck from the daily routine of negative thinking brought on by anxiety, resentments, shame and guilt. Good things happen to each of us every day. That's a fact. You may have heard the saying: *every day may not be good, but there's something good in every day.* By writing down those things for which you are grateful, your words become powerful weapons. Here's the catch. Only *you* can decide whether or not to be grateful. *Gratitude is a choice.*

Allow me to tell your future right here and now. I predict you will start this exercise convinced I am a raving, slobbering lunatic for suggesting there could be even one positive thing in your life at this moment. So, for the first few days, you will struggle mightily with identifying things for which to give thanks. Everybody does. It's always difficult to see the good when you're looking at life through a microscope, because at that magnification you can't help but see the imperfections in everything.

Dump the microscope. It's the wrong tool for this job. Better to use a telescope. Recovery is a lifelong commitment which you fulfill **"one day at a time"**; one *choice* at a time. Relax. Stop clutching so tightly to the notion that your life is totally and forever in the toilet. That's your disease talking, trying to keep you sick, afraid, hopeless and hemmed in. *Free your mind*, as Morpheus says to Neo in the movie: The Matrix. Work this program - no more or less - and in twenty-eight days, your daily gratitude list will be so long you'll be writing in the margins, guaranteed!

That is your future. Now, for your present... I took the liberty of completing your gratitude box for day one (yesterday.) From here on in, it is up to you.

> One day, an admirer looked at Michelangelo's finished statue of David and asked the sculptor how he had achieved such a masterpiece. Michelangelo replied: "David was always there in the marble. I just chipped away everything that wasn't him."

DATE	TODAY I AM GRATEFUL BECAUSE...
Day 1	I am alive, while so many other's with this disease are dead. I don't have to keep track of all my lies and be a phony anymore. Not everyone has given up on me. God has already forgiven every lousy thing I've ever done. I found a program that works if I work it. I only need to stay sober for today. My dog still loves me. I have a roof over my head. I'm told that when I get though this I'll be a better, stronger person than I've ever been. There's still time to have a good life. I haven't killed anyone. I know that I will feel better each day. I finally got rid of all the drugs and alcohol in the house.

Day 2	*The world breaks everyone, and afterward many are strong at the broken places. (Ernest Hemingway, A Farewell to Arms)*
Day 3	*If you always do what you always did, you'll always get what you always got. (A.A. saying)*
	Whatever the present moment contains, accept it as if you had chosen it. Always work with it, not against it. Make it your friend and ally, not your enemy. This will miraculously transform your whole life. (Ekhart Tolle, The Power of Now, page 29)
	Don't give up before the miracle happens. (A.A. slogan)
	Feelings aren't facts. (A.A. saying)
	When we are no longer able to change a situation, we are challenged to change ourselves. (Viktor Frankl, Man's Search for Meaning, page 112)

	Unless I accept my virtues, I will be overwhelmed with my faults. (A.A. saying)
	The power behind me is greater than the problem in front of me. (A.A. saying)
	Our challenges don't mold our character, our challenges reveal our character. (N.A., page 160)
	Willpower tells me I must, but willingness tells me I can. (A.A. saying)
	Humility is not thinking less of yourself, but thinking of yourself less. (A.A. saying)
	There are only two ways to live your life. One is as though nothing is a miracle. The other is as though everything is a miracle. (Albert Einstein)

	Whatever you put before your sobriety; you shall surely lose. (A.A. slogan)
	I can do all things through Christ who gives me strength. (Philippians 4:13)
	The task that we must set for ourselves is not to feel secure, but to tolerate insecurity. (Erich Fromm)
	You cannot depend on your eyes when your imagination is out of focus. (Mark Twain)
	Don't let the urgent get in the way of the important. (A.A. saying)
	A.A. is not for people who need it. A.A. is not for people who want it. A.A. is for people who do it. (A.A. saying)

	Criticism is something you can easily avoid by saying nothing, doing nothing, and being nothing. (Aristotle)
	Happiness is not a place you arrive at, it is a way you travel. (A.A. saying)
	Progress, not perfection. (A.A. saying)
	My sobriety depends on who God is, not who I am. (A.A. saying)
	Success is the ability to go from failure to failure without losing your enthusiasm. (Winston Churchill)
	Knowing when to walk away is wisdom. Being willing is courage. (Unknown)

	If you want to make God laugh, tell him your plans for the day. (A.A. saying)
	When the only tool you own is a hammer, every problem begins to resemble a nail. (A.A. saying)
	We are sick people trying to get better, not bad people trying to be good. (A.A. saying)
	Don't be afraid to take a big step. You can't cross a chasm in two small jumps. (A.A. saying)
	Everything can be taken from a man but one thing: the last of the human freedoms: to choose one's attitude in any given set of circumstances, to choose one's own way. (Viktor Frankl, Man's Search for Meaning, page 66)
	No God, no peace. Know God, know peace. (A.A. saying)

3. Autobiography of Substance Abuse

Have you hit **bottom?** Some of you will look with dour faces and exclaim: "YES, YES. I'M IN HELL." To those people I offer hearty congratulations on taking the first step out of bondage. Others will say: "HELL NO". They're *only* in recovery to satisfy the courts, their spouse, an employer, the military or even the Department of Motor Vehicles. To them I say, guess what… you're at bottom too!

Is it possible? Can it be, that all of you reading this page: regardless of your current situation, are at bottom? *Yes. Without a doubt!* The fact is, you don't need to want help in order to recover. *The recovery rates are the same regardless of whether you enter treatment enthusiastically or are dragged in kicking and screaming.* Just *being* in treatment of some kind, including this program, signals you are at a very serious crossroads in your life. That, my friends, is bottom!

What's that you say? You're still healthy, married, employed, able to drive, financially robust… you can't possibly be at *bottom*. Tell me then, what is bottom? Is it losing some of those things, or all of those things? Which things? From personal experience, I can tell you that the idea of one, almighty bottom is an utter myth. I lost my job and my marriage, and didn't believe I was at bottom. My house was in foreclosure and my friends walked away, and still I didn't believe I was at bottom. I was brought to the psyche ward after contemplating suicide, and that wasn't bottom. I was broke, had no credit and no gas for my car, and still didn't believe I was at bottom. On three separate occasions I was defibrillated back to life in the hospital emergency room. *Even then I didn't believe I was at bottom.*

The reality is that the only real bottom is death. Otherwise, "bottom" is a moving target, 100% of the time. One person's bottom is another's walk in the park. For me, bottom was the day I was handcuffed. But the truth is, I was ready for something different because I was sick and tired of feeling sick and tired. *Finally, the pain of using, was greater than the pain of not using.* If I had wanted to, I could have continued on. Thank God I *accepted* bottom.

Whether or not you've chosen to accept that you are at bottom doesn't change the fact that *you are.* As they say, just because you *don't believe* in the devil, doesn't protect you from him. One way to understand bottom, is to look at your history of substance abuse. It's something we alcoholics and addicts never do, because we're in **denial**. Seeing the entire arc of our disease at one time is a major buzz-kill, which is *exactly* the point of this exercise. The Twelve Steps and Twelve Traditions of Alcoholics Anonymous says: **"By going back in our own drinking histories, we could show that <u>years before we realized it</u> we were out of control, that our drinking even then was no mere habit, that it was indeed the beginning of a fatal progression" (page 23.)**

Now is the time to take a hard look at your own **"fatal progression"**, by documenting your history of substance use. Before you begin, read the Forward of this book. Then select any story from the back of your A.A. or N.A. book and read it over. Then, think back to your earliest memories of drinking or using. When did you start experimenting? Why? What chemicals have you used? How did your using become worse over time? How did you arrive at this point today? Be specific and as thorough as you can.

When you are done, look back and ponder the big picture. Prepare yourself, because *it's gonna get ugly.* Read your autobiography to your sponsor or one other person, and discuss.

My Life as a Substance Abuser

By _____

I first started thinking about drugs and alcohol when...

_____
_____
_____
_____
_____
_____
_____
_____
_____
_____
_____
_____
_____
_____
_____
_____
_____
_____
_____
_____
_____
_____
_____
_____
_____
_____
_____
_____

What does your substance use disorder look like? Draw or cut and paste from a magazine, website or newspaper.

4. Substance Use Disorder and Brain Drain

There are many ways to refer to someone who has a problem with alcohol and other drugs. Alcoholic, addict, abuser and dependent are urban slang for a person who has a **substance use disorder**, which is defined as "a pathological relationship with drugs and alcohol resulting in life-damaging consequences." **Pathological** means unreasonable or uncontrollable. When someone is a pathological liar it means they cannot ever be trusted. They lie for no good reason, they lie when they don't want to, and the lying never stops. It's the same when you have a substance use disorder.

The Insanity of It All
The American Medical Association recognized alcoholism as a physiological disease in 1956. Substance use disorder is a disease as much as schizophrenia and diabetes, though it is stigmatized by the public more like a sexually transmitted disease.

> **FACT: SUICIDE IS A LEADING CAUSE OF DEATH AMONG PEOPLE WHO ABUSE ALCOHOL AND DRUGS.**

Without help, addicts cannot stop using chemicals completely. *Chemicals become as indispensible as air or water.* The person is **compelled** to continue, even when they *despise* the drug and know *for certain* there will be **catastrophic consequences** as a result. What would examples of that be? You might leave the hospital after a near death experience and buy liquor on the way home. Or, you might experience chest pains yet continue using cocaine or meth, thinking; *"a little bit more will help <u>reduce</u> the pain!"* (I relate to that one.) When it comes to drugs and alcohol, *you have lost your ability to choose.*

DIFFERENT CLASSES OF ADDICTIVE SUBSTANCES

1. **Alcohol** (a sedative).
2. **Benzodiazepines**: Alprazolam (Xanax), clonazepam (Klonopin), diazepam (Valium), lorazepam (Ativan), temazepam (Restoril). Note that hypnotic properties occur at higher doses.
3. **Cannabis**
4. **Designer Drugs:** Bath salts, Ecstasy, GHB, Spice.
5. **Hallucinogens:** PCP, LSD.
6. **Hypnotics:** Sedatives and antidepressants including selective serotonin reuptake inhibitors (SSRIs), serotonin-norepinephrine reuptake inhibitors (SNRIs), tricyclics (TCAs), monoamine oxidase inhibitors (MAOIs).
7. **Inhalants:** Duster, gasoline, nitrous oxide, poppers.
8. **Opioid Pain Relievers:** Derivatives of the opium poppy such as codeine, Fentanyl, heroin, hydrocodone (Lortab, Norco, Vicodin), morphine, oxycodone (OxyContin, Percocet, Roxycontin), tramadol (Ultram).
9. **Other or unknown:** Steroids.
10. **Sedatives:** Antihistamines, antidepressants, barbiturates, benzodiazepines and sleeping pills such as Eszopiclone (Lunesta), trazodone (Desyrel), zolpidem (Ambien).
11. **Stimulants:** Amphetamine-type substances, cocaine. crack, methamphetamine, amphetamine (Adderall), methylphenidate (Ritalin).
12. **Tobacco** (a stimulant).

Most commonly abused illicit drugs: #1 Marijuana, #2 Opiates, #3 Cocaine, #4 Sedatives, #5 Stimulants

Substance Use Disorder is a D - I - S - E - A - S - E!
Substance use disorders share the very same characteristics as other diseases. They are:
- **Symptomatic.** The symptoms are not a mystery. They have been well defined.
- **Primary.** The disorder is the *cause* of other diseases or makes existing illnesses worse.
- **Predictable and progressive.** The disorder *always* gets worse if left untreated, even when the addict is not actually using or drinking. *Temporary periods of abstinence are not progress.*
- **Chronic.** Some diseases go away. Not this one.
- **Fatal if left untreated.** At present there is no known cure.
- **Treatable with 100% success.** You can put this disease into remission for life!

Substance use disorders are devastating for another reason. During the Civil War, Union General William T. Sherman marched through Georgia, stripping the land of food and setting fire to everything along the way. He called this tactic "total war". Nothing was spared. His strategy was to strike terror into people's hearts and bring about the end of the war. So it is with a substance use disorder. It is a total war, or **biological-psychological-social** disease. It attacks us physically, mentally, emotionally and spiritually. It radically alters behavior, ravages families, and is guarded by powerful **defense mechanisms**. For this reason, any successful recovery program must address all of these things.

FACT: IN 2015, 21.7 MILLION PERSONS NEEDED TREATMENT FOR A DRUG OR ALCOHOL PROBLEM, WHILE ONLY 2.3 MILLION RECEIVED IT.

Euphoria vs. Relief
Chances are, you use mood-altering substances for one of two reasons. You want to either feel good: that's called **euphoria**; or you want to cope with emotional pain: that's called **relief**. Eventually every person with a substance use disorder will use to relieve emotional pain. Painful feelings can serve as very powerful motivators to self-medicate.

> **We use chemicals to relieve emotional pain:** Anger, anxiousness, apathy, confusion, depression, desperation, disappointment, disgust, discouragement, embarrassment, exhaustion, fear, frustration, grief, guilt, hopelessness, insecurity, loneliness, powerlessness, regret, resentfulness, shame, terror, worthlessness

What is the Origin of My Disease?
The million dollar question! You've probably thought about this countless times. Obviously you didn't become this way overnight. Rather, it was the result of a gradual **progression** of increased drinking or drug use. It started with **experimentation**: perhaps sneaking a beer from the refrigerator, trying a joint with your friends, or popping a pain killer when absolutely nothing hurt. The experience was pleasant, so you took it up a notch and started using for **recreation**. But, you found that you weren't like your friends. It wasn't enough to use every so often. You used so regularly that it became a **habit**.

Up to now, it's been fun. However, habituation leads to **abuse**, which often results in negative consequences, like getting caught driving drunk, or testing dirty at work on a random drug screen. Most substance abusers *learn* from their mistakes. They can *connect the dots* between their drinking or drugging, and the negative consequences that follow. This **insight** leads them to change their behavior. For them, it's just not worth it. But, *your* substance us disorder prevents *you* from seeing things this way.

You are not alone. *Roughly 1 in 10 Americans cannot stop.* Science is not entirely sure why, though there is a genetic component and a behavioral component. Call it whatever you like... heredity, a brain condition, a disease, **"an obsession of the mind together with an allergy of the body", "a spiritual malady"**, being spanked as a child, not being spanked... It doesn't matter. Once past a certain point, there is no turning back. The real question is: *does it even matter* what triggered your disorder? Does it matter *why* someone has cancer in order for them to benefit from treatment? No! *What's important is that you accept your inability to manage drinking and drug using, now!* You are stuck because you have lost your ability to *choose*. You are **dependent** on mind-altering substances, using them pathologically, unreasonably, uncontrollably and dangerously. The progression to dependence looks like this:

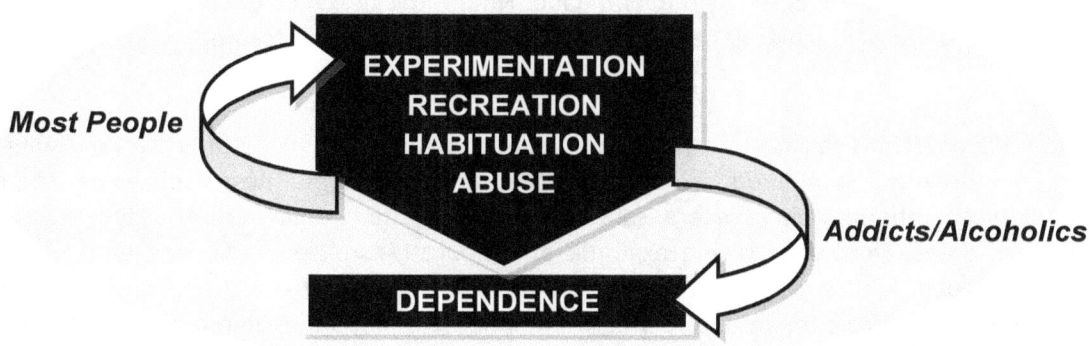

Once a person develops an unhealthy dependency on chemicals, **delusional thinking** keeps them that way. *A delusion is a false belief held with absolute conviction.* It's like holding up a mirror and not seeing reality. Why? Because for this disease to thrive, we must: 1.) lie to ourselves, and 2.) believe that lie. *Substance Use Disorder is a disease that convinces us we don't have a disease!* Why is it that so many of us don't seek treatment on our own? *It's because we simply don't believe we have a problem, despite all evidence to the contrary!* In other words, we don't see an addict or an alcoholic staring back at us in the mirror. Instead, we see someone who is: tired, overworked, hurting, stressed, unemployed, trying to find themselves, in control, the life of the party, blowing-off steam, victimized, losing weight, creative, successful, a failure, different from everyone else, no different than anyone else, etc. We see anything and everything but the truth, and actually believe these lies.

> **FACT: ALCOHOL IS ETHANOL: AN IRRITANT. IT REQUIRES NO DIGESTION, IS TOXIC, AND AFFECTS EVERY CELL IN THE HUMAN BODY. THE LIVER IS THE *ONLY* ORGAN THAT CAN DETOXIFY ALCOHOL.**

One expert calls this delusional state: "pathological mental mismanagement", accomplished through the use of *unconscious* lies, known as **defense mechanisms**. Defense mechanisms include: **agreeing, anger, avoiding, awfulizing, blaming, controlling, denying, euphoric recall, explaining, humor, intellectualizing, judging, justifying, lying, manipulating, minimizing, rationalizing,** and **withdrawing**. Distortions in thoughts, feelings and perceptions drive us to behave in ways that befuddle others. It is the thing that most frustrates our loved ones, who believe: "If only I love them enough they'll *see* they have a problem," which of course we cannot. They fail to understand that the problem is not with our eyesight.

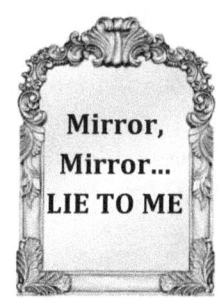

Co-occurring Disorders

Many of us are dealing with a substance use disorder and a mental illness simultaneously. This dual diagnosis is referred to as 'co-occurring disorders' The existence of co-occurring disorders will make it more difficult for professionals to assess the type and severity of either illness

There are a number of reasons why substance use disorders and mental disorders occur together. The most obvious reason is that certain substances can, at least temporarily, reduce the symptoms of mental illness, thus making us feel more "normal". Secondly, we might be predisposed to a mental disorder which is then triggered by chronic substance abuse. For example, research suggests that alcohol use increases the risk of post traumatic stress disorder (PTSD), and marijuana may contribute to schizophrenia. In this case it is particularly horrifying to know that the emergence of a potentially life-long mental disorder was triggered by our own hand. Finally, the presence of co-occurring disorders may be due to multiple factors such as genetics, brain injury, and exposure to trauma.

Why Can't I Just Stop?

To answer this question, you have to first understand a bit about how the brain works. When certain regions of the brain are stimulated, they produce pleasurable feelings. These feelings are the result of naturally occurring chemical messengers, called **neurotransmitters**, which are released between nerve cells in those areas. **Dopamine** is one example of a neurotransmitter associated with pleasure. For example, the good feeling associated with earning a promotion, having sex, eating chocolate or receiving some other kind of reward, is related to the release of dopamine in the brain. (Not surprisingly, the greatest *natural* dopamine release happens at the moment of sexual climax.) This process is part of the brain's **reward system.**

Dopamine is *also* stimulated by all those bad chemicals we abuse. A glass of wine is relaxing. The good feeling is short-lived. The body recovers, and that's the end. For *most people,* this is a natural process that occurs all throughout life. The dotted line, on the graph below, illustrates what happens to most people when they drink the occasional glass of wine. You can see how their mood is temporarily elevated by the stimulation of the brain's reward system. Afterward, their mood returns to normal as the dopamine is reabsorbed and recycled.

Notice I said "most" people. But we are not *like most* people. Those of us with a substance use disorder consume larger quantities, more frequently. The substances we shoot, snort and swallow, *cause a much more intense and longer lasting* surge in dopamine than the natural stimuli mentioned earlier. The behavior is self-reinforcing: meaning it feels *so euphoric... so magical... so orgasmic... so relaxing... so necessary...* that it reinforces the need to experience it again and again.

An article in Psychology Today Magazine explains the dopamine connection another way. It describes addiction as a collection of "powerful memories" created by the release of dopamine. These memories are so "intense", "lasting" and "important", that our brain is *commanded* to repeat the behavior. Recovery, therefore, is the process of weakening these memories.

By *conditioning* our brain to desire substances, we *alter* our brain chemistry. *We **hijack** the brain's reward system!* Dopamine helps explain why we can't stop using, despite knowing how destructive it is.

FACT: OVERDOSES INVOLVING PRESCRIPTION PAINKILLERS NOW KILL MORE AMERICANS THAN HEROIN AND COCAINE COMBINED.

Brain Drain and the Paradoxical Effect

As the disease progresses, we build up a **tolerance** to alcohol and drugs. Tolerance is the result of our brain cells becoming desensitized to, and depleted of, dopamine. So we receive less and less euphoria and relief, even though we are using more and more alcohol and drugs. We have *mismanaged* the reward process by draining our brain of natural feel-good chemicals like dopamine.

Brain scans prove that *brain drain* affects you long after you stop using. *That's why substance use disorder is a **brain disease**, of which drugs and alcohol are but symptoms.*

The greater the *brain drain,* the more anxious and depressed we feel whenever we are *not* high or drunk. Our compulsive substance use is now producing the *opposite* effect than intended. We call this *the* **Paradoxical Effect.** The Paradoxical Effect signals that the good times are over for anyone with a substance use disorder. The solid line on the graph below illustrates how the **euphoria** we receive from using alcohol or drugs, lessens over time. Instead of our mood returning to normal after being high, it falls short: we **crash**. Now the need to feel better is greater than ever: we **crave**. *The hopeless cycle of euphoria, crash and craving is the hallmark of substance use disorder.*

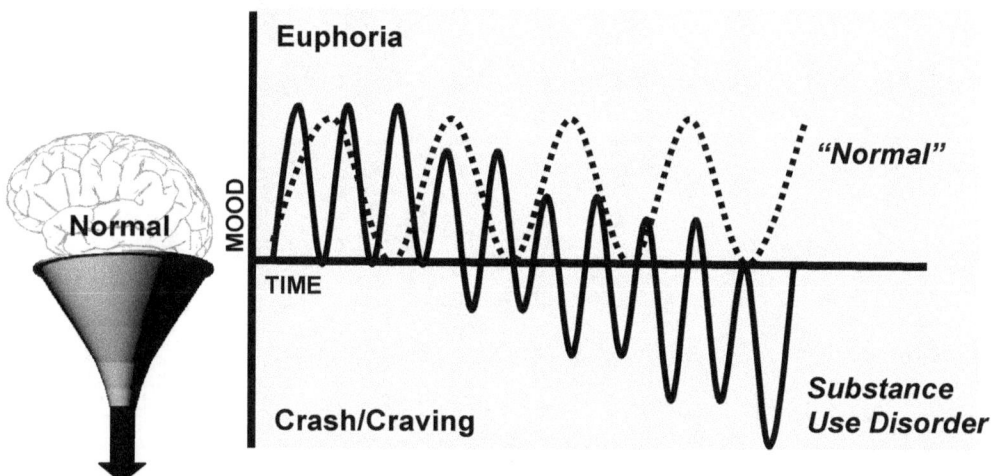

Paradoxical Effect: Short-Term Pleasure Leads to Long-Term Brain Drain

Looking at the above illustration it is easy to see how a high tolerance, also known as "chasing the high", can be fatal. Tolerance kills.

Now that you understand exactly what you're facing, perhaps you can draw more strength from your courageous decision to change. While **"cunning, baffling and powerful"**, this disease does not define who you are (contrary to what the "committee in your head" has been saying.) If you give yourself over to treatment, you too will rise above it. In Alcoholics Anonymous, the saying goes: **"If nothing changes, nothing changes!"** You can't possibly *hope* a disease away. But you can *help* put it into **remission** for life, one day at a time.

FACT: YOU DO NOT NEED TO HIT 'BOTTOM' TO RECOVER.

EXERCISES
1. **Think back over your history as you progressed through the stages of experimentation, recreation, habituation, abuse and dependence. What substance did you use, how much and how often? How did your using change over time?**

2. Describe all the reasons you drink and use drugs. Identify whether each cause is motivated by euphoria or relief.

3. Now that you understand delusional thinking, explain why each of your reasons for drinking and using drugs (above) really do not make sense.

4. Describe what each of the following feels like to you. Be specific:
   A. Euphoria i.e. the 'high'.

   B. Crash i.e. once the high is over.

   C. Craving i.e. the need to feel high again.

5. How has the 'high' you experience, changed over time? Is it as intense or lasting? What about side-effects?

6. You might be crazy, but you are *far* from lazy. People around you fail to understand how much time and effort it takes to maintain your lifestyle. Describe how your schedule is dominated by buying, hiding, using and recovering from chemical abuse.

7. Describe the catastrophic consequences you have experienced as a result of your chemical abuse. How have you suffered in your relationships, community, employment, self-esteem, finances, physical health, emotional well-being etc? Following are examples to get you going:
    - Arguments with family, friends and others due to substance use. Violence.
    - DUI and other citations, convictions, imprisonment etc.
    - Embarrassing behaviors. Morals compromised. Stealing. Lying. Disappointments. Betrayal.
    - Money spent and debts incurred.
    - Job opportunities lost. Days of work missed.
    - Putting your life at risk. Risking the lives of others.
    - Accidents or hospitalizations.
    - Physical conditions caused, or made worse, by chemical use.
    - Mental or emotional conditions caused, or made worse by, chemical use.

5. Delusional Thinking and Defense Mechanisms

Why is it so difficult to accept that we have a substance use disorder? Isn't using dangerously high amounts of substances every day enough? What about run-ins with the police, overdoses or emergency room visits? Or, all the money we spend and values we compromise? We worry about our hearts and livers, yet keep on using. We hide our alcohol and drugs, yet don't grasp this bizarre behavior. As time passes, the symptoms get worse and repeat themselves over and over again. Still we don't comprehend it.

We are suffering from **addictive thinking**: better understood as **delusional thinking**. What is a delusion, anyway? A delusion is a belief we hold to be true with all our heart, despite overwhelming evidence that it is false. What belief do *you* hold to be true despite all evidence to the contrary? Why, it is the belief that *you are not chemically dependent*, of course.

How can this sort of thinking continue? The answer is that we protect our delusional thinking with **defense mechanisms**. *Defense mechanisms are the things we say and do to protect our chronic abuse of substances.* They form a wall between our behavior, and the painful consequences that result.

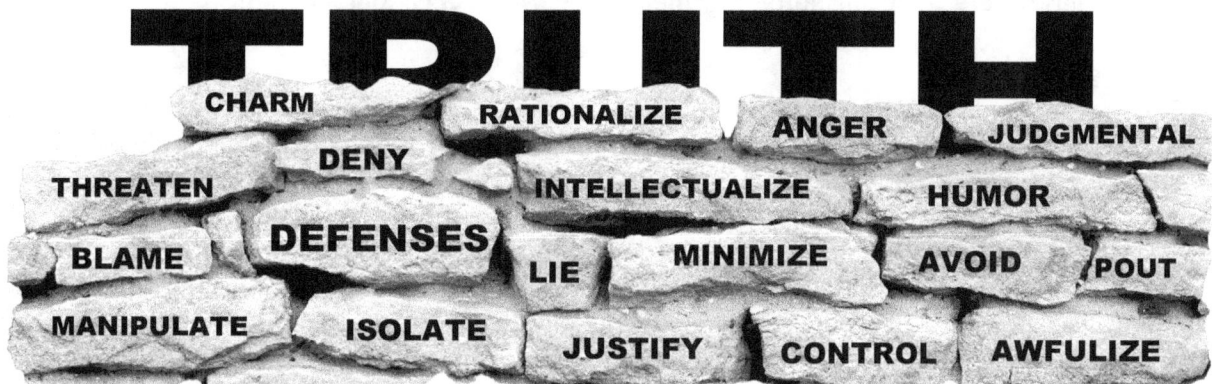

Defense Mechanisms Prevent Us from Seeing the Truth

Defense mechanisms shield us from pain. They change our perceptions so our lifestyle feels more comfortable. Rather than seeking help, *we continue a pointless search for new ways to abuse chemicals while avoiding the negative consequences.* Instead of just admitting *we can't control our drinking and using*, we say things like: "I only got wasted because I didn't eat before I drank. Next time will be different." Or, we might boast about drinking less, without acknowledging that we are also taking anti-anxiety medication like Xanax (i.e. alcohol in pill form.) If our substance is cocaine, we might convince ourselves that we don't have a problem because we never do coke on the weekends (although we drink heavily on those days.) We feed ourselves and others this bull, and believe it! Unfortunately, the wall built for protection becomes a prison, isolating us from reality and everyone in it.

Common Defense Mechanisms. Which are familiar to you?
- ❑ **Anger, Threatening and Intimidation**
   Anger is an ugly, multi-headed beast with a single purpose. It's sole function is to divert the focus off of ourselves. Simply put, we are being pushed. And, anger is the way we push back. One tactic is to *stubbornly refuse* all offers of treatment. We will say: "I don't need to go to rehab. Once I set my

mind on something, I get it done. I'll get sober on my own. " Another tactic is to turn the tables by *accusing* others of having the problem i.e. "How dare you tell me I have a problem with alcohol. You drink too." Yet another tactic is to become aggressive and *threaten* others to prevent them from talking about the problem. We say: "If you bring my drinking up one more time, I'm leaving." Anger is projected not just in what we say, but in how we say it. *Shouting* is meant to intimidate others. We learn early on that people back down right away when we get pissed. However, *silence* can convey feeling just as well.

❑ **Blaming, Projecting and Judging**
Pointing to others as the cause of *our own* behavior in order to avoid responsibility and feel better about ourselves i.e. "I wouldn't drink so much if you just quit nagging me", or "The cop is the one with the drinking problem!"

❑ **Controlling**
Or, more accurately, the *illusion* of control. For the addict and alcoholic, control is a fantasy. All of us eventually lose control over the chemical. Our lives become grossly unmanageable, yet we continue to insist we can stop any time we want. I often hear people say things like: "All I need to do to stop drinking is start working out at the gym." By claiming control, we cut God out of our recovery. A.A. states that since *we* have no control over our chemical use, we must obtain control from elsewhere. It is this "elsewhere" that constitutes a Higher Power. We **"Let go and let God."**

❑ **Denying**
To deny that our behavior is out of control is to deny reality. Denial is not a conscious lie. Rather, it is the *belief* that something is true when it is not. Once, during a group discussion on denial, a client stated that any child who believed in Santa Claus was in denial. He meant to be funny. Instead, he demonstrated a fundamental misunderstanding of denial and the addictive mind. Children who believe in Santa Claus do so because they wake up Christmas morning to find gifts under the tree. The tree is located in their home, which is locked at night. The cookies are eaten. The glass of milk is empty. Their parents deny any knowledge of the gifts, other than to credit the man in the white beard. Not to mention that, during the month of December, the entire country is transformed by the decorations, music and advertising. When presented with those facts, believing in Santa Claus is a rational, intelligent decision (which is exactly the point.) Unfortunately, that is not what's going on with us. In our case, there are no gift-wrapped boxes. The cookies and milk are untouched. Everyone is begging us to drop this fantasy of a Santa Claus. And, our lives have gone to hell. Yet, despite all evidence to the contrary, we continue to insist Santa is real and we don't have a substance problem.

Examples of denial include:
- Believing that we are different from "real" alcoholics and addicts.
- Thinking that we can get our substance abuse back "under control" by "cutting down."
- Refusing to believe that a secondary drug is also a problem.
- Believing that A.A. or N.A. will not be helpful because we are "not like those people."
- Continuing to hang out with "friends" who enable our using.

❑ **Euphoric Recall**
Substance Use Disorder is characterized by *short-term pleasure, followed by long-term pain*. Oftentimes we suffer from *selective memory* when thinking back on our drinking and drugging experiences. We dwell *only* on the brief periods of pleasure; we *romanticize the high,* while completely ignoring all the painful memories. For example, an alcoholic might focus on: the prestige

he feels when the bartender calls him by name, the tinkling sound of ice cubes tumbling round his favorite bar glass, the warm feeling of alcohol flowing down his throat to his belly, the instant relief of the day's chaos melting away etc. At the same time, he is able to block out: the sizable bar tab, driving home drunk, arguments with his wife resulting in their sleeping in separate bedrooms, constant abdominal pain, the necessity of drinking a few beers every morning to quiet the severe shaking of his hands, feelings of shame resulting from arriving to work every day reeking of alcohol etc. It is impossible to overstate the power of euphoric recall. People can lose their spouse, children, job, driver's license... you name it; and still look forward to relaxing after work with a drink or joint.

- ❑ **Extreme Thinking, also known as Awfulizing, Catastrophizing and Over-generalizing**
Extreme thinking is an example of a **cognitive distortion**; which is a fancy way of saying that we aren't thinking clearly. In this case, we magnify the importance of events and the chances of failure. It is the result of being negative, pessimistic and anxious. Extreme thinking convinces us that if something goes wrong, the result will be *impossible* to handle without drinking or using. We might say: "If I get a craving, it will be unbearable and I will never be able to resist it". The more we adopt this distorted way of thinking, the more we feel stuck in an endless pattern of hopeless failure.

- ❑ **Humor**
Making light of the situation and turning it into a joke.

- ❑ **Intellectualizing**
Using *false logic* to convince ourselves and others that we don't have a problem. Intellectualizing protects us from the stress we would feel by facing our problem. We might say: "Addiction is a genetic disease that runs in my family, so I was destined to get it anyway." In this example, the false logic assumes that *every* genetic disease is passed on to every descendent.

- ❑ **Isolating**
Among the *most* painful symptoms of substance use disorder, is that feeling of being *all alone*. *Human beings were not made to be loners.* We are hardwired for companionship. That is why people who donate their time, through service work, find the experience so deeply fulfilling. However, most of the family and friends in *our* world either criticize us or try to interfere with our drinking or drugging. To shut out reality, we avoid contact with anyone who lives in the real world. We isolate by physically restricting ourselves to the safety of our home, apartment or room; and we cut ourselves off emotionally. Then, our spark for living is extinguished, and we feel like zombies.

- ❑ **Lying**
Purposely changing the facts, distorting the truth or omitting important details.

- ❑ **Manipulating**
We manipulate people in order to get them to do things they wouldn't normally do, so that we get what we want. No doubt, you are a master manipulator. We manipulate by **agreeing, arguing, being sarcastic, charming, coaxing, crying, defiance, flirting, pouting, shaming, teasing, withdrawing** etc. Most defense mechanisms are a means of manipulating others. Many of us learned how to manipulate from our parents, having grown up in households where this was a parenting technique.

- ❑ **Minimizing**
Agreeing, *but* trying to make our addiction sound like it's no big deal. For example, we might say: "Sure I drink, but not nearly as much as my friends do."

- **Personalizing**
Blaming *ourselves* for anything bad that happens, even if it has little or nothing to do with us, is a common defense mechanism. Claiming responsibility is the quick way to avoid talking about our substance use disorder i.e. "No need for discussion. I already admit I'm guilty." By taking responsibility for other people's feelings and behavior, we feed into our already low self-esteem.

- **Rationalizing and Justifying**
All of us rationalize and justify our chronic abuse of chemicals. Synonyms for these words include: defend, diminish, excuse and reduce. When we rationalize or justify our behavior, we are providing a *good* reason for our action, not the *true* reason. Simply put, we are just making excuses i.e. "I'm not hurting anyone else", or "You can't be an addict if the medication is prescribed."

> **"Humility and intellect could be compatible, provided we put humility first."** (Twelve Steps and Twelve Traditions, page 30)

EXERCISES
1. Which defense mechanism(s) do you use to protect your addiction? Give examples for each.

2. **Let's look at this craziness in action. As you read, underline the defense mechanisms used by this binge drinker who can't connect the dots between his drinking and the consequences that result:**

FRANK SAYS HE "LOVES" DRINKING. He talks passionately of savoring the taste of a chilled, top-shelf vodka martini (with two olives). He says that his love of drinking quality vodka makes quitting extremely difficult. The only problem is that Frank is a binge drinker. Once he starts he cannot stop.

Even worse, somewhere in the process of each binge, Frank blacks-out. During the blackouts, he does and says things he would never dream of straight. He risks the lives of others by driving. He sleeps in parking lots, alleyways, even in the local cemetery; forgoing grooming and skipping days in the office without notice. He spends every dime he has, making numerous trips to the ATM until he can withdraw no more. To make his cash last longer, he switches to the cheapest vodka he can get, which he guzzles warm from the bottle. He steals. He pays for sex. He often awakens in a jail cell or hospital bed.

Yet, Frank is unwavering in his abiding affection for alcohol. Hearing him, even after a binge, you would think he was describing a beautiful painting or the perfect woman; certainly not a toxic liquid made from rotted farm produce. When you inquire of Frank about his pattern of binging followed by blackout, he disagrees. "I usually never black out. If you're referring to the last time it's only because I drank on an empty stomach is all."

Asked about the time before last, Frank grins. "Of course I remember. That was the day I drank this really expensive brand of vodka. Always wanted to try it, but the stuff is usually so expensive I can never afford the price. Then I was shopping at Costco, and saw it was on sale for the holiday." With a roaring laugh he adds: "I didn't know how strong it was until I was on my ass!"

Frank is pressed further to explain the time <u>before</u> the time before last; or three blackouts ago. Now he turns vicious. "Sometimes you are so stupid! Yeah, I was wasted. I smoked some killer weed my buddy had. So what? I have a medical marijuana card and pot helps with anxiety. Maybe I had a few drinks after, but what the hell! I'm allowed to get F-d up sometimes, just like anybody else. Stop treating me like you're my mother or you'll make me go out and drink right now."

It is brought to Frank's attention that he binged and blacked out 100% of the last three times he drank, which does not exactly support his account that this unhealthy behavior is far and few between. But Frank isn't ruffled in the slightest. "Well sure... if you look <u>only</u> at the last three times I drank. Try looking at the last three-hundred, and you will find the story is completely different."

Finally, when you inquire of Frank how he could love drinking when it causes him to suffer so, he replies: "Of course I love drinking. It's blackouts I hate!"

    A. **Frank's problem is not his drinking. It's his thinking. To him, "drinking" is the act of consuming the beverage, *period*. In reality, however, it's the entire experience; *the action PLUS the consequences.* Defense mechanisms allow Frank to enjoy alcohol while *separating* the pain out of the equation completely. Therefore, he continues to drink even though he blacks-out each time and ends up in jail or the hospital. What is Frank's delusion (i.e. the belief he holds to be true despite overwhelming evidence to the contrary)?**

B. When asked about his pattern of binging and blackouts, Frank says: "I usually never blackout." The dictionary defines the word "Never" as follows: *Something that will not happen at any time.* Based on the definition, why doesn't Frank's statement make any sense whatsoever?

C. Frank uses numerous defense mechanisms to shield himself from the truth (that he has a substance use disorder.) Identify the particular defense mechanism for each of the following:
   a) He talks passionately of savoring the taste of chilled top-shelf vodka.
   b) Love of drinking good vodka makes quitting extremely difficult.
   c) You would think he was describing a beautiful painting or perfect woman.
   d) I usually never black out.
   e) It's only because I drank on an empty stomach.
   f) With a roaring laugh he adds: "I didn't know how strong it was until I was on my ass!"
   g) He turns vicious.
   h) I smoked some killer weed.
   i) I have a medical marijuana card and the pot helps with anxiety.
   j) Maybe I had a few drinks after but what the hell.
   k) I'm allowed to get F-d up sometimes just like anybody else.
   l) Stop treating me like you're my mother or you'll make me want to go drink now.
   m) Look at the last three-hundred and you will find the story is completely different.
   n) Of course I love drinking. It's blackouts I hate.

(Answers: 1A. He is not alcoholic; 1B. "Usually" and "never" conflict with one another; 1C. a. Euphoric Recall, b. Rationalizing, c. Euphoric Recall, d. Denial, e. Denial and Justifying, f. Humor, g. Anger, h. Euphoric Recall, i. Justifying, j. Minimizing, k. Rationalizing, l. Manipulating and Blaming, m. Intellectualizing, n. Denial)

6. Sick and Tired of Being Sick and Tired!

By the time we get to the point that we need treatment, drinking and using have become a full-time occupation. We become sick and tired of devoting so much of our time to: earning money for drugs, buying drugs, hiding drugs, using drugs, hiding our being high or drunk, coming down, sleeping, and starting the cycle all over again with lots of smaller steps in-between. This is our pattern, day in and day out. It sucks the life out of us.

Don't ever let anyone tell you you're lazy or unmotivated, because we are devoted to chemical abuse. We are very good at it. We are expert! In fact, most of the people I counsel, who identify as addict or alcoholic, are above average in intelligence and creativity. That opinion is not alone. The A.A. text says this about the alcoholic: **"He often possesses special abilities, skills, and aptitudes, and has a promising career ahead of him."** Those gifts are hardwired into our DNA. When we apply them to a path or career that is both productive and fulfilling, we become expert as well.

In order to earn that privilege, your eyes must be opened. The extent to which drugs and alcohol have dominated your existence, must be revealed. Any delusion that you are different from other people who chronically misuse chemicals *must be shattered.*

You will use the next few pages to explain what it is like to exist in a world which revolves around drugs and alcohol. Focus on your thoughts, behaviors, priorities and problems. For example, what are the insane things you do over and over, day after day? What lies do you tell yourself and others to ensure the behavior continues? How do you feel about acting against your will? It's what we call *being sick and tired of being sick and tired.*

Later you will read this to your Twelve Step sponsor or a sober buddy. You will also find it useful to pull out and review whenever you need to remind yourself of why you don't *ever* want to drink or use again. Take your time. Be thoughtful and specific. Don't be surprised if you find yourself becoming emotional. Congratulations on taking the first step back to the real world!

Perhaps you can draw inspiration from the following passage, which describes a life out of control (or under the control of your disease):

> **"All these failings generate fear, a soul-sickness in its own right. Then fear, in turn, generates more character defects. Unreasonable fear that our instincts will not be satisfied drives us to covet the possessions of others, to lust for sex and power, to become angry when our instinctive demands are threatened, to be envious when the ambitions of others seem to be realized while ours are not. We eat, drink, and grab for more of everything than we need, fearing we shall never have enough. And with genuine alarm at the prospect of work, we stay lazy. We loaf and procrastinate, or at best work grudgingly and under half steam. These fears are the termites that ceaselessly devour the foundations of whatever sort of life we try to build."** (Twelve Steps and Twelve Traditions, page 49)

I am sick and tired of being sick and tired because...

> "People are not apt to consider being an addict highly desirable. But if we realize that the gains from recovery in a Twelve Step program *may not be easily found in other ways*, being addicted may not be the curse that we thought it to be." (Addictive Thinking, page 85)

7. Health Dangers of Your Drug(s) of Choice

Substance Use Disorder is a **bio-psycho-social** disease. It affects us *physically, mentally, socially and spiritually.* For the moment, let's focus on how the disease affects the body. In the space provided below, you are to list at least *five health dangers* of your drug of choice, with an explanation of each. If you have more than one drug of choice (such as alcohol and pot, or heroin and cocaine), list five dangers for each. Hopefully, after facing the reality of the poisons you ingest, you will never look at these substances the same way again!

Health dangers related to substance abuse are explained on countless internet sites. Start here:
- **DEA.gov/druginfo**   Drug Enforcement Agency (Fact Sheets for each drug)
- **DrugAbuse.gov**   National Institute on Drug Abuse (NIDA)
- **NCADD.org**   National Council on Alcoholism and Drug Dependence
- **NIAAA.nih.gov**   National Institute on Alcohol Abuse and Alcoholism
- **NIH.gov**   National Institutes of Health
- **RethinkingDrinking.niaaa.nih.gov**   NIAAA Rethinking Drinking
- **Teens.drugabuse.gov**   National Institute on Drug Abuse for Teens

_____
_____
_____
_____
_____
_____
_____
_____
_____
_____
_____
_____
_____

8. Substance Use Disorder Kills

Addicts and alcoholics do not usually dwell on death. No user starts a binge thinking that within a few hours, or even minutes, they will be dead and their family suffering. But we *should* think about it. We should think about it very hard, because the ways in which death can steal us away from this earth are many, painful and – honestly – gruesome. One thing they are not, however, is a secret. Death by chronic substance use is well documented. It's just that our disease causes us to rationalize or deny the danger. Prove it to yourself. Now is the time to face reality by understanding what a game of *Russian Roulette* we play whenever we indulge in our habit.

But first, let me share a true story. A former neighbor of mine really enjoyed drinking beer and smoking pot. Each afternoon I would see him drinking and smoking, and each morning he'd be dumping his empties in the recycle bin. He definitely was *not* what you would refer to as a 'sloppy drunk'. About forty-five years old, with long hair and bit of a belly cresting the top of his swim trunks, you could usually find him tan, shirtless and sitting in his front yard with the stereo cranked, or walking barefoot on the beach saying "Hey" to the girls. He was fun to talk to; amiable; easygoing; the kind of guy who would return stuff in better condition than when he borrowed it. If you had time to listen, he would talk your ear off about fishing, his dog... whatever. One day, after getting wasted at a friend's house, he decided to walk home. He was run-over by an Amtrak train and died.

How in the world do you plan for something like that? Can you? *Of course you can!* Stop deluding yourself. Understand the *reality* of what you are doing, and gain insight. Begin by reading about just a few of the countless ways in which your disease can end your life. The following list is by no means complete. Unfortunately, it can't make you feel the pain or the terror or sorrow. But I guarantee, you will learn something you did not know. Hopefully you will be frightened by the risks you have already taken, and humbled by how lucky you have been *thus far*.

When I was abusing drugs and alcohol, no one had the guts or the desire to get in my face with these facts. I can't say that I would have listened. But, I also cannot say I would have totally ignored them either, as I pray you won't.

During the two years prior to my recovery, I was a frequent flier at the hospital ER. Three of those visits required the crash cart to restart my heart. So it was obvious to me that I was in a great deal of danger. Of course, my solution to the problem was insane. During that period, whenever I felt like I had crossed the line and ingested too many chemicals, I would scribble on paper a makeshift Will which I would place in plain sight on the kitchen counter, where it wouldn't be overlooked. That way I could say "goodbye" and "I love you", to my family, and ensure that my dogs were cared for in the event I overdosed or was hit by a train. My hope was that someone would find me before the dogs were forced to nibble off my fingers and toes to survive. Later, after I straightened up, I would toss the paper out and wipe my brow, knowing I had dodged a bullet, only to do it all over again the next time. Sound familiar?

Like me, you have put a gun to your temple and squeezed the trigger many times without engaging a live round. But the odds are definitely stacked against you. Please, allow me to "get in your face" with some possible outcomes of your chemical abuse. Read each description and check the box if it might apply to you or your drug(s) of choice. Then, answer the questions that follow.

1. **Abdominal Aortic Aneurysm (also known as Aaortic Dissection)**
   Chronic alcohol abuse can precipitate a tear in the inner wall of the aorta (i.e. the main artery of the body). Blood flows between the layers of the wall of the aorta forcing the layers apart. This can quickly lead to death, even with optimal treatment. If the dissection tears the aorta completely open (through all three layers), massive and rapid blood loss occurs through every orifice. *Aortic dissections resulting in rupture have an 80% mortality rate and 50% of patients die before they even reach the hospital.* ❑ **May apply**

2. **Abscess**
   Skin and tissue infections are the *most frequent* cause of hospital admissions among IV drug users. Abscesses are associated with serious health complications throughout the body. ❑ **May apply**

3. **Aneurysm**
   An aneurysm is caused by the ballooning of a blood vessel wall. A stroke is the result of the blood vessel bursting. Brain and abdominal aneurysms have been linked to the abuse of alcohol, cocaine, methamphetamine and marijuana. ❑ **May apply**

4. **Angina**
   Reduced blood flow to the heart can result in chest pain. Angina is a symptom of an underlying heart problem, usually coronary heart disease. Stimulant drugs can trigger a coronary artery spasm, which is a brief and sudden narrowing of one of the arteries to the heart, resulting in pain. Alcohol can mask chest pain, meaning you will not realize you are having a problem. ❑ **May apply**

5. **Aspiration**
   Normally the body responds to breathing in a foreign substance, such as vomit, by coughing. if you are heavily sedated, such as when you overdose, you cannot respond because you have no gag reflex. If alone with no one to revive you, you *will* choke and die. ❑ **May apply**

6. **Binge Drinking (i.e. Alcohol Poisoning)**
   Binge drinking causes 80,000 deaths in the U.S. each year. Binge drinking increases the risk of stroke ten-times, and binge drinking just three or more times during pregnancy has been associated with an increased risk of stillbirth. ❑ **May apply**

7. **Cancer**
   Alcohol increases the risk of cancer multiple ways: it is metabolized into a toxic chemical which can damage DNA, it produces free-radicals, and it impairs the body's ability to process nutrition. Toxic contaminants can also be introduced during the fermentation process. Cancers related to alcohol include cancer of the oral cavity, tongue, pharynx, larynx, esophagus, , stomach, colon, rectum, liver, female breasts and ovaries. Marijuana smokers typically smoke fewer cigarettes per day then tobacco smokers, but consume more of the joint, inhale longer and more deeply, and hold the smoke longer in the lungs. *Marijuana has been found to have 75% to 95% more carcinogens than cigarettes.* ❑ **May apply**

8. **Cirrhosis and Liver Failure**
   Alcohol requires no digestion; 20% passes directly through the stomach, the remainder through the small intestines. Alcohol affects every cell in the body. Alcohol is converted by the body to a toxin called *acetaldehyde,* which is known to damage the liver. The liver is the only organ that can

detoxify alcohol. Cirrhosis is permanent scarring of the liver, resulting in poor liver function and end-stage alcoholic liver disease (i.e. liver failure). ❏ **May apply**

9. **Esophageal Hemorrhage**
Uncontrolled bleeding into the esophagus *can occur without warning*. Those individuals who have developed cirrhosis of the liver are particularly at risk, since the damage to the liver caused by scarring means that blood is unable to flow properly. The resulting increase in pressure causes the veins in the esophagus to bulge and eventually burst. ❏ **May apply**

10. **Gastrointestinal Bleeding**
Alcohol is an *irritant* that interferes with *all* parts of the gastrointestinal tract. Injury to the tissues in the mouth and esophagus occurs *with the very first sip.* ❏ **May apply**

11. **Hepatitis C**
A contagious liver disease that is spread through direct contact with infected blood. The condition is associated with intravenous drug use. It can lead to scarring of the liver and, ultimately, cirrhosis. Hepatitis C is known as a 'silent killer'. Although it starts to damage the liver immediately, many people feel few or no symptoms for years. Hepatitis C is the primary cause of cirrhosis and liver cancer, and is the leading cause of liver transplantation. *From 1990 to 2015, deaths from liver cancer in the US have increased by 60%, while deaths from other cancers have decreased.* Continuing to drink after being diagnosed with hepatitis C causes the disease to progress rapidly. It is curable if diagnosed in time! ❏ **May apply**

12. **Hemorrhagic Stroke**
Cocaine, methamphetamines, and other stimulants increase blood pressure. The extra pressure can cause blood vessels to rupture, allowing blood to leak into the brain. Heavy alcohol use is also linked to this type of stroke. *Every 4 minutes someone dies from a stroke. It is the fifth leading cause of death in America.* ❏ **May apply**

13. **HIV/AIDS**
HIV is contracted through contact with infected blood. It is associated with intravenous drug use as well as risky sexual behavior resulting from drug use. ❏ **May apply**

14. **'Hot Shot'**
Do you realize that your life is in the hands of your dealer? A 'hot shot' is a lethal dose of heroin, or a dose laced with poison *designed to kill the user.* A popular poison is strychnine; found in rodent bait. Strychnine is preferred for its bitter taste, making it undetectable to a heroin user tasting the product for purity. Why would your dealer do such a thing? To make more money! ❏ **May apply**

15. **Hyperthermia**
Cocaine, amphetamines, PCP, LSD and MDMA can cause the body to produce more heat than it can release. Excessive sweating – such as when you are dancing – without replacing fluids leads to dehydration, exacerbating the situation. Heart rate and respiration increase while blood pressure decreases. This condition can quickly escalate into a medical emergency requiring immediate treatment to prevent disability or death. ❏ **May apply**

16. **Hypoxia**
'Huffing' toxic vapors leads to a lack of oxygen, causing suffocation. *About 50% of deaths related to*

inhalant use occur with the very first use. ❏ **May apply**

17. Ischemic Stroke
Cocaine, methamphetamines, and other stimulants narrow the blood vessels. This can cut off blood flow to areas of the brain. Deprived of oxygen, those brain cells begin to die. *Two-thirds of stroke survivors have some type of lasting difficulty.* ❏ **May apply**

18. Kidney Failure
Every drug entering the body passes through the kidneys. Alcohol affects the kidneys by impairing their ability to regulate the volume and composition of fluid and electrolytes in the body. Other drugs that can damage the kidneys include heroin, inhalants, MDMA and PCP. ❏ **May apply**

19. Methamphetamine laboratory explosion (Including resulting burn injury) ❏ **May apply**

20. Motor vehicle accident
Eight teenagers die each day due to alcohol-related motor vehicle crashes. ❏ **May apply**

21. Myocardial Infarction (i.e. Heart Attack)
Most street drugs, including: heroin, cocaine and ecstasy, can cause high blood pressure, stroke, heart failure and death; in some cases from only one use. According to the National Institutes of Health, *even a single session of huffing can disrupt heart rhythms and lower oxygen levels*, which can lead to death. ❏ **May apply**

22. Overdose
According to the Center for Disease Control, *overdoses involving prescription painkillers now kill more Americans than heroin and cocaine combined.* ❏ **May apply**

23. Pneumonia and Acute Lung Injury (i.e. Acute Respiratory Distress Syndrome)
A serious lung infection leading to pneumonia can result from the spread of bacteria and/or a weakened immune system. Alcohol and drug abuse have long been recognized as a significant risk factor for pneumonia. For example, alcohol abuse promotes the spread of bacteria by depressing the cough mechanism while increasing the risk of aspiration of gastric acid into the throat. According to the Centers for Disease Control, *pneumonia is the eighth most common cause of death in the United States.* Alcohol abuse also makes a person four-times more likely to develop acute lung injury following a trauma, such as an auto accident or gunshot wound. Acute lung injury has a 40 to 50 percent mortality rate. ❏ **May apply**

24. Respiratory Failure
Drugs that depress the central nervous system, such as opioids and benzodiazepines, can interfere with the area of the brain that controls the rate and depth of respiration. Too much and you simply stop breathing. ❏ **May apply**

25. Risky behavior related to substance abuse
Judgment is frequently the first mental capacity affected. Poor or impulsive decision-making is common. Risky behavior includes: violence; unprotected sex; accidental injury to self (such as trauma to the head); sharing needles; driving while under the influence; and being struck by a car, bus or train. ❏ **May apply**

26. Seizure

The central nervous system is so depressed by chronic alcohol abuse, binge drinking or mixing drugs and alcohol, that it can *rebound* if alcohol is suddenly removed, causing a grand mal seizure. A grand mal seizure affects the entire brain, and can be fatal. ❏ **May apply**

27. Sepsis and Septic Shock

'Blood poisoning' is a serious infection occurring when bacteria produce toxins that cause the immune system to attack the body's own organs and tissues. The most common cause is the sharing of a dirty needle. Studies show that alcohol-dependent critical-care patients are more likely to develop sepsis. ❏ **May apply**

28. Suicide

Suicide is the leading cause of death among people who abuse alcohol and drugs. Teens who consume alcohol are almost three-times as likely to make a suicide attempt. ❏ **May apply**

29. Violence

i.e. Assault, homicide, manslaughter, murder, resisting arrest, prison violence etc. ❏ **May apply**

30. Withdrawal

Alcohol is the most dangerous drug to withdraw from. One in three people who experience alcohol withdrawal seizures also experience delirium tremens (DTs.) Delirium tremens can be fatal. Symptoms include high blood pressure, fever, terrifying hallucinations, tremor, rapid heartbeat and respiratory depression. ❏ **May apply**

EXERCISES

1. **Are you *predisposed* to certain disorders based on your family history, including parents, grandparents, aunts, uncles? For example, does Alzheimer's, cancer, dementia, diabetes, schizophrenia or addiction run in your family? (If you are unsure, ask family members.) List each illness below. Perform an online search and write a simple description for each.**

2. Please describe your complete current and past physical and mental health history. What in your medical history is cause for concern? What *physical conditions* do you have? For example do you have a heart murmur, diabetes or high blood pressure? Are you pregnant? What about *mental conditions?* Do you suffer from anxiety, bipolar disorder, borderline personality disorder, depression, post traumatic stress, schizophrenia? What medications are you currently prescribed?

3. Please describe how continued substance abuse can worsen the physical and mental conditions you identified in your medical history. Perhaps you are predisposed to an undiagnosed illness you identified in your family history. Please describe how the chemicals you abuse can affect these conditions. How could it affect any medications you are currently taking?

4. **If you don't stop drinking or using, you may die. An obituary may be the last thing anybody will remember about you. So, who better to write it than you. Besides, you did this to yourself. Why burden someone else with the sad task. As distasteful an exercise as it may be, use the space below to write a brief and concise obituary which your family can submit to the newspaper in the event of your demise. Include your biographical and survivor information:**

The family is sad to announce that _____, age _____ passed away suddenly and tragically as a result of an addiction to _____.

9. Do Twelve Step Programs Work?

The success rate of a Twelve Step program like Alcoholics Anonymous is difficult to define because it depends on *who* you ask. It is in fact a moving target. The data is available; but from different sources using different definitions for "members" and "sobriety", resulting in *vastly* differing results. To further complicate matters, the results continue to evolve over time as our population grows and changes. Read on. It's important for you to know the truth about this thing that's saving your life.

Some Reliable Numbers on Addiction, Relapse and Recovery
To begin to understand the issue, it's best to start with a broader perspective of addiction itself:

1. According to a 2009 article in Wired Magazine, entitled *The Secret of A.A.: After 25 Years We Don't Know How It Works,* an estimated 23 million people grapple with severe alcohol or drug abuse. That's more than twice the number of Americans afflicted with cancer. Some 1.2 million people belong to one of A.A.'s 55,000 meeting groups in the U.S., while countless others are introduced to the Twelve Steps at one of the nation's 11,000 professional treatment centers.

2. According to an oft quoted study by Hunt, Barnett and Branch published in a 1971 edition of the Journal of Clinical Psychology entitled *Relapse Rates In Addiction Programs*, 33% of all recovering addicts relapsed within two weeks of leaving treatment, 60% within three months, and 67% within one year

3. Another popular reporting is a 1989 Alcohol Alert published by the NIAAA (National Institute on Alcohol Abuse and Alcoholism) which is part of the NIH (National Institutes of Health,) stating that 90% of alcoholics are likely to experience at least one relapse within four years. And they calculate similar relapse rates for alcohol, nicotine and heroin addiction.

Decades of Conflicting Success Rates
In a famous 1941 Saturday Evening Post article, cofounder Bill W. claimed A.A. enjoys a 50% success rate immediately, and another 25% success rate after a relapse or two. The figures were published three years later in the American Journal of Psychiatry. Bill W's admission has become a time-honored statement. These articles - and success rates - have been cited repeatedly over the years by supporters of Twelve Step programs (as indicative of their success) and critics of the program (as indicative of their deliberate misinformation.) Today we can actually look to A.A. itself for more insight.

A.A. has in fact conducted anonymous member surveys every three years since 1968, called the Triennial Survey. The 1989 survey reported that only 9% of new members remain for four months, and 5% remain for twelve months, which equates to a 95% drop out rate! A.A. presented these figures with a 99% degree of confidence based on random samples taken throughout each year.

A 1996 A.A. membership survey reported that 45% of members *(again, what does that mean?)* had at least five years sobriety. And, according to the report, if 6% - 8% of all alcoholics are A.A. members, then you can conclude that 2.5% - 3.5% of alcoholics stay sober. Based on 26,000,000 addicts in this country, that equates to at least 75,000 sober people. *Around the same time, a study by the Betty Ford Center indicated that 35% of A.A. members stay sober five years, 34% from one to five years, and 31% for less than a year. Overall they found that A.A. works for one-third of those involved.*

An even more recent assessment of success and failure was published by A.A. in 2008. *Alcoholics Anonymous Recovery Outcome Rates: Contemporary Myth and Misinterpretation* reported:
- Of those in their first month of meetings, 26% will still be attending at the end of that year.
- Of those in their fourth month, 56% will still be attending A.A. at the end of that year.
- The length of sobriety is increasing. (As has every triennial survey since 1983.)
- 50% of A.A. members remained sober over five years.
- The survey found the average A.A. member stayed sober for more than eight years.

Best of the Bunch: Project MATCH
This landmark study compared three popular therapies: **Twelve Steps, Cognitive Behavioral Therapy (CBT)**, and **Motivational Enhancement Therapy. The conclusion was that all three of these therapies were more or less equally effective at reducing alcohol intake among subjects.** It also showed that following the Twelve Steps was more effective for alcoholics without other psychiatric problems, and did a better job of inspiring total abstinence as opposed to a reduction in drinking. *In other words, the Twelve Step program designed by alcoholic stockbroker Bill W. works slightly better than the therapies offered by the medical community.*

Making Sense of It All
There are significant research flaws you should be aware of:
- Studies fail to account for members moving from one Twelve Step program to another. The open-door policy of most Twelve Step meetings, which is one of its greatest strengths, causes the greatest barrier to measuring success.

- Studies fail to consider the "intent" of the member. No differentiation is made between members who are serious about working a recovery program, and members who just attend meetings because they are required. For example, 270,000 individuals each year are accused or convicted of a drunk driving or an alcohol related crime, and are *forced* into A.A. programs. It is unreasonable to assume the same rate of dedication as that among *willing* volunteers.

- Studies vary as to the definition of "member". In a 1965 article published in the Quarterly Journal of Studies of Alcohol, a member is someone who attends *ten* A.A. meetings. In a 1990 survey by Robin Room of the Addiction Research Foundation, he reported that 9% of Americans have been a member of A.A. by attending *at least one* A.A. meeting.

- Similarly, what defines "sobriety". A.A. defines sobriety as: *life-long abstinence.* According to other sources, such as the Hunt study, sobriety is considered to be only one year of abstinence.

And the Moral of the Story is...
Twelve Step programs work. They save lives every day. According to Tonigan & Rice (2010), those who attend A.A. have a reduced drinking intensity and greater abstinence. Anyway, even if it were only one life - *your life,* what value would you assign? Your life is precious. Richard Halverson, former chaplain of the U.S. Senate, writes: *"In the economy of God, one man is of inestimable worth."* The dictionary defines inestimable as; *impossible to put a value on.*

Programs like A.A. perform miracles on a daily basis. To the person delivered from misery, that's better than pitching a no-hitter every single game you play. While you can analyze Twelve Step programs quantitatively, you should judge their effectiveness *qualitatively*, and when you do, the fact that they work at all is *all* that matters. Now it's up to you. Will yours be the life that is saved?

EXERCISES

If you work a Twelve Step program, the Twelve Step program will work for you. Now that your head is full of statistics, it's probably a good time to change gears. Let's actually take a look at how Alcoholics Anonymous worked for someone addicted to alcohol and drugs. Turn to page 407 of your Alcoholics Anonymous book, and read the personal story entitled: "Acceptance Was the Answer." Then answer the questions below.

1. The writer states:
    "If you had my problems, you'd drink too, was my feeling"
    "If you had my wife, you'd drink too."
    "If you had my responsibilities, if you needed the sleep like I do, you'd drink too."

    A. The writer suffered from a delusion. What was it?
    _____

    B. The statements above are examples of two defense mechanisms. Name them.
    _____ and _____

2. The writer states: "The longer the drinking continued, the shorter the time the alcohol would keep me asleep. I would have to drink myself back to sleep again and again throughout the night. But I never became a morning drinker." Here, the writer is protecting his addictive thinking with the following defense mechanism. _____

3. The writer began using alcohol in pharmacy school as a means of helping him sleep. For a while, it worked. But, eventually, drinking interfered with his responsibilities as a physician. The problem got so bad that he would wake up in the middle of the night, then couldn't fall asleep again unless he drank more. Simply put, he drank in order to sleep, but couldn't sleep because he drank.
   - ❏ Drinking was *solving* his problem
   - ❏ Drinking was *causing* his problem

4. "My drinking kept increasing. But I thought it was because my responsibilities were increasing." This is an example of a classic symptom of alcoholism called _____.

5. Many alcoholics continue to drink, even when their drinking results in terrible problems. This behavior is another classic symptom of substance use disorder. Use the space below to list some of the problems created by the author's drinking.

6. "I had a pill for every ill, and I was sick a lot", is an example of the defense mechanism known as _____.

7. The author learned how to give up alcohol completely, while saving prescription drugs for emergencies only.
   - ❏ True
   - ❏ False

8. During his recovery, the writer learned that if he focused on the _____ environment, the _____ environment would take care of itself. He accomplishes this via the _____.

9. The writer goes out of his way to emphasize the benefits of living in the present. For example, he strives to live in the *solution* instead of the problem. He also states: "Nothing, absolutely nothing, happens in God's world by mistake." He talks about being grateful instead complaining, focusing on the good qualities rather than the defects, acting rather than waiting, and, living life on life's terms. All of these things are used to describe what the author believes is the key to recovery. That key is _____.

10. What does accepting life on life's terms, mean to you?

(Answers: 1A. He was not an alcoholic; 1B. Justification and Blame; 2. Rationalization; 3. Drinking was <u>causing</u> his problem; 4. Tolerance; 5. Not knowing whether he was coming or going from work, Forgetting advice he'd given patients on the phone, Trouble getting up in the morning, Risking his career, Using drugs to manage the drinking, Convulsions, Mental ward, Marriage trouble; 6. Justification; 7. False; 8. Internal, external, Twelve Steps; 9. Acceptance.)

10. Principles of Recovery

For ten years straight; right in the prime of my life, I indulged my darkest desires. Like Robert Louis Stevenson's character Dr. Jekyll, the more chemicals I consumed, the scarier I became. Though the specifics of your experience may differ, the characteristics of any substance use disorder are *exactly* the same for all of us with the disease.

Same Story, Different Players
Stevenson's tale is well known, of course. The kindly and respected Dr. Jekyll ingests a chemical concoction that transforms him into the darkest parts of himself: the horrible Mr. Hyde. The more the good doctor indulges his addiction and escapes into Hyde, the more powerful Hyde becomes. Inevitably the elixir stops working altogether, and he is Hyde *for good.* Isolated, paranoid, miserable... he ends his life in the same way many chemical abusers die: some intentionally, some unintentionally, all unnecessary.

Contrary to what you might think if you haven't read the story, the horror was not in the character of Hyde himself. No. It was in Dr. Jekyll's *uncontrollable craving* for the *high* of Hyde, despite the *certain knowledge* that it was getting harder to transform back. Simply put, Dr. Jekyll was terrified of what he was becoming, yet *couldn't stop* his compulsive behavior. Remind you of anyone?

Alcoholics Anonymous
Substance Use Disorder can be defined as the continued repetition of a behavior despite adverse consequences. *The Strange Case of Dr. Jekyll and Mr. Hyde* was published in 1886, but timeless are the concepts of addiction which it illustrates. If only Dr. Jekyll had met Dr. Silkworth and Bill Wilson.

Dr. Silkworth was the Director of Charles B. Towns Hospital for Drug and Alcohol Addictions, in New York City in the 1930s. He was a medical doctor specializing in the treatment of addictions. One of his patients, Bill Wilson, would go on to co-found Alcoholics Anonymous. Dr. Silkworth was influential in helping Bill Wilson realize that *alcoholism should be considered a **disease**, rather than a lack of willpower or morals.* He theorized that alcoholism had two components; an **"obsession of the mind"** together with an **"allergy of the body."** The **obsession** guarantees the alcoholic will keep drinking even when they don't want to. The **allergy** dooms the sufferer to death, insanity or jail. His revolutionary approach is so important, that his thoughts are included at the beginning of the Big Book of Alcoholics Anonymous, in the chapter entitled: The Doctor's Opinion.

Bill W (aka Bill Wilson) is a name you will hear often. As co-founder of A.A., he helped formulate the Twelve Steps and author the text. But what made all that possible was a *hopeless* dependence on alcohol. Bill Wilson was a self-described **"alcoholic of the worst sort"**; which means, you and I have much in common with him. His life and death struggle, and miraculous recovery, are described in: Bill's Story, the first chapter of the Alcoholics Anonymous text.

Initially the A.A. Big Book was used by alcoholics and addicts. As Alcoholics Anonymous grew in popularity, Narcotics Anonymous was formed, which published a text written specifically for addicts. These books contain identical concepts and principles, because Twelve Step wisdom is universal. Each book, however, contains different personal stories by alcoholics or addicts. Other basic texts that are available to you include Cocaine Anonymous: *Hope, Faith and Courage;* and Marijuana Anonymous: *Life with Hope.* As part of your recovery, you *must* read the Alcoholics Anonymous text. Purchasing a hardcopy allows you to highlight and mark. (Always read the literature with a pen and highlighter handy!) Alternatively, you can view the book *free* at www.aa.org. I strongly encourage you to read the others as well, if these drugs are trouble for you. No doubt the personal stories will hit uncomfortably close to home.

Good Person, Bad Disease
Reading The Doctor's Opinion and Bill's Story will help you understand why compulsive chemical use is a disease, and how the basic principles of recovery work. (These two chapters only appear in the Big Book of Alcoholics Anonymous.)

Many years before I got sober, a close friend gave me a copy of the Alcoholics Anonymous text. On the inside front cover he inscribed: "To my dear friend. Read this book. You will find wisdom and freedom." I looked at him cross-eyed. *What a nut-job*, I thought, as I tossed the book to the bottom of my closet where it gathered dust for the next eight years.

Unfortunately, no amount of time would cure my addiction. Eventually I was Hyde all the time. (It's weird how 'Hyde' and 'High' are so similar!) Everything good about me was stuffed so deep down inside that I feared I would never return to normal. With nothing left to lose, I rummaged through the closet and pulled out that dusty book. Then a funny thing happened. Once I started reading, I couldn't stop. I had stumbled upon a step-by-step instruction manual for happiness: No chemicals necessary. Over time, the Twelve Steps of Alcoholics Anonymous, Narcotics Anonymous and Cocaine Anonymous became the solution to all my problems. It turns out my friend wasn't the nut-job: *I was the nut-job.* Chapter two of the A.A. book is entitled: There is a Solution. Could it have been any more obvious?! Though the solution to all my problems lay on the closet floor for nearly a decade, I thank God I gave it a try when I did.

Like me, you are a good person with a bad disease. So, believe me when I say that it's never too late. Twelve Step programs like Alcoholics Anonymous saved my life, and are still the solution to all my problems as well as yours. Give it a try. What do you have to lose?

EXERCISES
Read: The Doctor's Opinion and Bill's Story (Chapter 1), and answer the questions below. Then, starting tomorrow, you are to read at least *4-pages in your book each day.* **Your objective over the next twenty-eight days is to read the first 164-pages of the A.A. Big Book. This is in addition to your daily worksheet assignment and Twelve Step meeting.**

1. Dr. Silkworth regarded his patient (Bill Wilson) as _____.

2. Alcoholism/addiction is a disease of the _____ and _____.

3. When Dr. Silkworth's patient requested permission to tell his story to other patients, he stated that he considered it a _____ to do so.

4. The effect of alcohol on chronic alcoholics is likened to an _____ of the body.

5. Alcoholics can never safely use alcohol in any form.
   ❑ True
   ❑ False

6. Emotional appeals to stop drinking or using drugs *usually* work.
   ❑ True
   ❑ False

7. A power greater than yourself is required to recover.
   ❑ Never
   ❑ Sometimes
   ❑ Most of the time

8. People drink and use drugs essentially because they like the _____.

9. When substance abusers *aren't* using, they feel _____, _____, _____.

10. After consuming alcohol or drugs over and over, the phenomenon of _____ develops.

11. When an alcoholic or addict experiences a "psychic change", they find they can easily control their desire for chemicals so long as they follow a _____ simple rules.

12. Human power alone is enough to produce this "psychic change".
    ❑ True
    ❑ False

13. The doctor believes substance abuse is more than a problem of willpower.
    ❑ True
    ❑ False

14. The one symptom shared by *all* substance abusers is the phenomenon of _____.

15. It is possible to *permanently cure* alcoholism/addiction.
    ❑ True
    ❑ False

16. According to Dr. Silkworth, recovery begins when you *believe* the plan outlined in this book.
    ❑ True
    ❑ False

17. Bill W describes how liquor ceased to be a luxury and became a _____.

18. Bill lacked the *willpower* to get sober.
    ❑ True
    ❑ False

19. Bill wasn't *smart* enough to beat alcoholism.
    ❏ True
    ❏ False

20. Bill didn't have the *guts* to get sober.
    ❏ True
    ❏ False

21. According to Bill W, *religion* is essential to recovery.
    ❏ True
    ❏ False

22. Bill learned that the power to recover originated from deep within him.
    ❏ True
    ❏ False

23. The foundation of Bill W's recovery was built on:
    ❏ Complete *belief* in a power greater than himself, or
    ❏ Complete *willingness to believe* in a power greater than himself

24. Sobriety requires:
    ❏ Humility
    ❏ Pride
    ❏ Money
    ❏ Faith
    ❏ Service
    ❏ Perfection
    ❏ Honesty
    ❏ A recovery program
    ❏ Something more powerful than you
    ❏ A life without trouble and misery
    ❏ Religion

25. Through A.A. or N.A., you will learn a way of living which answers _____ your problems.

26. The solution is simple, *but not easy.* The *price* to be paid is the destruction of _____.

(Answers: 1. Hopeless; 2. Body and mind; 3. Privilege; 4. Allergy; 5. True; 6. False; 7. Most of the time; 8. Effect; 9. Restless, irritable, discontent; 10. Craving; 11. Few; 12. False; 13. True; 14. Craving; 15. False; 16. False (Accept); 17. Necessity; 18. False; 19. False; 20. False; 21. False; 22. False; 23. Complete willingness to believe in a power greater than himself; 24. Humility, Faith, Service, Honesty, A recovery program, something more powerful than you; 25. All; 26. Self-centeredness.)

11. Is My Life Really Out of Control?

TWELVE STEP CONCEPT
STEP ONE - We admit we are powerless over our addiction - that our lives have become unmanageable.

INSPIRATION
"What sort of thinking dominates an alcoholic who repeats time after time the desperate experiment of the first drink? Friends who have reasoned with him after a spree which has brought him to the point of divorce or bankruptcy are mystified when he walks directly into a saloon. Why does he? Of what is he thinking?" (Big Book, page 35)

According to the American Psychiatric Association, substance use disorder is characterized by the eleven criteria specified below. Indicate which have applied to you over the past twelve months:

- ☐ **Compulsion.** Do you sometimes use more or for a longer time than you would like? Do you sometimes drink to get drunk? Do you stop after a few, or does one lead to more?

- ☐ **Persistent desire to quit or unsuccessful efforts to quit or control substance use.** Have you wanted to quit? Have you tried and failed to quit or cut down?

- ☐ **Much time/activity to obtain, use, recover.** Have you spent excessive amounts of time planning to use, obtaining, using, concealing and recovering from drugs and alcohol? Do you daydream about getting drunk or high? Have you spent time scheming of ways to avoid getting caught?

- ☐ **Craving.** Do you experience an overwhelming desire or urge to use? When you think of alcohol or drugs do you experience a physical reaction such as increased heart rate, sweaty palms, a burst of pleasurable feelings etc.

- ☐ **Failure to fulfill major role obligations.** Has substance use interfered with your responsibilities at work, school or home? Do you blow off events, or call in sick in order to use or recover?

- ☐ **Use despite recurrent social or interpersonal problems.** Have you continued to use chemicals even though it interferes with your ability to interact with others?

- ☐ **Isolation.** Has substance use caused you to withdraw from participating in social, occupational or recreational activities?

- ☐ **Use in physically hazardous situations.** Have you continued to drink or use even though it places you in physically dangerous situations? Have you gotten a DUI?

- ☐ **Use despite recurrent physical or psychological problems.** Do you continue to use even though you have a physical or psychological ailment that is likely to have been caused or worsened by the substance?

- ☐ **Tolerance.** Do you continue to need more of the substance to get the same high?

❏ **Withdrawal.** When you stop using, do you ever experience 1.) characteristic withdrawal syndrome including irritability, anxiety, shakes, sweats, nausea or vomiting; or 2.) the need to take the substance (or a closely related substance) to relieve or avoid withdrawal symptoms?

_____ *Total boxes checked. Interpret your score as follows: 2 – 3 = Mild substance use disorder, 4 – 5 = Moderate substance use disorder, and 6+ = Severe substance use disorder.*

Willpower Is Way Overrated
As you can see, to be diagnosed as having a substance use disorder you need answer *Yes* to only *two* of these questions. Think for a moment. Before today you may have gone quite a long time abusing drugs and alcohol. In fact you might not even remember just how long other than knowing they have always been there for you. All this time you've suffered under the misconception that others possess the strength, smarts, courage, fortitude, character, self-control and common sense to manage their drug and alcohol use, while you were born weak-willed, defective, a dummy or hopeless loser It's time now for you to know the truth. None of these labels apply, because *substance use disorder has nothing to do with willpower or any other personal quality.*

In 1956, the American Medical Association recognized alcoholism as a physiological disease. Like other diseases, alcoholism is **chronic, progressive, symptomatic with a predictable pattern or course, and can be fatal.** Did it strike you odd that at least two of the eleven criteria (specified above) fit your behavior exactly? After all, don't you believe your circumstances, childhood, career or lack of employment, marriage, finances, health, anxiety, legal trouble, etc. to be entirely unique? How could anyone possibly know you so completely? Are both the American Psychiatric Association and the American Medical Association wrong and you right?

The Framework Provided by Alcoholics Anonymous
Doctor Bob, co-founder of Alcoholics Anonymous, reframes the disease concept in: The Doctor's Opinion, found at the beginning of the Big Book of Alcoholics Anonymous. He writes that addiction can be thought of as: **"An allergy of the body, together with an obsession of the mind".** Though written decades ago, this way of thinking is wholly compatible with the disease model and still just as valid today. Simply put, your body doesn't react to alcohol and drugs like others. You are in the minority of drinkers and drug users who, over time, experience **catastrophic consequences** yet continue to ingest larger and larger quantities.

Many recovering alcoholics and addicts are shocked to find they are not alone. They become overwhelmed with relief to learn their personal struggle is so well documented in so much literature and shared experience. Like others before you, you might find yourself powerfully drawn to know more about the disease that's killing you. You are encouraged to read about the allergy and obsession of every addict and alcoholic in great detail in the A.A. Big Book as well as countless other books. Start with the list of recommended sources in the appendix. Such efforts will be greatly rewarded. Education leads to a new attitude, making it possible to forgive, even love yourself once more. For now it is enough to know that the fellowship of A.A. joins with the American Psychiatric Association and the American Medical Association in agreement that *addiction is not a matter of willpower*. It is a treatable disease.

> "When I first got sober, the feeling of waking up with a clean and clear mind was the ***best*** experience I had *ever* had; certainly better than any high on drugs. What a waste of so many years!" (Hope, Faith & Courage, page 70)

Can You Get 100% Honest?
If you are reading this, you are already sober. Likely you're reminded of this fact as each hour of these first days drag on. You might be going through detox, in pain, exhausted, groggy, pissed off, fearful, anxious or highly emotional; possibly all of these things at once and more. But you are *not* drinking and using. We call this: **abstinence**, which is the same as being **sober**, and it is to be entirely free from drugs and alcohol. *But sobriety isn't the same as recovery.* Believe it or not, quitting alcohol and drugs was the easy part. Now the work can really begin.

In the big picture of things, compulsive substance use was never really the main problem, only a *symptom*. You use to feel "normal" by numbing yourself to emotion. So, when you refrain from drinking and drugging how are you to feel… Ab-normal? *That is a lie you tell to protect yourself from the truth because if you knew the truth you would have to face the fact you are delusional.* Lying makes you feel more comfortable, but in the long run you just feel alone. The A.A. Twelve Steps and Twelve Traditions book labels this underlying feeling **"soul-sickness."** The Big Book calls it a **"spiritual malady."** In simplest terms it is the part of you that feels like you're different from other people, you don't fit in, and you just can't cope like others can. This is the heart of your *DIES-ease* as well as your recovery.

Recovery can be thought of as what takes place when soul-sickness is finally confronted. It is a lifetime of living to the fullest, overcoming life's challenges in a healthy manner without drinking, *one day at a time*. It is learning how to stop, think and plan before acting. There is *no* known cure to this disease, but you can force it into **remission** and keep it there starting right now. That's good news. You are now a *recovering* addict and alcoholic. Your counseling, therapy, homework assignments, fellowship, meetings and other treatment tools are designed to help you break through your addiction, challenge beliefs, change behaviors and heal. Don't be surprised if you flourish in a short time.

The Big Book says: **"To drink is to die."** Addiction kills! You will recover, go to jail or die. That's it. Stop beating up on yourself. Any thought of *controlling* your alcohol and drug use is an utter illusion, or shall we say **delusion!** You have as much chance of reversing your male pattern baldness or eradicating hypertension by simply wishing it away.

EXERCISES
1. **Describe the last time you used drugs or drank when you did not want to.**

2. Describe all the different ways in which you tried to limit your drinking and drug use.

3. How have you lied to cover up your chemical use? How did you feel about yourself afterward?

4. People who are insane lose control over their behavior. They do things when they are under the influence that they would never do when sober. Describe three times you lost control over your *behavior* when drunk or high.

5. Circle the number that best represents where you fall on the following scale:

Measuring Your Self-Worth Today

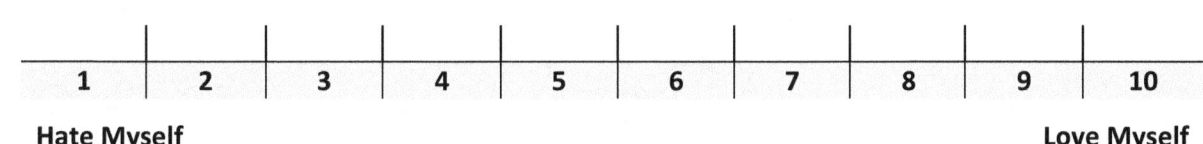

Hate Myself   Love Myself

6. Describe what a "10" (on the scale above) would look like.

7. What are the legitimate responsibilities you blow off when you are drinking or using?

8. You must have worthwhile reasons to work toward a clean and sober lifestyle. List all your reasons for wanting to recover, and why. Start with reasons related to health, legal, relationships and employment.

12. Why is Spirituality So Important to Recovery?

TWELVE STEP CONCEPT
STEP TWO - Came to believe that a Power greater than ourselves could restore us to sanity.
STEP THREE - Made a decision to turn our will and lives over to the care of God as we understand Him.

INSPIRATION
"It is only when a man has tried everything else, when in utter desperation and terrific need he turns to something *bigger than himself*, that he gets a glimpse of the way out. It is then that contempt is replaced by hope, and hope by fulfillment." (Experience, Strength & Hope page 130)

Lasting recovery from a substance use disorder requires you plunge into the sober lifestyle with both feet. Of course, it would be a lot easier if you were merely standing on the side of the pool rather than stepping out on the precarious end of the high-dive platform. But the high-dive platform is where you find yourself, and *its decision time*. Will you crawl back down the ladder into your bottle of booze or pills to stay stuck, afraid and alone, exactly where you are? Or will you close your eyes, place yourself in the hands of a *stronger something* than you, and step into the unknown?

If you choose to follow the Twelve Steps of Alcoholics Anonymous, you will quickly find it to be a spiritual program. The Big Book says on page 45: **"Its main object is to enable you to find a Power greater than yourself which will solve your problem. That means we have written a book which we believe to be spiritual as well as moral."** Did you catch that? According to the text, its "**main objective**" is to help you find a higher power. Why so important? Because your higher power will "**solve**" your problem.

"But you have to be *religious* to have a higher power", I often hear. Wrong. *Religion is for people who are afraid they'll go to hell. Spirituality is for people who have been there* goes the saying. Spirituality is the understanding that you have *inestimable worth*: that you are *priceless* at the cellular level. The dictionary defines *priceless* as "impossible to put a value on." And exactly what is it you do that makes you so precious? Nothing! You are valuable for who you are, because you *are*. Therefore, you are neither the sum of your accomplishments *nor* your screw-ups. Isn't that fantastic news! *Learning to redefine yourself as a child of God: however you understand Him, will bring you positive self-esteem, freedom from shame, and power to change!* Translation... One moment you're at the end of the high-dive platform; the next you're flying through the air under God's protection. That's exhilarating.

> "Belief in a higher power takes you out of your universe and offers peace of mind and serenity by awareness that there is a power that is *not restricted* by *your* weaknesses and limitations." (Staying Sober, page 78)

You should also know that once you take that step, there is no going back. Why do you think it's called a *leap* of faith! The Big Book of Alcoholics Anonymous says: **"Half measures availed us nothing"**. It talks about being **thorough, complete, fearless, rigorously honest** and to **"let go absolutely."** The end of the high-dive platform is what the Big Book calls the "**turning point.**" It's where you ask your higher power for His protection and care with *complete abandon,* then release yourself. Millions of fellow alcoholics and addicts before you took the very same course, and became sober and happier than they ever dreamed because of it. Why not you?

What Is a Higher Power?
Many people already have **a god of their own understanding**, though the relationship may need rekindling. If the concept is unfamiliar or unwelcome to you, remember it must be a god of *your own personal* understanding. Many people defer to the collective wisdom of their A.A. or N.A. group as god, which is a nice benefit of working a Twelve Step program. Others select the majesty of the mountains or the sea. The Big Book affords great leeway in your selection: "**We found that God does not make too hard terms with those who seek Him. The Realm of Spirit is broad, roomy, all inclusive; never exclusive or forbidding to those who earnestly seek.**" That doesn't sound like religion to me.

Chapter 4 of the A.A. text is entitled: We Agnostics. It is devoted specifically to answering questions about a higher power and what that relationship is supposed to look like. Page 55 sums it up as follows: "**We finally saw that faith in some kind of God was a part of our make-up, just as much as the feeling we have for a friend. Sometimes we had to search fearlessly, but He was there. He was as much a fact as we were. We found the Great Reality deep down within us. In the last analysis it is only there that He may be found.**"

Building Your Recovery Plan from the Ground Up
Turn to page 59 of your Big Book. Draw a line beneath the Third Step. In the margin to the right of the first three Steps, write **"TRUST GOD,"** because sobriety begins with a stronger something than you. After all, how long have you failed at being your own rehab center: months, years, decades?

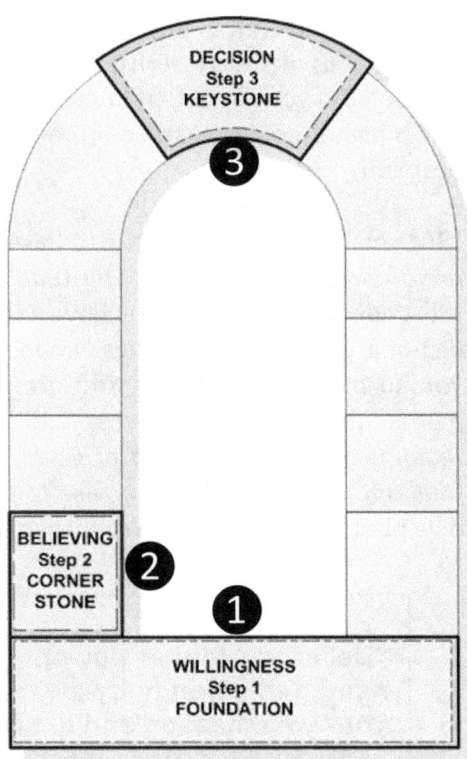

Let's look at it another way. Putting together your recovery plan is a lot like constructing a building. The first step is to lay the **foundation**. The foundation of A.A. is a **willingness** to try. To the left of Step One, on page 59, write **"Foundation"** (1).

Once the foundation is complete its time to lay the first stone, called the **cornerstone**. The cornerstone is the very first stone laid in any construction. It is critical, since all other stones will be set in reference to that one stone. Thus, the single cornerstone determines the position of the *entire* structure or your lifetime of sobriety. On page 59, to the left of Step Two, write **"Cornerstone." Belief** in a higher power is the cornerstone of your recovery. That *stronger something* loves you unconditionally despite your shortcomings, is supremely dependable, and **"will *solve* your problem"** (2).

To raise your sobriety from the dirt into the air, you will need a **keystone**. A keystone is the larger stone at the tippy-top of an arch. As the last stone to be set, it locks the whole arch together. On page 59, to the left of Step Three, write **"Keystone"** (3). The keystone of your recovery is your **decision** to forgo your ego, and turn this whole business of recovery, and your place in the world, over to God.

Surrender Trumps Understanding!
Perhaps you're still uncomfortable with the whole *God thing.* Your skepticism might be made all the worse due to your current state of mind. Likely your brain is still too foggy to make an informed decision on such an important issue. This is to be expected. For now, however, *to save your life,* you must abandon your best thinking and **"let go absolutely"**, **"think yourself into a new way of acting"** and **"fake it till you make it"** if you have to, for good reason. A.A., N.A. and other recovery fellowships are a living history of continued success. Every day, in meetings all over the world, recovering alcoholics and addicts recount brutal stories of addiction, desperation, humiliation and near-death, followed always by their miraculous rebirth and freedom from bondage. Having made so many *insane* choices in the past, surrendering now to whatever you choose to call divine: *based solely on the overwhelming evidence available*, seems surprisingly reasonable. Yes? Each day, people step onto airplanes without possessing a shred of knowledge as to how they fly, don't they?

What Keeps *You* Frozen, Afraid and Alone At the Turning Point?
The strongest opponent in your fight for sobriety is *yourself.* The Big Book says: **"the root cause of drinking and drugging is selfishness,"** which is also referred to as **"self-will run riot"** (page 62.) It keeps you sick, stuck and scared, while draining every last drop of hope, joy and self-esteem from your life. And while you're busy obsessing, your focus is off of the big picture: your value in the universe. All day long you're listening to the toxic tape recorder in your head telling you that you're a failed mother or loser of a son; that the world would be a brighter place if you just crawled up and died; that you will never dig yourself out of the hole you're in; that God isn't big enough etc. *Lies, lies and more lies.* Fear prevents you from **letting go and letting God**. No wonder God's most frequently repeated command is **"Fear Not"**, appearing 366 times in the Bible. (One for each day of the year!)

Why Is Spirituality so Important?
Your fear is *irrational,* just as your obsession with self is *delusional. Selfishness is killing you!* But where you have made a mess of your life, God, or a power greater then you, can make a miracle. You can break free of this miserable, Groundhog Day lifestyle. You can be restored to sanity, one day at a time. Success is *guaranteed,* if only you make the decision and then act. It is wise to remember: **"God is God and you aren't."** Why is Spirituality so important? *Because it will save your life!* It's time to take a leap of faith!

EXERCISES
1. Describe the religious environment of your childhood. What was it like? What did you learn.

2. What are some of the things that have greater power than you do?

3. Who or what do you choose to call the *cornerstone* of your recovery, and why?

4. What decision have you made that will serve as the *keystone* of your recovery, and why?

5. Who was the most trustworthy person you ever knew? How so? How did they treat you?

6. What do you need to see happen in order to prove to yourself that you are trustworthy?

7. Describe three characteristics or qualities of God or your higher power.

8. Give examples of your willingness to trust in a higher power. What are you willing to entrust to your higher power? When, why and how?

9. Addicts and alcoholics are terrible at playing god. How has your own self-will run riot?

10. List the things you have to gain and to lose by turning your will and life over to a higher power:

THINGS I HAVE TO GAIN	THINGS I HAVE TO LOSE

11. If you already draw strength from The Bible, then it's important to know exactly where to find those words of comfort when they're needed most. An optional assignment: *The Big Book and The Good Book*, is included in the appendix. It can help reconnect you to the ultimate power source, or plug you in for the first time.

13. The Serenity Prayer

TWELVE STEP CONCEPT
"God, grant me the serenity to accept the things I cannot change;
The courage to change the things I can;
And the wisdom to know the difference. Amen"

The Serenity Prayer is as much a part of Alcoholics Anonymous as the Big Book itself. It is recited daily at every Twelve Step meeting worldwide. Chances are, you will memorize the verse without much effort. That's a good thing. It's rare that you find so few words that embody principles which people hold so dear. Compare the Serenity Prayer to the Star Spangled Banner or the Gettysburg Address. They are simple yet eloquent, noble, and most of all, powerful.

The history of A.A. is meticulously documented. Far less is known about the Serenity Prayer. For example, do you realize that the Serenity Prayer appears nowhere in the Big Book? Don't be a robot, mechanically grasping hands and reciting empty words at the conclusion of a meeting. It's not about words. It's about what the words *mean to you*. We know what serenity did for Bill Wilson: co-founder of Alcoholics Anonymous. In the chapter: Bills Story, on page 14 of the Big Book, he describes the exact moment he found serenity: "**…the effect was electric. There was a sense of victory, followed by such a peace and serenity as I had never known. There was utter confidence. I felt lifted up; as though the great clean wind of a mountain top blew through and through.**"

How extraordinary Bill Wilson must have felt, to be renewed after years of punishing drinking and catastrophic loss, and at a time when there appeared to be no hope whatsoever! Only a few pages before (on page 8), he paints the grim picture of where his life was headed as a result of alcoholism. He states: "**No words can tell of the loneliness and despair I found in that bitter morass of self-pity. Quicksand stretched around me in all directions. I had met my match. I had been overwhelmed. Alcohol was my master… Everyone became resigned to the certainty that I would have to be shut up somewhere, or would stumble along to a miserable end.**" Understand? When all was said and done, Bill Wilson was faced with just two choices; serenity, or hellish pain.

Do you want that extraordinary feeling described by Bill Wilson? What are you willing to do to get it? If you are sick and tired of being sick and tired, *and are willing to do anything to change,* then you will find serenity: electric, victorious, peaceful, certain, uplifting, clean serenity. How can I be sure? Because 100% of the folks that work a rigorous program of recovery, do. I am one of them. Understanding the Serenity Prayer will provide unique insight into recovery, as you tap into the power behind the prayer.

Origin of the Serenity Prayer
American theologian Dr. Reinhold Niebuhr is credited with first committing the Serenity Prayer to paper, as part of a sermon in 1943; although it was used in prayers as early as 1934. They were always printed as a single sentence. The earliest published form of the prayer attributed to Niebuhr, is from a Christian student publication which states: "Father, give us courage to change what must be altered, serenity to accept what cannot be helped, and the insight to know the one from the other."

Bill Wilson modified the prayer, and began distributing it through the fellowship in 1941. Notice that the original version asks first for *courage,* followed by *serenity.* However, the modern version juxtaposes the first two lines, asking for serenity first, followed by courage. I suspect the difference is due to the enormous ego that afflicts all of us with a substance use disorder. We take on so much, push so hard and are so charged-up by addictive thinking that it becomes impossible to recognize when we run into something we cannot change no matter how much effort we throw at it. Consequently, we need to *change the way we think altogether*. Acceptance of reality must become a way of life if we want to recover. *Acceptance must become our new drug!*

Understand What You are Asking For

1. **God...** Not a *religion*, but a *relationship* with something more powerful than you. It can be God, Jesus the ocean, the wind etc. In early recovery, many people select their Twelve Step group or sponsor. Why? Because people with more sobriety then you are wiser than you when it comes to recovery. For example, once a trial is concluded and turned over to the jury, the jury becomes the higher power. Why? Because a dozen brains are better than one. Do you need a higher power? *Twelve Step based programs make it clear that nothing else will remove the obsession to use chemicals.* Page 44 of the Big Book states: **"If a mere code of morals or a better philosophy of life were sufficient to overcome alcoholism, many of us would have recovered long ago. But we found that such codes and philosophies did not save us, no matter how much we tried. We could wish to be moral, we could wish to be philosophically comforted, in fact, we could will these things with all our might, but the needed power wasn't there. Our human resources, as marshaled by the will, were not sufficient; they failed utterly. Lack of power; that was our dilemma. We had to find a power by which we could live, and it had to be a Power greater than ourselves. Obviously."**

"Failed utterly." Remember that. It's time to open your eyes. Are all of those people, who recovered before you and around you, any different from you? Many were worse off then you are now. So how did they get sober? Are they smarter, better looking, or do they have more willpower than you? Go to meetings. Listen to their stories. Ask them when the miracle began. They'll tell you it began with the acceptance of, and reliance on, a higher power.

Nor are you any different than Bill Wilson. He believed *something* was out there. He just didn't know what. He says, he: **"had little doubt that a mighty purpose and rhythm underlay all"** in the universe. **"But that was as far as I had gone"** (page 10.) Then, something happened to radically change his thinking. One day his old drinking buddy dropped by for a visit. Bill looked forward to an afternoon of binge drinking together. But, when his friend arrived, he was much different then Bill remembered: **"The door opened and he stood there, fresh-skinned and glowing. There was something about his eyes. He was inexplicably different. What had happened?"** (page 9.)

Bill's friend was sober, and Bill finally began to understand what it takes: **"...my friend sat before me, and he made the pointblank declaration that God had done for him what he could not do for himself. His human will had failed. Doctors had pronounced him incurable. Society was about to lock him up. Like myself, he had admitted complete defeat. Then he had, in effect, been raised from the dead, suddenly taken from the scrap heap to a level of life better than the best he had ever known! Had this power originated in him? Obviously it had not. There had been no more power in him than there was in me at that minute; and this was none at all"**. **"That floored me"** (page 11.)

2. **Grant me...** Not a *free gift*, but something earned working a program of recovery.

3. **Serenity...** Viewing reality free of delusional thinking. It is the serenity that goes along with having a sane mind.

4. **Accept the things I cannot change...** The key word is "cannot", which means *impossible* no matter how much effort. Alcoholics and addicts don't like these words! We bang our head against the wall trying to change the impossible, rather than simply acknowledging reality. We like to "die on every hill", as the saying goes, rather than pick and choose the fights that are really worthwhile and that can be won. For example, if we are involved in a traffic accident in which we are not at fault, then there is no way: absolutely no way on God's green earth, that we could have changed things. *Yet, we become full of resentment anyhow.* We yell at the other driver, as if they could take it all back and leave us to go on our way untouched. Why? Because of our GINORMOUS egos. We think that *giving in* is the same as *giving up. It's not!* It is a healthy decision based on the evidence in front of our noses.

5. **Courage to change the things I can...** *You are never powerless.* That is reality also. You have *some* control in *any* situation, even if that means controlling nothing but your *attitude. We are what we choose to be.* For example, choosing to be calm after being hit by another driver means you changed the one thing over which you had control. It takes real courage to make these sorts of changes, because change is uncomfortable. We'd rather **sit in our dirty diaper.** For Bill Wilson, radically changing his attitude took nothing short of a miracle. Faced with the reality of his sober friend, Bill states: **"My ideas about miracles were drastically revised right then. Never mind the musty past; here sat a miracle directly across the kitchen table."**

6. **Wisdom to know the difference...** Wisdom is gained by experiencing life. It is what you learn from mistakes and earn from triumphs. It is an insight into reality. It is a filter, yardstick and roadmap combined. It is your Swiss Army knife. Wisdom is invaluable because *you paid for it dearly* with every mistake you've made. *For that reason, I advise you to never forget what you've been through.* Hold on to painful memories. Hold them tightly. Wear your battle scars proudly. No longer are they mistakes. They have been transformed. Now they are wisdom.

The Power Behind the Prayer
This particular worksheet contains more direct quotes from the Big Book of Alcoholics Anonymous than any other assignment in your AT HOME RECOVERY HANDBOOK treatment plan, with the majority coming from Bill's Story. Why? Am I simply cramming as much A.A. down your throat as I can get away with? Certainly not... You'll either get through the material or you won't.

Because Bill Wilson so vividly describes his transformation from delusional mind to serene mind, you can live the experience through *his* eyes. In trusting his friend, Bill found that a higher power could succeed: and succeed spectacularly, where he failed so miserably, so long as he didn't let his ego get in the way.

EGO = Edging God Out

If you believe his retelling of events, *then Bill Wilson is a power greater than you.* And, if that's true, then so is the fellowship of A.A. and N.A. That's great news. It means you are not stumbling around in the dark. The path to serenity is clear. It also means *you don't have to make all the mistakes yourself!* You can add to your own wisdom the wisdom of Bill Wilson, your group, your sponsor and everything A.A. and N.A.

Have you ever played an old vinyl LP album that is marred by a small scratch? What happens when the phonograph needle hits the scratch? It can't advance any longer, so it keeps playing the same phrase over and over and over. If you don't act, the needle will eventually turn that tiny blemish into a deep groove. Then the only way to play the rest of the record is to physically lift the needle out of the groove.

That is exactly where you are at this moment. I encourage you to rely on something greater than yourself for the courage to remove the needle from the groove in your life caused by drugs and alcohol. Beyond the abyss is a future where buying, using, hiding, lying, resenting, fearing, losing and doing it all over again the next day, isn't a full-time job. The serenity described by Bill Wilson and experienced by countless others is available to you too. Now *that's* power!

EXERCISES
1. **Using a dictionary, define the following words:**
    A. Serenity.

    B. Courage.

    C. Wisdom.

2. **Use your imagination and describe in detail what serenity looks like physically, mentally, socially and spiritually.**

3. Give examples of things you have NO control over and that cause you frustration. (God, grant me the serenity to accept the things I cannot change.)

4. Give examples of things you DO have the ability to control, but have not. (The courage to change the things I can.)

4. How can knowing something *ahead of time*, save you pain and expense? (The wisdom to know the difference.)

5. **Nothing in life comes easy. Bill Wilson says; "Thus was I convinced that God is concerned with us humans when we want Him enough" (A.A. Big Book, page 33.) The Big Book also says; "half measures availed us nothing" (page 59.) Would you believe that the Bible says the exact same thing? Using a Bible, turn to Deuteronomy 4:29. The writer says that if you look for God you will find Him. But only if you search with all your _____ and all your _____.**

6. **In your own words, describe what it takes for you, personally, to connect with a Higher Power.**

14. The Meaning of Recovery

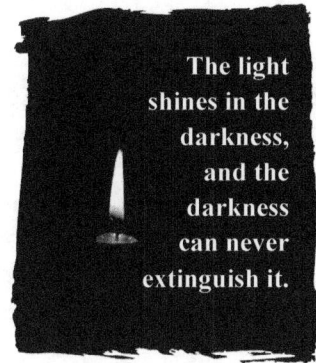

The light shines in the darkness, and the darkness can never extinguish it.

As you undertake your journey to recovery, it's important to understand what it is you are working so hard to attain. There are many definitions of **recovery**. As professionals learn more about substance use disorders, our understanding of recovery evolves too. Recently, the Substance Abuse Mental Health Services Administration (SAMHSA) released a new definition of recovery from substance use disorders. It states: "Recovery is a process of change through which individuals improve their health and wellness, live a self-directed life, and strive to reach their full potential." What does that mean for you?

The Spark of Hope
There is really only one reason why you have bought into the promise that your life can change when, previously, that notion seemed impossible. The reason, is because you now have *hope*. Hope is defined as: "A *feeling* that something desirable is *likely* to happen." Hope resides within each of us. It lives even though we do our best to drown it with alcohol, smother it beneath powder and pills, and use negative thinking to forget it even exists.

Somehow, the spark of hope was ignited within you. Maybe you were inspired to hope by someone close to you who believes in you, just as you might inspire someone who feels as hopeless as you once did. Many people in recovery are convinced that it was a **divine** spark that put them on the road to recovery. Otherwise, they are at a loss to explain how they could have stumbled upon something as precious as hope, while trudging the desolate landscape of hopelessness. You will regularly hear them speak of recovery as a "gift" and a "miracle". The very idea that God would give you such a gift, *especially* when you are doing... well... all those disgraceful things we do when we are in our disease, may be laughable. However, it is absolutely true.

Recovery is All-Consuming, Enduring and Addictive
As you learned, substance abuse is a whole body, or **bio-psycho-social** disease. No part of your life is left untouched. You become physically rundown and emotionally sick. Sometimes the damage is irreversible. Spiritually, you become disconnected from God. Distorted thinking causes you to repeat the same destructive behaviors again and again, impairing the brain's chemical reward system and stealing away your joy and purpose for living. As a result, you cannot function productively at your job, nor can you maintain healthy relationships with family and friends. You end up isolated, broken and empty. That's if you live through it at all.

Therefore, recovery is nothing if not a complete **rebirth:** a *make-over* of the body, mind and spirit. By rejecting the old lifestyle, you are taking a stand. No more: **"sick and tired of being sick and tired."** Accepting that your life is out of your control, and that your best thinking got you into this mess, is the first step of a program designed to free you of lies, shame, pride and isolation.

Hope cannot be confined to your brain or your heart, contrary to what you might read in greeting cards. Rather, it grows into a flame that alights your whole being. In doing so, it becomes tenaciously difficult to kill off. When you recover, *your entire life will be affected for the better*. The thought of returning to the old lifestyle will make you feel so disgusted that you will want to run the other way.

It feels *good* to have hope. You nurture the spark by taking action. You take action by learning about recovery and acting on what you learn, with the confident assurance that God will do the rest. As a result, the more hope you feel, the more you want. You will get greedy for hope!

Recovery Requires Forgiveness and Love
Start with yourself! Family members, friends and employers love you. So do the people in the rooms of Alcoholics Anonymous and other programs. Surround yourself with people who believe you can recover, and who offer hope, support and encouragement. Substance use disorders meet all the criteria of a *disease,* and are recognized as such by the medical community. **"You are a good person with a bad disease."** Don't allow shame to defeat you. Your substance use disorder is a part of you, but it does not *define* you. Tools like the Twelve Steps allow you to shed toxic feelings and regain self-worth. They also provide the means to forgive others who have wronged you. If you want to gain the serenity that comes with working a recovery program, then you cannot afford to hold on to resentments.

Recovery is an Individual Sport *and* a Team Sport
In recovery, **your side of the street** won't look the same as anybody else's. That's because you have unique needs, strengths, character flaws, preferences and experiences. For example, oftentimes people abuse substances because they are self medicating another disorder. In fact, this is always a possibility, since fifty-percent of those with a substance use disorder have a co-occurring mental disorder.

While the range of support tools and programs are the same for everyone, more emphasis should be placed on mastering some topics or skills over others. Besides mental health, your particular needs may differ from the needs of others in the areas of anger management, communication, physical health, spiritual health and financial health. (AT HOME RECOVERY HANDBOOK includes all of these topics as either essential or optional subject matter.)

Who decides on your customized course of treatment, is what makes recovery a *team* sport. Take advantage of all you can. Your team members can include: physicians, psychiatrists, psychologists, therapists, certified alcohol and drug counselors, Twelve Step programs, alternative programs such as Practical Recovery, alternative faith-based programs such as Celebrate Recovery, sponsors, sober fellows, clinics, rehabs, detox facilities, places of worship, career counselors, fitness coaches, financial planners, Zen masters. All of these resources are available in your community. Many are available at no charge. For a list of resources, see the appendix.

The Unopened Gift
If recovery is, indeed, a gift from God, then it is here, waiting to be opened by you. *Not* opening the gift would be a terrible, terrible waste. Why? Because, you don't know what's inside it! If you don't open the gift, then you will never know what you can truly accomplish. All that intelligence, creativity and drive will be lost; ignored because of your disease. It will be as if you never possessed them at all. And, you will miss out on knowing *real* peace, *in your own skin*, *without* the need for drugs or drink.

Go on. Open your gift.

> **GOLDEN RULE OF RECOVERY:**
>
> *You don't recover from addiction by not using. You recover by creating a new life where it is easier to not use.*

EXERCISES

1. How does the dictionary define: "rebirth"?

2. How has your disease attacked you physically, mentally, socially and spiritually:
    A. Physically.

    B. Mentally.

    C. Socially.

    D. Spiritually.

3. Recovery empowers you to reach your full potential. Describe the goals you've set for yourself.

4. List the major steps to achieving each of your goals?

15. Finding and Working with a Twelve Step Sponsor

Now that you know something about Twelve Step programs, it's time to ask someone to sponsor you.

You probably have a hard time believing that anyone would actually *volunteer* to spend time with you, given the things you've done to feed your disease, the chaos you've cultivated, the pain you have caused; even the mood you are in at this particular moment. It's difficult to understand why someone who is further down the road of recovery would be willing to double back just to help *you*: a total stranger. *I must have to pay them, or do their laundry, or at least walk their dog;* you're thinking. *Nobody does anything for free, right?!*

Most people in early recovery, find the idea of sponsorship very uncomfortable. Odds are good that you are, *at this very moment*, questioning whether you need a sponsor too, or whether you're the *exception to the rule* and can recover without one. Such is the nature of our disease that we automatically rebel against anyone giving us direction. We say it's beige when they say it's white. We ignore them when they tell us to turn, and continue going straight ahead. When they tell us to get a sponsor, we reassure them that we don't need to cozy up to some stranger. Can you relate? I certainly can.

Here's the problem. Working with a sponsor is a *vital* part of recovery. In fact there isn't a single, sound reason to go it alone. The only thing standing between you and recovery, is your disease. Substance use disorder prevents you from thinking logically. **Logical thinking** is the process of collecting facts and making an informed decision. Instead, you make decisions based on **superficial reasoning**, which is also called **addictive thinking**. Superficial reasoning is the opposite of logical thinking. You start with the decision *first*, and then come up with facts supporting that decision. So, *you* start with the decision that you *do not* need a sponsor, and then invent reasons that support your decision. Unfortunately, you can't trust your head, because your best thinking got you here!

Characteristics and Responsibilities of Sponsors
Alcoholics Anonymous defines a sponsor as **"an alcoholic who has made some progress in the recovery program, and who shares that experience on a continuous, individual basis with another who is attempting to attain or maintain sobriety through A.A."** So you see, sponsors don't attend a school or training program to learn how to work with others. They become sponsors the same way you will, one day, become a sponsor: by working their own recovery program and passing it on.

Each sponsor is the product of his or her own unique experience, so their style and stories will vary. However, you can expect every sponsor to share the same responsibilities. *Your sponsor's primary duty is to help you work the Twelve Steps!* A sponsor will walk you through the A.A. or N.A. text, educating you on the program and answering your questions. They will help you work each of the Twelve Steps, one at a time, by giving you assignments, holding you accountable, and motivating you.

A sponsor is supposed to be a safe person whom you can learn to trust and count on. When you're experiencing a craving or facing a crisis, your sponsor will answer the telephone *when nobody else will*. They act as a *mirror*, helping you to look at yourself honestly. A sponsor has *been* where you are. They are straight-shooters who will call you on your bull. At the same time, they understand your pain and frustration, and *won't judge* you.

What you learn from your sponsor, you will one day pass to someone *you* sponsor. Sponsors model healthy behavior. In that respect, think of your sponsor as a **mentor**. One characteristic shared by all sponsors, is the desire to remain sober themselves. Hence, they are willing to do *anything* to support their own recovery. According to A.A. **"you keep sobriety by giving it away"**. It means that someone will sponsor you because the act of sharing their **experience, strength and hope** is as important to *their* recovery as it is to *yours*. So, sponsors don't volunteer for *free*. Their payoff is a stronger recovery for themselves. That's how we stay humble.

Sponsors provide a non-threatening means for you to step out of your comfort zone. I found this characteristic of sponsorship to be especially important to me, personally, because I was so used to avoiding other people. You will meet with your sponsor to do Step work. Oftentimes, the meetings will occur in a public place with a social atmosphere, like a coffee shop or food joint. Or, you can meet at your house or theirs. Perhaps you will arrange to drive together to and from meetings. Simply interacting with your sponsor, will help you develop the communication skills necessary for building relationships. Sponsors act as a gateway to friendships with others in recovery, as well. Through him or her, you will meet *safe* people who may, over time, prove to be worthy friends.

What Sponsors DO NOT Do
As you can see, it's hard to argue against working with a sponsor.

Remember that members *volunteer* because it is important for *their own* recovery. However, sponsors *will not* do the heavy lifting for you. That would rob you of your dignity. They will not *force* you to stay sober. If you want to go out and get loaded again... go right ahead. If you don't, pick up the phone and call your sponsor.

A sponsor is not your therapist, substance abuse counselor, priest, *BFF,* or the parent you never had. They won't try to trick you or get inside your head. (They already know what's there!) They should never try to control you. Of course, they should never take advantage of you.

The Human Connection
By now, you have been to enough meetings and observed enough members to have some idea as to who might be a good fit for you. Likely you're also feeling extremely uncomfortable with the idea of letting someone *you barely know* into your rather complicated life. You might be embarrassed or think you are so screwed up that no one will want to deal with you. That's normal. However, the disease (or *DIS*-ease) that lives inside you will likely seize on those feelings and blow them way out of proportion.

The worst thing you can do is over-think the sponsor thing. Identifying people who might make a good sponsor, couldn't be easier. They sit all around you every day at Twelve Step meetings. Listen for someone with more sobriety than you, and with whom you have something in common (such as your drug of choice, circumstances, occupation, hobby, pet etc.) That will make relating to them much easier. *They must also be of the same sex.* Oftentimes, the meeting secretary will ask sponsors to raise their hands. Many meetings also make available a list of sponsors and contact information.

You might have to ask a half-dozen people before finding the right person. That's normal, too. After you start working with a sponsor, you may decide that he or she isn't a good fit. Again, normal. People's circumstances change. Sponsors are "hired" and "fired" all the time. Your sponsor will have a sponsor, too. Perhaps they've had *many* sponsors during the course of their recovery. It's ingrained in the Twelve Step culture. So long as you are honest, it's no big thing.

Don't ever forget that your addiction is fighting for its rotten life. Sponsorship attacks at the heart of the behaviors that nourish it. A sponsor is your connection to another human being, representing the beginning of the end to your self-imposed isolation. They are a light in the darkness; representing, perhaps, the first person in a very long time with whom you can be totally honest, *and who can be totally honest with you.* Because they are also in recovery, you can be yourself without feeling judged. All you have to do is ask.

> **FACT: INDIVIDUALS WITH AN A.A. SPONSOR THREE MONTHS INTO RECOVERY ARE *3 TIMES* MORE LIKELY TO ABSTAIN FROM ALCOHOL AT SIX MONTHS, COMPARED TO THOSE WITHOUT A SPONSOR.**

<u>**EXERCISES**</u>

1. Please indicate which of the following characteristics of a Sponsor are most important to you. Afterward, explain why:
   - ❑ A straight-shooter that will call you on your bull.
   - ❑ Background similar to yours.
   - ❑ Dependable. Available for telephone calls and meetings with little notice.
   - ❑ Emphasizes the spiritual aspect of the program.
   - ❑ Has his or her own sponsor.
   - ❑ Has more time in recovery than you, and worked some/all of the Twelve Steps.
   - ❑ Lives in the solution, not the problem.
   - ❑ Open to including you in his or her social circle.
   - ❑ Owns a car.
   - ❑ Punctual.
   - ❑ Same gender and/or age.
   - ❑ Walks the talk. Is willing to remain sober no matter what.
   - ❑ Won't judge you.

2. A sponsor is like a mentor. How does the dictionary define "mentor"?

3. Chronic substance abusers do not use logical thinking. How does the dictionary define "logic"?

4. We use superficial reasoning instead. How does the dictionary define "superficial"?

5. A sponsor is vital to your recovery. How does the dictionary define "vital"?

6. List the things you have to gain and the things you have to lose by working with a sponsor:

THINGS I HAVE TO GAIN	THINGS I HAVE TO LOSE

7. Where will you look for a sponsor?

8. List possible candidates.

9. How and when will you approach them?

(Complete the remainder of this section after getting your sponsor)

10. How did it feel to ask? List specific statements that encouraged you.

11. When and where will you meet?

12. Sponsor information:

   Name _____

   Phone _____

   E-mail _____

- Jimi Hendrix

16. Saying Goodbye

Dear Dummy,

You know me very well. You can always count on me. Through the worst of times when you are confused or down or need a reason to keep moving forward, I am there for you. Through the best of times also, when you feel undeserved of success and unworthy of love, I am the one who says "yes, you are right". Nobody understands you better than I do. All I ask in return is... everything.

They call me cunning, baffling and powerful. They claim that to know me is to know suffering and death. They say that millions have perished under my yoke; people like you, with families like yours; and they back up these claims with proof. It is all true. I am not in the business of hiding anything.

I am a puppeteer. You are the puppet dancing from my strings. As you hop from left foot to right I pretend to be your friend. "I am the solution", I whisper. "I am dependable." I am indispensable." "You deserve me." "You control me." And you listen like the dummy you are, dancing harder, trampling over your dreams.

You worry about cancer, chest pains, diabetes, liver disease and such; but cannot accept that I am the one responsible for these things, even when it is so obvious. Instead you keep choosing me over and over in an endless cycle like so many other dummies that have chosen to put their sanity last. What a perfect heaven you have made for yourself in the bowels of my Hell.

Young, old, rich, poor, smart, famous, dumb as dirt... you are all the same. What I provide is instant gratification; something which you find as vital as water and are willing to trade for your soul. "What about consequences", you ask from time to time? "Never mind that", I reply. Why focus on the negative, dummy, when you live thrill to thrill? Besides, you have willpower. You are intelligent. You will be the one person in the entire world to get the better of me. "Trust me".

Alas, not everyone dances as faithfully as you do. Hard as I might try, some folks are just not interested in my slice of heaven. Instead they have chosen honesty and sanity and Programs and... (ugh)... *God!* No matter. Right now I am busy, busy, busy with the performance of a lifetime, starring you. Dance dummy, dance.

Sincerely,

Your Addiction

You have tossed out the drugs, poured the alcohol down the drain and deleted the dealers from your contact list. But, you haven't *officially* closed this painful chapter in your life for good.

Though you started out as great friends, your **drug-of-choice** has been unmasked as a wolf in sheep's clothing. It has wrought devastation to your life, and misery to the lives of those around you.

If your disease could speak to you, I imagine it would communicate a message similar to the letter above. It would be **rude,** because your disease does not need to *earn your business.* (Sadly, you are already a loyal client.) Not surprisingly, it would be **puffed-up** due to the utter lack of respect you have for yourself. The message would be **devoid of all hope,** since chronic substance abuse does not subside on its own, and those who refuse treatment are assured of a tragic demise. Finally, regrettably... *disturbingly*... it would be a message of **truth.**

Imagine addiction as the puppet-master who controls your every move. Without control strings, you would collapse on the floor. Just as you cannot control your addiction, you are at the mercy of the master who manipulates your controls. As addiction jerks the controls up and down, you head to the store for a bottle of booze, or to the drug dealer's. *You do this even though you know for a fact that you will suffer negative consequences.* For example, you know you will not be able to hide the ATM or credit card receipt from your spouse, making a bad situation at home even worse. Or, you know you will be unable to stop yourself from drinking alcohol or snorting cocaine while driving back home, putting yourself and others in peril. Or, you know that once you are high or intoxicated, the people around you will notice immediately, resulting in feelings of guilt and betrayal.

> ### Attitude
> By Charles Swindoll
>
> "The longer I live, the more I realize the impact of attitude on life. Attitude, to me, is more important than facts. It is more important than the past, than education, than money, than circumstances, than failures, than successes, than what other people think or say or do. It is more important than appearance, giftedness, or skill. It will make or break a company... a church... a home. The remarkable thing is we have a choice every day regarding the attitude we will embrace for that day. We cannot change the inevitable. The only thing we can do is play on the one string we have, and that is our attitude... I am convinced that life is 10% what happens to me, and 90% how I react to it. And so it is with you... we are in charge of our attitudes."

If you have a substance use disorder, then you are tethered to your master's controls. Your master despises you. You represent life and hope. He represents selfishness, pride and death. His only goal is to inflict pain on you and your loved ones. This is no fairy tale. It is a nightmare that will not end by making a few changes here and there. Snipping one or two strings will not save you. In fact, it will probably make things worse because you will be forced to overcompensate in other areas. Cutting all the strings will only work if you have implemented a new plan for living. Otherwise, you will just be a lifeless lump on the floor: **restless, irritable and discontent.**

But, all is not lost. With a new **attitude,** you have begun a process of **renewal** that will evict this demon-master and restore every area of your life to a glowing vigor: just as others have been restored.

You have written *about* your addiction before, but never *to* it. Here, for the first and last time, you will speak to your disease *directly.* Use this opportunity wisely. *Unleash the beast inside of you,* which is your sane self... *the good person beneath the bad disease.* Find your authentic voice and let the emotions flow. Finish the following goodbye letter:

AT HOME RECOVERY HANDBOOK

Date _____

Dear _____,

GOODBYE AND GOOD RIDDANCE!

NOW, HIT THE BRICKS!!

Signed _____

17. Changing Old Behaviors

INSPIRATION
"If nothing changes, NOTHING CHANGES!"

Substance Use Disorder affects us physically, mentally, socially and spiritually. Though it affects the whole person, we mistakenly focus only on the alcohol or drugs as being the problem. To be effective, treatment must address the whole person as represented by the Recovery Wheel below. Either we have a program that is healing to our whole selves, or we risk returning to our old lifestyle.

A Bio-Psycho-Social disease requires that you treat the whole person.

Being "Grateful" For New Behaviors
Do you realize that you might otherwise have gone your *entire life* without changing your unhealthy behaviors, had it not been for substance abuse treatment? Likewise, many of the new behaviors you are developing now, will result in a stronger *faith* in someone or something more powerful then you.

Please do not tell me that you have *no faith*. The fact you have this book in your hands, proves you do. The fact that you attend support meetings and read the literature, proves you do. Not only is your faith growing, but your faith is growing *you*, too, by constantly being put to the test. Of course, right now you are none too happy about that. Things are difficult enough! However, this is exactly what you need.

Let me illustrate. When raw gold is melted down, the impurities rise to the surface and are skimmed off. These impurities are called "dross". The process is repeated until there is nothing left to skim. The dictionary defines dross as: "Something that is worthless." In similar fashion, each time your faith is tested some of your *doubt* is skimmed off. As a result, your faith becomes ever purer, ever stronger and ever more valuable. In doing so, you grow closer to your **Higher Power.**

As a direct result of your *worst* fault, you get to enjoy this phenomenal gift of faith. From that point of view, the process of recovery serves as a direct conduit to God.

ABUSE → NEW BEHAVIORS → FAITH → RECOVERY → GOD *(of your own understanding)*

The A.A. Big Book makes this point over and over. The chapter entitled: We Agnostics, states the following about our disease and how it keeps us disconnected from God:

> **"We were having trouble with personal relationships, we couldn't control our emotional natures, we were a prey to misery and depression, we couldn't make a living, we had a feeling of uselessness, we were full of fear, we were unhappy, we couldn't seem to be of real help to other people."** (Big Book, page 52)

Can you relate? It goes on to say that a **"simple reliance"** on **"the God idea"** *solved* this problem for others. The Big Book "promises" (a key word!) that the god of your understanding, *through the program of Alcoholics Anonymous*, is the answer to what has been frustrating and killing you all this time.

How do you access this power? Are you asked to crawl over cobblestones or starve for days? *No.* Are you required to read the Bible cover to cover? *No.* Are you asked to knock on the doors of strangers or speak in foreign tongues? *Heck no.* Are you asked to be baptized or attend church? *NO!* Are you asked to practice any of the world's religions or any religion at all? *NO, NO, NO!* According to A.A., giving your recovery over to *something more powerful then you* starts with nothing more than **"childish faith"**; and, that faith starts with *new behaviors*.

It doesn't take much to receive what's promised: *faith*... a toe in the water creating ripples that broadcast over an entire lake. Waving your fist at a giant mountain and declaring: "I will no longer be afraid of you"; and the vibrations from your voice building against the rock walls causing a landslide that lays waste to that mountain. *Faith* is not a new concept. You have been growing in it since the moment you were born. Every breath demonstrates your faith that oxygen is present, despite the fact you cannot see oxygen molecules. Every night, you lay down to sleep having faith that the world will keep spinning, even though you will be oblivious as to what is happening while you slumber. Over the years, our faith in air and earth has been strengthened by the repetition of breathing, waking and watching others do the same. So it is with those of us who misuse chemicals. Our faith is tested, gets stronger, and we share the experience with others, while others share their experiences with us. We learn that we are only as crazy as the person seated beside us. And, if that person recovered, so can we.

Substance abuse *can* lead to *new behaviors*, which lead to *faith*, which leads to *recovery* and all the *promises* that go along with it. The Promises are found on page 85 of the A.A. Big Book:

> **"We are going to know a new freedom and a new happiness. We will not regret the past nor wish to shut the door on it. We will comprehend the word serenity and we will know peace. No matter how far down the scale we have gone, we will see how our experience can benefit others. That feeling of uselessness and self-pity will disappear. We will lose interest in selfish things and gain interest in our fellows. Self-seeking will slip away. Our whole attitude and outlook upon life will change. Fear of people and of economic insecurity will leave us. We will intuitively know how to handle situations which used to baffle us. We will suddenly realize that God is doing for us what we could not do for ourselves."**

Though found in two different chapters, separated by thirty-three pages, the message couldn't be clearer. Substance use disorder **disconnects** you from God. When it does, life sucks in every way. In fact, the life of a chronic substance abuser is the *exact opposite* of the kind of life you can lead by living in harmony with God *through the Twelve Steps*. Coincidence? I think not. That's because the Twelve Steps are a **conduit** that make it possible for you to tap directly into the inexhaustible power of God.

So, the next time you hear someone at a Twelve Step meeting say they are a "grateful" alcoholic or addict, you will know why.

New Behaviors and the Myth of the 'Pink Cloud'
Have you heard of the **"pink cloud"**? It's a popular term in the rooms of Alcoholics Anonymous. Everyone recovering from an addiction *rides* the pink cloud at some point. Many don't understand it. So now is the perfect time to learn the truth about this thing called the pink cloud.

Check the color wheel and you'll find that pink is not a primary color. It doesn't exactly match up to the majesty of blue or righteousness of green. Pink appears on only one national flag in all the world. (The Turks and Caicos Islands flag includes a pink shell.) Things that come to mind as being associated with the color pink include: piggy banks, pink eye, pink elephants, cotton candy, pink-o communists, Pink Floyd, receiving a pink slip when you're fired, Barbie's™ pink camper, pink roses, soothing pink stomach relief, and ordering your steak *pink in the middle please.* Consequently, pink has a hard time inspiring confidence. So when you hear mention of the *pink cloud,* you might not assign much importance to it. That would be a mistake.

Of course, we aren't talking about an *actual* pink cloud: that intensely beautiful mass of water vapor hanging in the sky at dusk. Rather, in the context of recovery, the pink cloud refers to *a state of mind.* Mention of the pink cloud is found on page 113 of the **Twelve Steps and Twelve Traditions**, which describes the way you feel when you finally admit that you are powerless over chemicals, and your life has become unmanageable. A.A. calls this Step One, or **Surrender**. But the concept is universal. So if you don't relate to Twelve Step programs like A.A. or N.A., that's okay. Think of it as the way you feel after you finally hit **bottom** and know in your heart you are done. (I call this being *done-done.*)

Owning the fact you are powerless over your addiction, marks the beginning of recovery. When your ego quits calling the shots, horror gives way to hope. An enormous feeling of relief follows surrender. The bricks you have shouldered for so long, fall away, awakening intense emotions long anesthetized with chemicals. You enter the *miracle* phase of recovery. *You're floating on a beautiful pink cloud.*

However, there is a tendency in early recovery to feel so victorious that you *stop working* for it. Instead, you celebrate your newfound freedom by shouting out to anyone who will listen. A.A. calls this phenomenon the **"two-step illusion"**, which refers to a person who completes Step One and immediately skips to Step Twelve, or **Sharing the message with others**, without doing any of the work in-between. Or, you can just think of it as being naive, lazy or overconfident. You might be sober, but you haven't identified your triggers or cravings, nor learned healthy coping skills; you haven't set things right with the people you wronged; and, you haven't developed a new way of living. This is tough stuff that takes time. A.A. puts it this way: **"We temporarily cease to grow because we feel satisfied that there is no need for *all* of A.A.'s Twelve Steps for us. We are doing fine on a few of them."**

Eventually, life tap-dances on your head. You're jolted back to reality by issues; both good and bad, which you haven't the skills to handle. A.A. states: **"Then perhaps life, as it has a way of doing, suddenly hands us a great big lump that we can't begin to swallow, let alone digest... Sooner or later the pink cloud stage wears off and things go disappointingly dull. We begin to think that A.A. doesn't pay off after all. We become puzzled and discouraged."** The Urban Dictionary defines a pink cloud as follows: "Twelve Step recovery jargon referring to someone new who talks about how great life is now that they're sober. Usually meaning that the person is out of touch with reality."

Pink clouds showcased by Mother Nature are intensely beautiful, but they only last long enough to snap a few good photos. In the same way, your initial gung-ho enthusiasm for recovery will eventually fizzle. When it does, you will lose faith in the recovery process, sink into depression, and relapse...

Or not! With all due respect to Alcoholics Anonymous, that is a myth! The truth is, *you can ride your pink cloud for the rest of your life.* I am! Of course there are challenges. At times, things have gone to hell in a hand-basket. But, recovery teaches that you can overcome absolutely anything so long as you adopt new, healthy behaviors. Let me assure you with the utmost certainty; my worst day sober is *infinitely* better than the best day I *ever* had trashed.

Regardless of your convictions, or whether you have yet to find a god of your own understanding, recognizing your shortfalls affords you the opportunity to *eliminate them*. The Bible explains it this way: "...I delight in weaknesses, in insults, in hardships, in persecutions, in difficulties. *For when I am weak, then I am strong.*" (2 Corinthians 12:9-11.) Weakness can be transformed into wisdom. Work a program of recovery, and in no time you will find yourself floating atop your own pink cloud. Then, whether or not you ever give up this intensely beautiful state of mind will be your choice alone. But I warn you, pink clouds, like recovery and cotton candy, are addicting!

<u>EXERCISES</u>
1. **Using the spaces provided, suggest new behaviors you can adopt which will support your recovery spiritually, physically, mentally and emotionally:**

SPIRITUALLY	PHYSICALLY	MENTALLY	EMOTIONALLY

2. **What people, places and things remind you of drinking and using drugs? List them in the top row. In the bottom boxes come up with new behaviors that can replace them:**

OLD PLAYMATES	OLD PLAYGROUNDS	OLD PLAYTHINGS
NEW PLAYMATES	**NEW PLAYGROUNDS**	**NEW PLAYTHINGS**

(Suggested answers to Exercise 1)

SPIRITUALITY	PHYSICAL	MENTAL	EMOTIONAL
Twelve Steps, Animal sanctuary, Bible study, Big Brother/Sister, Botanical gardens, Church, Drive in the mountains, Fellowship, Habitat for Humanity, Hiking, Inspirational literature, Listen to worship music, Look at the stars, Prayer, Sing in choir, Spend time outdoors, Volunteer, Watch the sunset, Whale watching	*Bike ride, Camp, Clean the house, Dance lessons, Dental exam, Diet, Gardening, Hike, Home improvement, Haircut, Horseback riding, Hygiene, Manicure, Jogging, Paddle boarding, Pedicure, Physical exam, Picnic, Psychological assessment, Racquetball, Rafting, Rock climbing, Sailing, Skiing, Sleep, Sports, Surf, Swim, Take a nap, Tennis, Walk, Wash the car, Weight training*	*Twelve Steps, Bowling, Cooking, Counseling, Education, Exercise class, Fishing, Go to a concert or play, Golf, Gratitude list, Hobbies, Job training, Jogging, Kite flying, Massage, Medication, Meditate, Painting, Photography, Poetry, School, Sponsor, Stretching, Support meetings, Write a book, Yard sales*	*Cold shower, Communication tools, Counseling, Deep breathing, Emotional movies, Family, Friends, Help a friend, Journaling, Learn to play an instrument, Listen to music, Meetings, Pets, Prayer, Read recovery books, Relaxation techniques, Service work, Sponsor, Warm bath, Work Twelve Steps*

(Suggested answers to Exercise 2)

OLD PLAYGROUNDS	OLD PLAYMATES	OLD PLAYTHINGS
Abandoned building, Adult bookstore, Apartment, Automobile, Bar, Campsite, Casino, Dealer's house, Drugstore, Emergency Room, Head shop, Hotel, Jail, Liquor aisle, Public bathroom, Store, Topless bar, Train, Urgent Care	*Bartender, Chat room, Dealer, Escorts, Facebook friends, Followers, Inappropriate websites, Significant other, Unhealthy family members, Using friends*	*Air freshener, ATM machine, Bong, Cash, Cocktail glass, Cotton, Drink cozy, Foil, Gatorade, Hand sanitizer, Lighter, Mirror, Mouthwash, Paper money, Pill dispenser, Pipe, Razorblades, Rig, Spoon, Straw, Texting, Video games, Water bottle, Wine glass*
NEW PLAYGROUNDS	**NEW PLAYMATES**	**NEW PLAYTHINGS**
Twelve Step meetings, Aquarium, Beach, Bowling alley, Campgrounds, Church, Club meetings, Dog park, Golf course/Driving range, Gym/Yoga/Pilates, Hobby shop, Job, Kitchen, Local events, Movie theater, Nature, Ocean, Park, Pool, Rehab, Restaurant, School, Sightseeing, Start a business, Tennis court, Zoo	*Classmates, Community activists, Coworkers, Dating sites, Exercise class, Fellowship, Gym members, Healthy family members, Join a club, Neighbors, Other pet owners, Participate in team sport, Pet, Physician, Service work friends, Sober friends, Sponsor, Stranger(s) at the table next to you, Supportive friends, Therapist, Time with children*	*Art, ATM card and Checkbook, Bicycle, Board game, Boat, Books (Recovery and general interest), Build a website, Camping equipment, Cards, Chewing gum, Clothing, Coffee, Collectibles, Computer, Crochet, Crossword puzzle, Exercise equipment, Favorite new non-alcoholic beverage (i.e. root beer, Arnold Palmer), Golf clubs, Magazines of interest, Music, Musical instrument, Pet, Phone call, Rollerblades, Sewing*

18. Managing Stress

Stress is your body's way of responding to a challenge. The stress response involves the brain, glands, hormones, immune system, heart, blood and lungs. Stress can have either a positive or a negative effect. For example, lifting weights creates stress on the muscles that results in positive growth. On the other hand, stress created by chronic worry can *overwhelm* the body's resources, leaving you physically and mentally exhausted.

Fight, Flight... or FRIGHT
The body reacts to stress by triggering a cascade of hormones which drains our energy, attacks our immune system, and weakens our muscles. *Up to 80% of all illness have their origins in stress!* Heart attacks, strokes, hypertension, cancer, diabetes, and respiratory disease all have strong stress-related components. Stress is frequently a root cause of ulcers, colitis, asthma, skin eruptions, insomnia, headaches, anxiety, menstrual problems and impotence, too.

Early man's ***fight or flight*** response was an important means of survival. However, fight or flight has evolved over time, what we experience now is ***fight, flight... or fright;*** with most of us being victimized by this third response. It is clear that stress is killing us, where it once helped keep us alive.

Addicts and alcoholics cope with *fight, flight or fright* by chronically abusing alcohol and other drugs. This unhealthy coping mechanism quickly backfires. Eventually, every anxious thought, no matter how small, is magnified to the extreme, resulting in a reaction that is wholly out of proportion to reality. Envision the person who works hard all day pleasing other people then comes home and *kicks the dog*. Was the dog at fault or just in the wrong place at the wrong time?

Never is this toxic chain-reaction more apparent than in early recovery: before healthy coping skills are learned, as you try to deal with the uncomfortable sensations resulting from abstinence. Throughout your recovery you risk switching addictions. **Cross-addictions** are just another addiction used to cope with losing the original addiction. Like the original addiction, they are an unhealthy means of managing stress. Some of the most common cross-addictions are addictions to food, gambling, work, exercise, sex/porn, buying stuff, relationships, and other mind altering substances.

Only by confronting anxiety, and learning that you can safely get through each and every situation, can you *truly* become healthy. Anxiety can *even* be a means to learn, grow and become a better person. Perhaps it would be helpful to remember that: *courage is fear in action.*

HALT to Buy More Time
Don't get steamrolled by people or issues which you are not prepared to deal with at that moment. Give yourself the gift of *time*. The simplest way to do that is to literally hold up your hand and say **HALT**. Remember to HALT when you are **Hungry, Angry, Lonely** or **Tired**. These are four common precursors to relapse:

1. **Hungry**
If you're like most substance abusers you probably neglected good nutrition. You habit could have been going days without eating, or subsisting on fast food. In fact proper nutrition may have been lacking from your diet for years! But recovery gives you time to reset your eating habits. *Regular, nutritious meals are essential to regaining your physical and mental health.*

   When it comes to eating, pay attention to some simple do's and don'ts:
   - **Do** schedule meals at specific times. Make them a part of your daily routine.
   - **Don't** overeat. Avoid snacking. Cut down on the amount of salt and fats consumed.
   - **Do** avoid fast-food restaurants. Most of the food is loaded with fat and salt.
   - **Don't** load up on caffeine and energy drinks. Choose tea instead.
   - **Do** live it up in the morning! Breakfast is the most important meal of the day because your body has been starved overnight. *Breakfast is not coffee, a pastry and a cigarette!* Eat a substantial breakfast with moderate portions. Breakfast should also be the most fun meal. Since you have all day to digest, quantity is less of a concern then at lunch or dinner.
   - **Don't** try for too much at once. Resist fad diets, energy supplements and steroids. As someone who is chemically dependent, you'll tend to look for the quick-and-easy fix.
   - **Do** eat more fruits and vegetables. They are filling and provide fiber and other nutrients.
   - **Don't** depend on processed carbohydrates, refined sugars and high glycemic index foods that spike blood sugar. Instead, eat a balance of protein, carbohydrates and fat *each* meal.
   - **Do** try nutritional supplements such as protein drinks.
   - **Don't** starve yourself or binge and purge. If you think you have an eating disorder, get help from a healthcare professional.

2. **Angry**
The radical changes you make during recovery can heap stress on your life. You may become short-tempered and resentful. Something which you would normally react to with four units of anger, now gets eight units. Follow through with any mental health referrals and practice developing a spiritual nature that accepts life on life's terms. Anger invariably leads to **resentment,** which leads to relapse.

3. **Lonely**
When you withdraw and deprive yourself of human companionship you fail to benefit from the connection with others that is so important to mental and spiritual health. Isolation leads to a lack of perspective, allowing your mind to conjure up irrational and self-defeating thoughts. Remind yourself: "My head is a dangerous neighborhood to be in alone."

4. **Tired**
Stress can be exhausting. The early months of recovery are by definition times of great stress. Much energy is expended resolving financial, vocational, and relationship issues, all the while struggling with the discomfort of exploring defects of character. *Seldom will you have the stamina to cope with all of the stress generated.* That's the time returning to drugs and alcohol might actually look to you like a pretty good alternative. Getting a good night's sleep is important. Many times in early recovery, sleep patterns are still influenced by old habits and residual chemical effects. *You must be rested and well fed to make the most of each day.* This means getting to bed early and not indulging in late-night TV, DVD's, video games or texting. You're changing to a healthier lifestyle, which

includes being alert and rested. Perhaps you're thinking about making up for lost time and immediately jumping back into a schedule of long work days. Don't you dare! Resist the urge to do too much too fast. Seek **moderation** instead. There is no deadline for your recovery.

Exercise; The Natural High
Substance use disorders devastate the body; not just in the damage they cause internally, but in our desire to care for ourselves. I once worked with an ultra-marathoner: the elite of endurance athletes, who spent most of his time on the couch in front of the television, drinking. The only running he did was to the liquor store or his dealer's house.

Why? As you previously learned, compulsive substance use drains the brain of "feel good" chemical messengers like dopamine. It's part of the hopeless cycle of euphoria, crash and craving which is the defining characteristic of substance use disorder. First, we use alcohol and drugs to stimulate massive amounts of **dopamine**, creating a feeling of **euphoria.** But because we have abused these substances for so long, we don't produce very much dopamine. So when we aren't high on something, we *crash,* and are likely to be total jerks **craving** our next high. We called this the **Paradoxical Effect.**

It is impossible to overstate the importance of exercise to your recovery. *Exercise naturally stimulates the release of dopamine.* It produces a natural high, improving the way you think and feel. It helps combat depression, especially during early recovery. It reduces stress. Exercise improves self-image, self-worth, motivation and energy. What else can you say about the benefits of exercise?! Walking, biking, jogging, running and aerobics are all great. Treat yourself to a yearly membership at a health club for a hell of a lot less money than you spent in *one month* on drugs and alcohol. Refer to the bonus chapter on health and nutrition to log your exercise results.

Diaphragmatic Breathing
Your breathing is a tipoff as to how much stress you are under. When stressed, breathing becomes more rapid and shallow, and takes place higher in the chest. This is known as **chest breathing.** Rapid and shallow chest breathing can cause anxiety, or can make your existing anxiety worse. You can slow down your breathing using a simple technique known as **diaphragmatic breathing.**

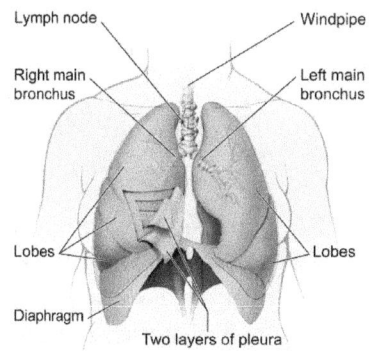

To breathe diaphragmatically, you must draw in air with your *belly* rather than your chest. The diaphragm is a dome-shaped muscle that assists in breathing, and separates the heart and lungs from other organs. The surface of our diaphragm moves downward as we inhale, and upward as we exhale. When we breathe diaphragmatically, the diaphragm moves *farther down* into the abdomen, and the lungs are able to expand more completely into the chest cavity. We benefit from more oxygen, while releasing more carbon dioxide.

What are the Benefits of Diaphragmatic Breathing?
When your breathing is full and deep, the diaphragm *massages* the liver, stomach and heart. Breathing with your diaphragm does the following:
- **Relaxes your nervous system.** Diaphragmatic breathing stimulates the **parasympathetic nervous system,** promoting calmness. It works in an opposite fashion to the sympathetic branch of your nervous system, causes emotional arousal and the very physiological reactions underlying a panic attack.

- **Aids circulation and digestion, improves your immune system, and reduces high blood pressure.** Diaphragmatic breathing increases the supply of oxygen to the brain and musculature.
- **Heightens your sense of well-being.** Anxiety and worry keep you *in your head*. Just a few minutes of deep, abdominal breathing will help bring you down.
- **Detoxifies your organs and expels waste through the lungs more efficiently.**
- **Improves concentration.** It's difficult to focus your attention when your mind is a locomotive of anxious thoughts. Abdominal breathing will help to quiet your mind.
- **Slows your breath.** Abdominal breathing by itself can trigger a relaxation response.

Focus On Your Breath, Takes the Focus Off Your Stress
Whenever you feel anxious you should check to see how you're breathing. Anytime you focus on your breath, you take the focus off your stress. The more you practice, the more of a habit it will become, and the more you will breathe diaphragmatically without even thinking about it; even when talking with someone. Practice diaphragmatic breathing as follows:

1. Lie down flat or sit up straight. Place one hand on your abdomen right beneath your rib cage.

2. Inhale slowly and deeply through your nose into the *bottom* of your lungs. Imagine a balloon inside your abdomen. Each time you inhale, imagine the balloon filling with air. If you're breathing from your abdomen, your hand should rise as the balloon fills.

3. After you've taken in a full breath, pause, and then exhale slowly and fully through your nose or mouth. Imagine the balloon collapsing. As you exhale, allow your whole body to just *let go.*

4. Each time you inhale, say; "in comes the healthy air" silently to yourself. Each time you exhale, say; "out goes the stress."

5. Continue breathing like this for five breaths or longer.

6. With the aid of a heart rate monitor you can utilize biofeedback to actually watch your heart rate slow.

7. Sometimes when I practice diaphragmatic breathing, I listen to music. I also found it helpful to download one of the many sound machine apps to my phone, so I can listen to nature, the ocean waves or the rain. Rather than using my hand, I find it especially comforting to place my mp3 player on my abdomen, to feel it rise and fall with my breathing.

Guided Meditation, Safe Place Imagery and Mindfulness
Diaphragmatic breathing can be used in conjunction with techniques that enhance the experience of relaxation, including **guided meditation, safe place imagery** and **mindfulness.**

Guided meditation and safe place imagery are **visualization techniques** that engage all your senses, in order to deepen your level of relaxation. These techniques require someone else to lead you through the experience. Search the internet and YouTube for recordings, and download those you like best so you can practice relaxing anywhere.

Mindfulness is a technique used to block out **automatic thoughts** that can be toxic and lead to anxiety. Twelve Step programs refer to automatic thoughts as: **"The committee in your head."** Mindfulness forces you to replace toxic thoughts with safe thoughts. To practice mindfulness, all you need to do is become **mindful** of your surroundings, using all of your senses. By doing so, *you can use the present to force the past and future from your mind.*

For example, the committee in *my* head often gets rambunctious when I'm driving and my mind wonders. That's when mindfulness works for me. The way I become hyper-aware of my present surroundings is by reporting, *aloud,* information about the cars and drivers around me. It might sound like this: "In front of me is a white Ford F-150 pickup truck with a black plastic bed liner and chrome bumper with a decal of a surfboard. It looks like the driver has his phone to his ear talking. (Idiot!) To the left of me is a dark blue foreign car that looks like a Toyota. It has rust on the front bumper and no hubcap on the front wheel. The driver is wearing a dark baseball cap backwards on his head. A pine tree air freshener is hanging from the rearview mirror. The front passenger window is down and I hear the radio playing. Someone around me is smoking a cigarette because I smell the smoke... " Just by reading these few sentences, you can already see how concentrating fully on the present moment diverts your attention from everything else. Sounds stupid, right? Who cares! I'd much rather talk out loud then infect myself with useless negative thinking, or worse, have a panic attack.

Anxiety and Alcoholics Anonymous
Alcoholics Anonymous provides a solid foundation for dealing with anxiety. The Twelve Steps themselves are a powerful tool for identifying anxiety and changing behaviors, so you can see stress from a more realistic and healthy perspective. Sponsors, meetings, fellowship with others, and the wealth of learning materials available, are also tools at your disposal. As you read the A.A. text and work the Twelve Steps with your sponsor, these tools will become second nature to you. By using these tools, you can **"uncover...discover...discard"**.

Reviewing the Promises of A.A. is another method you can use to quickly rebalance your mood. They can be found on pages 83 and 84 of the A.A. Big Book. They are a reminder of what is **guaranteed** to you by the fellowship, *so long as you do the work:* **"If we are painstaking about this phase of our development, we will be amazed before we are half way through. We are going to know a new freedom and a new happiness. We will not regret the past nor wish to shut the door on it. We will comprehend the word serenity and we will know peace. No matter how far down the scale we have gone, we will see how our experience can benefit others. That feeling of uselessness and self-pity will disappear. We will lose interest in selfish things and gain interest in our fellows. Self-seeking will slip away. Our whole attitude and outlook upon life will change. Fear of people and of economic insecurity will leave us. We will intuitively know how to handle situations which used to baffle us. We will suddenly realize that God is doing for us what we could not do for ourselves."**

A Precious Gift
A stable recovery lifestyle includes taking care of yourself emotionally and physically. Take the time to practice the relaxation techniques described: meditate, pray, exercise, read, attend meetings etc. A little goes a long way. You'll be amazed at how smoothly things will run without your constant supervision! *Remember, out of all the things in life, time is the one thing you cannot get more of.* So taking the time to care for yourself is a precious gift indeed.

EXERCISES

1. Describe a decision you made while hungry, angry, lonely or tired that you later regretted, and why you regretted it.

2. What could you have done differently?

3. Why is it so difficult to think rationally when you are emotional?

4. List any physical sensations that accompany your anxiety?

5. **Often times we use extreme thinking ("awfulizing or catastrophizing") to convince ourselves that our situation is much worse than it actually is. Describe three *anxiety lies* you've told yourself:**

   A.

   B.

   C.

6. **Anxiety is fear driven. In what areas of your life is fear causing anxiety?**

7. **When has anxiety caused you to blow a minor situation *way* out of proportion?**

8. Anxiety and compulsive substance use go hand-in-hand. However, using drugs and alcohol to cope eventually backfires. This is the great paradox of addiction. Please list specific, painful *experiences* in your life that *made* you anxious and triggered your using. Then, list the painful *consequences* (which resulted in even more anxiety):

PAINFUL EXPERIENCE LEADING TO DRINKING/USING	PAINFUL CONSEQUENCES
1.	1.
2.	2.
3.	3.
4.	4.
5.	5.

19. Anger and Substance Use Disorder

Everybody gets angry. It's natural to feel angry. Anger only becomes a problem when it turns into a behavior. The key, is to *manage* your anger. Healthy anger, is anger *within limits*. We are only able to get as angry as the law allows, society accepts and common sense dictates. The ability to manage anger and stop ourselves from doing something we will regret later, comes with **maturity.**

Wearing an Angry Mask
Often we lash-out as a way to **cope** with feelings like fear, shame, hurt, jealousy and embarrassment. What are some of the ways *you* express your anger (or others express their anger towards you):

- ❏ Abuse substances?
- ❏ Blaming?
- ❏ Button pushing?
- ❏ Controlling?
- ❏ Emotional abuse?
- ❏ Property damage?
- ❏ Rage?
- ❏ Self harm?
- ❏ Threatening?
- ❏ Verbal abuse

You're Frightening Me
Intimidation is defined as: "persuading by frightening." Intimidation is not about **intention!** What makes a threat *real* is how the receiver *interprets* the threat. **Perception** is the key. This is *very important* to understand. You may *not* be trying to intimidate. You might be anxious, in a hurry or frustrated. You might be the gentlest soul on planet earth. Yet none of that matters whatsoever, because *it's not about you, it's about them* and what *they* perceive. And if someone *feels* threatened, regardless of your intentions, there will be consequences! Can you see how a situation can spin totally out of control because of a misunderstanding? Misunderstandings can destroy your life.

Anger played out to its conclusion, results in **violence.** *Substance abusers are likely to be more violent, faster.* "Violence never solved anything." Is it true? Absolutely not! Violence works. We use it to manipulate others into doing what we want them to. It can also earn us respect. The act of violence can reward us with a *high* of good feelings, too. But there are consequences to violent outbursts, including: serious injury, arrest, incarceration, restraining orders, loss of children, loss of a relationship or job, guilt, shame, low self-esteem, financial penalties, the effects of stress on the body, and relapse.

> The constant flood of stress chemicals resulting from anger can harm the body. **Health issues linked to chronic anger** include:
> - Anxiety and depression
> - Digestive problems, ulcers and colitis
> - Headache and chronic pain
> - Heart attack
> - High blood pressure
> - Immune system problems and cancer
> - Insomnia
> - Stroke

Is violence worth it? Does aggression bring *real* change when human nature is to push back when pushed? *Resistance breeds resistance,* goes the saying. The problem is that we were born with free will. As a result, we are compelled to exercise our right to choose. Why? Because that is what brings us fulfillment. That's why reasoning with someone, getting them involved in the process and coming to a resolution *together*, is the only way to bring *lasting* change.

What is Maturity?
At what age do you become an adult? If you think the answer is 21, then you are wrong. That's just the legal drinking age. Twenty years ago it was legal to drink at 18. Does that mean some people became adults at 18 and some at 21? And, while on the subject of age, let's not forget the minimum legal age you can enlist in the military, the legal age of consent, the legal age to vote, the age at which you don't legally have to listen to your parents anymore and so on. Do any of these criteria make you an adult? Absolutely not. What are they then? They're *arbitrary boundaries* set by governing laws: laws which *vary widely* all over the world. Were you aware that the legal age of consent is 13 in Argentina, and that the United Nations guidelines for military service allow those over 15 years old to serve?

So what makes you an *adult*, really? An adult is a person who is fully grown and no longer needs to be cared for like a child: in other words, **independent**. Therefore, **adulthood** is more accurately based on characteristics like *emotional maturity,* not age. To be adult is to be mature. They go hand-in-hand.

Maturity is defined as: "showing the qualities gained by development and experience." Notice that maturity is an *action*. It is *showing,* not simply *knowing*. Maturity is *wisdom in action.* It's *using* what we know. In simplest terms, maturity means that our personal experiences help change the way we think and act. Another word for "change" is **evolve**. As we mature, we get more and more skilled at emotional regulation, and better at reducing *impulsive, compulsive* thoughts and behaviors. *Unfortunately, those of us with a substance use disorder are at a serious disadvantage, because we stop maturing when we start relying on drugs and alcohol.*

Characteristics of a Mature Adult
You might be thinking; *this sounds good and all, but Maturity will happen when it happens. It's a "natural" thing.* For *most* people, yes, but not for us. We must work at maturity. A mature adult:
- ACTS, rather than RE-acts, and is *accountable* for their actions.
- Avoids dwelling on the negative (i.e. stinking thinking.)
- Doesn't allow character defects like jealousy, pride or insecurities to drag them down.
- Grows more mature all the time.
- Handles pressure with self-composure.
- Is considerate of others and tries *not* to be self-centered.
- Is honest and accepts that they cannot *always* win.
- Is open to the opinions of others, and looks at every situation as an opportunity to *compromise*.
- Learns from mistakes instead of complaining.
- Manages their temper.
- Practices basic conflict resolution skills.
- Understands that open communication is the key to diffusing conflicts.

Resentments *Are* Anger
Resentment is unresolved anger that has a very long life expectancy. It keeps you stuck in the past and even contributes to long-term health problems. I love the saying: **Holding onto grudges and bitterness is like letting someone you don't like live inside your head for free.** Alcoholics Anonymous warns us over and over about the dangers of anger and resentment:
- **"Resentment is the 'number one' offender. It destroys more alcoholics than anything else."** (Big Book page 64)

- **"This business of resentments is infinitely grave. We found that it is fatal. For when harboring such feelings we shut ourselves off from the sunlight of the Spirit. The insanity of alcohol returns and we drink again."** (Big Book page 66)

- **"Few people have been more victimized by resentments than have we alcoholics. Anger, that occasional luxury of more balanced people, often leads straight to the bottle."** (Twelve and Twelve, page 90)

- **"When we harbor grudges and plan revenge for such defeats, we are really beating ourselves with the club of anger we had intended to use on others."** (Twelve and Twelve, page 47)

Another popular A.A. saying goes: **Holding onto resentments is like drinking poison and expecting** *someone else* **to die.** So why do we? Because we *love* our anger! We believe it gives us an *edge* by making us more powerful and in control, and thereby superior to others. We become fifty-feet tall and bulletproof. And anger is a **defense mechanism** that keeps us conveniently stuck in **addictive thinking**.

The Twelve Steps were designed to deal directly with your resentments. Step Four talks about **"a searching and fearless moral inventory of ourselves"**, in which we uncover character defects and resentments and become accountable for them. We **uncover, discover, discard**. Step Eight and Step Nine ask us to become accountable for the harm we've caused others. This is done in the form of making amends.

Making amends is not the same as apologizing. In fact one of the most powerful amends is **forgiveness.** Forgiveness challenges you to put *yourself* first, knowing that holding on to resentments hurts *you* more than anyone else. Forgiving is not the same as forgetting. The particular issue may always be a part of your life (often as a useful learning experience.) It doesn't mean that you deny another's responsibility for their part, and it doesn't minimize or justify the wrong. You can forgive the person without excusing the act. You can keep the memory and lose the pain. *Your life depends on it!* Saying, "it's hard," is not an excuse. In the past, we drowned these emotions in alcohol and drugs, so we won't stay sober very long if we don't deal with them properly.

Honestly, Count Me In
Accountability is such an important part of being an adult, getting sober, remaining sober and managing anger. We can't talk about accountability without also mentioning **honesty**. Do they mean the same thing? No. *Honesty takes courage. Accountability takes humility.* How important are these two words to addicts and alcoholics? Critical! *It is impossible to be an addict or alcoholic if we are being honest and accountable.*

How did you avoid being honest and taking responsibility? Did you isolate, make light of things, deny, blame others, rationalize or lie? You probably did just about *everything* to avoid the truth. Addicts and alcoholics are saturated in this **delusional thinking**.

Conflict resolution skills allow you to stand up for yourself without being aggressive or disrespectful:
- Agree to disagree.
- Avoid name calling.
- Compromise.
- Respect someone's physical and emotional boundaries.
- See their side.
- Take a time-out (HALT) when things get heated.
- Validate the opinion of others.

To whom are we accountable? We are accountable to: God, family, friends, support groups, sponsors, employers, and the community. When are we accountable? All the time! We are *always* responsible for what we do: not just when the kids are home; not just we're sober; not just when we are out in public; not just when we *feel like it*. When it comes to accountability, there are two things to remember. First, accountability is about *us*. It's *not* about holding *someone else* accountable. A.A. says: **"Keep your side of the street clean"** Second, accountability equals *power*. When we start to accept that our actions result in **consequences,** then we can immediately begin to change for the good. That's called **recovery.**

Start by Being Honest with Yourself
If we can't be honest with ourselves, then we certainly can't be honest with others. One definition of **character** is: *What we do when no one else is around to witness it*. It's how we act in the *unseen moment*. Recovery builds character. Character comes with maturity. Character is *priceless*. A.A. says; **"If nothing changes, nothing changes."** Without being honest and owning the problem, we will never change. But if we are able to take an honest look at ourselves, listen to others, own our feelings and be willing and courageous enough to make changes, we can master our anger as well as sobriety.

> **"The alcoholic is like a tornado roaring his way through the lives of others. Hearts are broken. Sweet relationships are dead. Affections have been uprooted. Selfish and inconsiderate habits have kept the home in turmoil."** (Big Book, page 82)

EXERCISES
1. An adult is someone who is independent. In what ways are you independent and dependent:

HOW AM I IN-DEPENDENT?	HOW AM I DE-PENDENT?

2. What characteristics of a mature adult (listed above) are most appealing to you, and why?

3. How is your anger and substance abuse related? (Check one of the following and explain):
   - ❑ I drank/used to make my anger go away.
   - ❑ I drank/used to express my anger.
   - ❑ I drank/used to get back at others.
   - ❑ I drank/used when I got angry because I didn't care about anything.
   - ❑ I drank/used to punish myself.

4. Describe how resentment has caused you problems.

5. Give one example of an amends you need to make.

6. Choose a conflict resolution skill and describe how you would use it.

7. Make a "grudge list" of people, institutions and principles that you resent, and why.

> **The Bible expresses a universal truth about anger: "Don't sin by letting anger control you. Don't let the sun go down while you are still angry, for anger gives a foothold to the devil."** (Ephesians 4:26-27)

20. STOP to Communicate

The ability to be **assertive** when you communicate, empowers you to successfully set healthy boundaries. Being assertive does not guarantee you win every situation, but it does mean you take responsibility for your feelings and express what you see to be your rights. *Assertion* is a **behavior**. Effectively asserting yourself is a **skill** which happens to be lacking in many of us grappling with substance use disorder. Rather than being assertive, we often act **aggressively** or **submissively**.

Different Communication Styles
1. **Aggressive** - To *win* at any cost. Only looking out for *your own rights and feelings,* while trampling on the rights and feelings of others. Typified by spontaneous, over-the-top outbursts.

2. **Submissive** - The opposite of aggression. Being on the losing side of an argument with someone who is aggressive, because you *ignore* your own rights and feelings in favor of theirs. To be clear, ignoring your own needs is *not* the same as *sacrificing* them. The difference is that when you sacrifice, you put aside your needs *on purpose*. Your needs have *value*. So by ignoring your needs, you communicate that they have no worth at all.

3. **Assertive** - Exercising your own rights and expressing your own feelings *while, at the same time, respecting the rights and feelings of others. In other words, you declare yourself firmly, clearly and respectfully.* Anger is **expressed,** but not wielded like a weapon.

Rights and Responsibilities
Communication goes both ways. Know your rights and responsibilities as a communicator:

RIGHTS AND RESPONSIBILITIES TABLE	
YOU HAVE THE RIGHT TO...	IT IS YOUR RESPONSIBILITY TO...
1. Make your own decisions.	1. Allow others to make their own decisions.
2. Be treated with respect.	2. Treat others with respect.
3. Refuse requests by others.	3. Refuse courteously and assertively.
4. Make mistakes.	4. Ensure mistakes don't harm others.
5. Change your mind.	5. Act reasonably.
6. Take time to consider requests.	6. Allow others this courtesy.
7. Make reasonable requests.	7. Do not impose upon others.
8. Have personal opinions .	8. Respect the opinions of others.
9. Control your own destiny.	9. Allow others to control their own destiny.
10. Express your feelings.	10. Consider the feelings of others.

Respect and Understanding

Asserting yourself successfully requires more than respect. It requires **understanding.** Keeping communication channels open, and trying to understand *why* people act in certain ways, is useful in helping us to respond sensibly. President Harry S. Truman dropped the only nuclear bombs ever used on civilians. In Hiroshima alone, the bomb killed an estimated one-third of the population of 300,000. Using nuclear weapons ended World War II and made the United States victorious, yet President Truman said; "It is *understanding* that gives us an ability to have peace. When we understand the other fellow's viewpoint, and he understands ours, then we can sit down and work out our differences."

Want more proof? Turn on your television. Whether you realize it or not, you are constantly on the receiving end of *assertive* communication in the form of *advertising*. Think about it. To be effective, advertisers have to *understand the needs* of their target audience, and then assertively position their product such that it is perceived as the best and only choice. On the other hand, turn to any news channel. *Aggressive* communication seems like it is the only way our politicians relate to each other nowadays. One reason government turns off so many people is because the major political parties seek to "win" at the expense of the other's rights and feelings. There is little effort made by one party to understand the other. And, rather than respecting each other, both parties are openly hostile. As a result, precious little gets accomplished.

'STOP', To Express Yourself

Whether you will use an *assertive* style of communication, or not, is your **choice.** Remember, effectively asserting yourself means a better outcome for everyone. The best way to be assertive is simply by *expressing your feelings*. Why? Because it is difficult to argue with *how* someone feels! For example: "I feel sad", can be *neither* right nor wrong. "Sad", is a feeling, not an opinion or fact.

A simple tool can help you to express your feelings firmly and clearly every time. You can use this tool in virtually any situation. Practice till it is second-nature. Think **STOP...**

S: **STATE** the action or behavior that led to the conflict.
T: **TELL** the person how it made you feel without blaming.
O: **OFFER** a suggestion so the person can act.
P: **PROPOSE** positive outcomes that could result.

Assertive communication using the STOP tool looks like this:

STEPS TO ASSERTIVE ACTION	YOU MIGHT SAY
1. **S**tate the action or behavior that led to the conflict (Use "I" statements rather than "you" statements)	*When (I saw/ gave/ said)...*
2. **T**ell the person how it made you feel without blaming	*I felt (angry, disappointed, upset, hurt)...*
3. **O**ffer a suggestion so the person can act	*I would prefer that...*
4. **P**ropose positive outcomes that could result	*If that happens I/we (will, can, be,)...*

Let's look at an example. Say that you have been sober and in recovery for over two months. Most days you spend looking for a job. Lately you notice that when you return home after filling out applications all day, your parent or spouse has been asking more and more questions about where you've been and what you've been doing. They ask questions like: "Why did it take you so long to apply for only a few jobs. Are you sure that's what you did today?" As a result, you become angry because you have been working very hard and doing everything asked of you. In the past, you probably would have responded by having a temper-tantrum and drinking or using. Nothing would have been resolved. Now, using the STOP framework, you might respond as follows:

STEPS TO ASSERTIVE ACTION	YOU MIGHT SAY
1. **S**tate the action or behavior that led to the conflict (Use "I" statements rather than "you" statements)	*When I hear you question where I've been...*
2. **T**ell the person how it made you feel without blaming	*I get angry and hurt, and I feel like a failure.*
3. **O**ffer a suggestion so the person can act	*I suggest you remember that it takes courage to keep going out there day after day, despite being rejected for every job opening. Next time I suggest you encourage me for what I did manage to accomplish, and deal with your anxiety another way, like talking to a friend or a therapist.*
4. **P**ropose positive outcomes that could result	*A little motivation goes a long way. If you can make these simple changes, it would help me stay positive and continue to find the strength to look for a job, rather than relapsing.*

Refuse to Use
Assertive action is important in social situations, where a decision to use or not use drugs may influence whether or not your friends will accept you. Some friends deserve to be lost. Others are not. You don't want to convey that being **clean** makes you weak or boring. In addition, you do not want to appear as if you are judging them or are better than they are because you are in recovery. You simply do not want to participate in that unhealthy behavior.

STOP, is a simple way to **refuse to use.** For example, suppose you make plans to drive your friend to the mall to go shopping. On the way, your friend asks you to make a short detour so she can pick up some weed. Spending the afternoon getting high and shopping is one of the regular, fun things you used to do together. But everything has changed now that you are in recovery. You can refuse to use by following STOP, as follows:

STEPS TO ASSERTIVE ACTION	YOU MIGHT SAY
1. **S**tate the action or behavior that led to the conflict (Use "I" statements rather than "you" statements)	*When I hear that you want me to stop for weed...*
2. **T**ell the person how it made you feel without blaming	*I feel afraid, disrespected and hurt, because you know that I'm trying to live sober, and one more dirty test at work will get me fired.*
3. **O**ffer a suggestion so the person can act	*So, in the future, I prefer you not think of me as your "drug taxi" and put me in the position where I might be tempted.*
4. **P**ropose positive outcomes that could result	*If you can help me to stay safe, then we can keep hanging out. In fact, let's come up with something else we can do at the mall today that's crazy and fun.*

Practice, practice, practice this technique. You can use it just as effectively in all areas of your life. Not only is it a means by which you can effectively communicate your needs, but in doing so, you will make it n*early impossible* for the other party to refuse to give you what you want!

EXERCISES
1. **Recall three incidents where you were dissatisfied with an outcome because of how you acted or failed to act, or what you said or failed to say. Complete the following:**

STEPS TO ASSERTIVE ACTION	#1 YOU MIGHT SAY
1. **S**tate the action or behavior that led to the conflict.	*When I...*
2. **T**ell the person how it made you feel without blaming.	*I felt...*

STEPS TO ASSERTIVE ACTION	
3. **O**ffer a suggestion as to how you would like the person to act.	*I prefer...*
4. **P**ropose positive outcomes that could result.	*If that happens then I...*

STEPS TO ASSERTIVE ACTION	#2 YOU MIGHT SAY
1. **S**tate the action or behavior that led to the conflict.	*When I...*
2. **T**ell the person how it made you feel without blaming.	*I felt...*
3. **O**ffer a suggestion as to how you would like the person to act.	*I prefer...*
4. **P**ropose positive outcomes that could result.	*If that happens then I...*

STEPS TO ASSERTIVE ACTION	#3 YOU MIGHT SAY
1. **S**tate the action or behavior that led to the conflict.	*When I...*
2. **T**ell the person how it made you feel without blaming.	*I felt...*
3. **O**ffer a suggestion as to how you would like the person to act.	*I prefer...*
4. **P**ropose positive outcomes that could result.	*If that happens then I...*

> "Being positive does not mean ignoring the negative. Being positive means overcoming the negative." (Unknown)

21. Guilt and Shame Are Not the Same

Whenever you talk about guilt and shame you strike at the dark heart of substance use disorder. In a broader sense these feelings fall under the topic of morals, principles, ethics, honesty and decency. To those of us suffering from compulsive substance use, these things are as far away as the moon is from the earth. Like the moon, we can see morality very clearly because we are painfully aware of our sins. Yet we just cannot touch the honest light of truth. It is too far away.

If you think that shame and guilt are the same, then you are wrong. It is important for you to understand the reason why they are different. *Shame* is the belief that *you are* defective as a human being. Shame can involve feelings of humiliation or disgrace. *Guilt,* on the other hand, refers to feeling bad about something *you did or failed to do.* For example, you may feel guilty for any or all of the following:
- Abusing loved ones (including pets) physically or verbally.
- Acting irresponsibly as a parent or spouse.
- Being dishonest and cheating family, friends and others.
- Committing adultery or sleeping with prostitutes.
- Committing crimes such as theft, prostitution or assault.
- Driving under the influence.
- Going deep into debt.
- Ignoring your parents, spouse or children.
- Losing a job.
- Spending family income on alcohol and drugs.

Guilt is the way you feel about your **behavior.** *Shame* is a **belief** about yourself. Guilt says: *I've done something wrong;* while shame says: *There is something wrong with me.* Guilt says: *I made* a mistake; while shame says: *I am a mistake.* Guilt says: *What I did was not good;* while shame says: *I am no good.* Got it?!

You may have lied, but that doesn't make you a liar. You might have stolen, but you are not a thief. By the way, you should be aware that our society uses the terms "addict" and "alcoholic" as *shorthand.* They are not, in fact, *accurate.* Your disease doesn't **define** you. Therefore, you might have a **substance use disorder**, but are not an alcoholic or addict. (That would be like saying: "You are diabetes.")

I Hate Myself That Much!
Substance use disorders produce feelings of guilt and shame that can be overwhelming. *Obsessing* on these negative feelings wears us down. It eats away at our self-worth, bruising our souls like the rotten inside of an apple laying on the ground. Low self-esteem can be a powerful motivator to continue abusing alcohol and drugs in order to feel better, at least *temporarily.* It's easy to get caught in the death-spiral of feeling disgusted with ourselves, using drugs to feel better, feeling disgusted about using drugs, using drugs to feel better about being disgusted etc.

Any time I counsel on guilt and shame, I'm reminded of the novel *The Scarlett Letter,* by Nathaniel Hawthorne. The story concerns an adulterous woman in the year 1642. She is a Puritan. Puritans were a strict religious group that considered adultery a very serious sin.

The woman will not name the father. As a result, she is forced to wear a large, red "A", which is sewn onto her dress. The "A" stands for *adultery*: an outward sign of her inner sin. It is a sign of shame. The letter "A" could just as easily represent *Alcoholic* or *Addict*, because too many people struggling with substance abuse live as if there was a big red "A" on their chest. They live in shame, allowing a past action to define who they *are now*. This is a *lie* we tell ourselves to stay stuck in our disease.

The woman in the story is more or less a victim of her times. Back then, committing adultery made you *an adulterer*. You *became* your sin. Consequently she wore the "A" until she died, at which time the "A" was chiseled into her tombstone. End of story.

What about *your* story? Do you *have to* wear your "A" until you die? Shame sucks. You can't change history or *undo* something you've already done. It's impossible. Think about it. So you may have lied cheated, but you're not a *cheater*; or abused drugs and alcohol, but you're not an *addict* or *alcoholic*, not anymore. Turning shame into guilt, removes the "A".

You are a *good person* with a *bad disease*. Are you willing to stop punishing yourself for being something you are not? If so, you can transform your shame into guilt, then address each guilty act in a healthy way until your conscious is clear.

As a person in recovery, it was essential for me to go through the process of turning my shame into guilt, then dealing with the guilt. I was great at chronically abusing drugs and alcohol, lying and manipulating. For me, it was a 24-hours a day, 7-days a week job. I am not proud of the many things I did to fuel my habit. But if I thought for one minute that any of those appalling behaviors *defined me*, I would jump off of a tall building. They were that bad. I couldn't breathe under the weight of my shame. Instead of jumping, I chose to **act myself into thinking**, as goes the A.A. saying. I turned to A.A., N.A. and C.A.. I prayed. I got honest. I changed my friends. I became responsible for my actions. I dealt with the consequences of my past. I didn't drink or use no matter what. I was forgiven by others *and* by myself.

I now choose to believe I am a good person, as you are. I am not the sum of my sins. Nor are you. The "A" that I know, stands for *apology, absolution and action*.

Overcoming Feelings of Guilt and Shame
You can't possibly feel good about yourself while you are wallowing in booze and drugs. That is why we cannot tackle this subject until now, after you have stopped. *Chemical dependency and negativity go hand-in-hand.* The more you use, the worse you feel about yourself. Fortunately, the reverse is also true. The more sober time you accumulate, the better your outlook becomes. Therefore, if you want to overcome guilt and shame, you cannot use drugs or alcohol, *no matter what.*

In order to overcome guilt and shame, you must **recognize** these feelings. Being **rigorously honest** with yourself can be the most painful thing of all, particularly when it concerns the things you did, or did not do. Avoiding emotional pain is probably the reason you self-medicated in the first place. Start by talking about your feelings. As they say in A.A.: **"our secrets keep us sick."**

Without the benefit of alcohol and drugs, we are forced to **confront** these negative feelings. Let me save you some time, here. You cannot *take back* the things you've said or done, regardless of what you do.

Punishing yourself for things that occurred in the past is a supreme waste of time. You have already wasted enough time. Agreed? Accept the fact that you are a good person with a bad disease. No matter how terrible your actions might feel, they do not define *who* you are. Feelings aren't facts! Therefore, you must **forgive** yourself. If you are a person of faith, it would be good to remember Psalm 103:12: " He has removed our sins as far from us as the east is from the west."

To truly overcome guilt and shame, you must also **seek** forgiveness from others. A.A. calls this process: **making amends.** While the thought of facing the people you lied to, stole from, disrespected and harmed in countless other ways may be overwhelming, take heart. This is a **process** you complete a little at a time. *How* and *when* you do it, is not as important as *why* you do it. Apologies cannot turn back the clock and undo what you have done. In fact, there will always be people who simply cannot forgive you, no matter how enthusiastically you apologize. The purpose of an apology is to help *you* come to terms with *your* beliefs and behaviors. **"Clean your side of the street"**, as they say in A.A. Rather than force an apology on someone, you can pray for that person afterward.

Many of the Twelve Steps deal with the issue of morality. They serve as a vehicle for transforming your shame (a behavior) into guilt (a belief), which is much more easily corrected. For example, Step Four helps you take stock of character defects like **fear, resentment, dishonesty and selfishness.** It also helps you overcome resentments against others. Steps Eight and Nine enable you to receive forgiveness from others on a day-by-day basis.

Be thorough, sincere and humble as you go through this cleansing process. As you do, be *kind* to yourself. Give yourself *time* to heal. There is no instant gratification to be had here. Overcoming guilt and shame takes time and work, but the process will work if you work it.

Overcoming Guilt and Shame:
1. No chemicals, no matter what!
2. Be honest with yourself.
3. Talk about your feelings.
4. Forgive yourself.
5. Seek forgiveness from others.
6. Work a Twelve Step program.
7. Give yourself time to heal.

EXERCISES
1. **Using a dictionary, define the following words:**
   A. Shame.

   B. Guilt.

   C. Fear.

   D. Resentment.

   E. Dishonesty.

   F. Selfishness.

2. List the things you feel most guilty about doing as a result of your addiction.

3. List the things you feel most guilty about NOT doing as a result of your addiction.

4. In what ways has addiction caused you to feel ashamed?

5. Use this page and the next to make a list of your character defects. Character defects are those beliefs and behaviors you dislike in yourself. Be thoughtful and brutally honest (what A.A. calls: "**searching and fearless**").

"Nothing goes right on the outside when nothing is going right on the inside."
(Matthieu Ricard, French Buddhist Monk)

22. Boosting Your Self-Esteem

Most people feel bad about themselves from time to time. Feelings of low **self-esteem** may be triggered by being treated poorly by someone else, or by a person's own judgments of themselves. It's normal. However, self-loathing is a *constant companion* for those of us with a substance use disorder. We go through life feeling bad about ourselves when it is undeserved. Low self-esteem prevents us from enjoying life, doing what we want to do, and accomplishing our goals. Low self-esteem keeps us stuck in the mud of our disease.

You have a **right** to feel good about yourself. However, that becomes very difficult when you are abusing drugs and alcohol. Then, it is easy to be drawn into a downward spiral of lower and lower self-esteem. For instance, you may begin feeling bad about yourself when someone insults you, you are under a lot of pressure at work, you are experiencing physical pain from withdrawal, or you are having a difficult time getting along with someone in your family. You begin to give yourself **negative self-talk** like, "I'm no good", or "Nothing is ever going to get better for me." Negative self-talk is an utter waste of your energy. Nothing can ever be gained from it. Negative self-talk fuels the downward spiral that results in you having to turn to chemicals in order to feel better.

Negative Self-Talk
Are you feeding yourself a steady diet of pessimistic messages? You may have developed this behavior when you were young. You could have learned these messages from all around you, including other children, teachers, family, caregivers, the media, and from prejudice and stigma in our society. You might also have invented these confidence-killing messages all on your own.

Once you learned them, you may have repeated these lies over and over to yourself, especially when you were having a hard time and were emotionally vulnerable. They became part of your **belief system.** Why? *Because no one is tougher on you then you are.* You are your own harshest critic, judge and abuser. *And you punish yourself not once, but over and over again for the same mistake*. You make a mistake, judge yourself, declare your guilt and execute sentence. Every time you *remember* the incident, you judge yourself *again*, find yourself guilty *again* and punish yourself *again!* All this hurt and pain and punishment for a negative message that *isn't true in the first place!*

Common examples of negative messages that people repeat over and over to themselves include: "I'm damaged goods", "I never do anything right", "I can never be forgiven for what I've done", "No one would like the real me." Most people believe these messages, *no matter how untrue or unrealistic they are.* They pop into our brain immediately upon being triggered. For instance, if you answer a question incorrectly, your automatic reaction is to think: "I am so stupid."

Negative self-talk includes words like "should", "ought", or "must". We call this **musterbating.** The messages imagine the worst in everything, especially you, resulting in feelings of guilt and disappointment, particularly if these thoughts are unreasonable. For example: "I **must** not get angry", " I **must** be perfect", "He **should** always be on time", "**Shouldn't** he be more considerate", "I **ought** to be strong enough to ignore cravings."

You may think these thoughts or feed yourself these negative messages so often that you are hardly aware of them. You are especially prone to negative thinking when they are tired, sick, or dealing with a lot of stress (i.e. remember to HALT when hungry, angry, lonely or tired.) Start paying attention. As you become aware of your negative thoughts, you will notice more and more of them.

A women was well known for making a fabulous roast beef. She reserves the dish for special occasions. Relatives and friends never fail to show up when roast beef is on the menu. She learned how to make the meal from her mother, who had learned it from *her* mother. Now, it was time to pass the family secret to her daughter.

One day, mother and daughter gathered in the kitchen. The daughter watched as her mother carefully sliced off the butt of the roast, rubbed the remainder with butter, added a combination of seasonings, then placed it in the oven. The result was delicious, as always. To show her gratitude, the daughter hosted her mother for dinner the following week. She carefully prepared the roast exactly as she was taught. Dinner was a success. Afterward, mother and daughter were discussing the meal over coffee. Unexpectedly, the mother asked: "I noticed the end of the roast was missing. Was there a reason for that?" Shocked, the daughter responded: "Mom, I followed your directions from start to finish. The roast was prepared *exactly* as you have been doing it ever since I can remember. The first thing you *always* do is slice off the end of the roast." The mother sat back and laughed, then replied: "Yes, because I don't have a big enough pan to fit the whole thing!"

As far as the daughter could tell, removing the butt of the roast didn't appear to have any effect on the taste of the meal. It also seemed like a waste of good food. However, she had watched the meal prepared the very same way her whole life. She accepted what she observed as *fact*. She simply didn't know any other way. Had she challenged her mother, she could have done away with her old belief and served a bigger meal.

What about you? What is it you believe about addiction, recovery, and especially yourself? Are you seeing things as they really are, or is there a better world right under your nose that you're missing simply because you've never lived any other way.

Changing Negative Thoughts to Positive
The best way to change your thought pattern is to stop believing every old thing you say to yourself. Start questioning each one of your toxic thoughts. Ask yourself:
1. Is the thought *true?*
2. Is it *reasonable?* Would one person say this to another? If not, why am I saying it to myself?
3. What is the *purpose* of this thought? If it makes me feel badly, why not stop thinking it?

You can change your unhealthily thinking by replacing negative thoughts with positive statements, called **positive affirmations**. The reason is simple. You cannot be thinking a positive thought *and* a negative thought *simultaneously.* You must cultivate this habit, so that replacing negative thoughts with positive ones becomes automatic. In developing positive affirmations, use positive words like: *happy, peaceful, loving, enthusiastic,* and *warm*. Avoid negative words such as: *worried, frightened, upset, tired,* *bored, not, never* and *can't*. Instead of: "I am *not* going to worry anymore", you can say: "I *will* focus on the positive". Always use the present tense, as if the condition *already* exists i.e. "I *am* healthy", or, "I *have* a good job".

In order for a positive affirmation to be effective, you must **believe** it. Once you have developed a positive affirmation, you should repeat it often to yourself, aloud and in writing. You can make the statement into signs you post on the bathroom mirror and refrigerator door. You can share the positive thought with another person, such as saying: "This color looks good on me."

How Can a Water Glass Be 100% Half Full?

Here is a simple experiment designed to prove that your **perception** of yourself is your **reality,** and also, that you can change your thinking easier than you think, if only you try. Just because you *believe* a thing doesn't make it true. That goes for even the most stubborn, most negative thoughts about yourself and your situation. For example, say you are thirsty and only want to drink a half-glass of water. In that situation a glass filled half-way to the top is full, isn't it? Perception is reality.

Now it's time for a demonstration. Get two identical water glasses. Fill one to just below the top, and the other only half-way. Place them side-by-side on the counter. If I were to ask you if these two glasses were the same, you would say "absolutely not. One is full. The other is only half full." But If I am right, then just by getting you to *think* differently, your reality will change. Now answer the questions below:

Using Your Eyes
When observing the glasses next to each other do they appear the same or different?
- ❏ Same
- ☑ Different

Using Your Nose
Bring each glass to your nose and inhale. Does the water smell the same or different?
- ❏ Same
- ❏ Different

Using Your Mouth
Take a sip from each glass. Do they taste the same or different?
- ❏ Same
- ❏ Different

Using Your Touch
Stick a finger into each glass. Is the water in one glass wetter than the water in the other?
- ❏ Same
- ❏ Different

Using your Ears
Finally, pour the water from each glass slowly into the sink. Is the sound of the water hitting the basin from the first glass different from the sound of the second?
- ❏ Same
- ❏ Different

If you were honest, you marked the four remaining boxes: "Same". Although the glasses looked very different initially, they are much more alike then you first perceived. What you first believed to be 100% *different* is, in fact, 80% *the same* according to 4 of your 5 senses! And, the *only* thing you changed was your thinking. Perception is reality. It's time to begin seeing yourself in a kind and loving way. Is your life an empty glass, or is it 100% full of the things that matter?

EXERCISES
1. **List three negative thoughts you have about yourself, then answer each of the questions:**
    A. **Is the thought** *true?*
    B. **Is it** *reasonable?* **Would one person say this to another? If not, why am I saying it?**
    C. **What is the** *purpose* **of this thought? If it makes me feel badly, why not stop?**

NEGATIVE THOUGHT #1:
A. TRUE?
B. REASONABLE?
C. PURPOSE?

NEGATIVE THOUGHT #2:
A. TRUE?
B. REASONABLE?
C. PURPOSE?

NEGATIVE THOUGHT #3:
A. TRUE?
B. REASONABLE?
C. PURPOSE?

2. Practice the *skill* of developing positive statements to replace negative thoughts. These are called *positive affirmations.* The reason is simple. When thinking a positive thought about yourself you can't be thinking a negative one. Complete the following positive affirmations:

   - A positive characteristic I have is...

   - I am loved by...

   - I am most happy when...

   - I feel good about...

   - I have a natural talent for...

   - I know I will be successful in life because I will...

   - I like myself because...

   - I look good when...

   - I'm told I have attractive...

   - My favorite place is...

- My goals for the future are...

- People often compliment me about...

- The color that looks great on me is...

- The person I look up to most is...

- The person that makes me feel most worthy is...

- What I enjoy most is...

3. Take the three negative thoughts you identified above, and convert them to positive affirmations:

AFFIRMATION #1:

AFFIRMATION #2:

AFFIRMATION #3:

23. Triggers and Cravings

A **trigger** is an experience, person, situation, event, or thing (object) that **stimulates** a desire or **craving** to drink or use drugs. Triggers result from strong **memories** of past using. Alcohol bottles, a syringe or friends you partied with, are all obvious examples. However, triggers can be insanely subtle. Many people have told me that *sunshine* is a huge trigger for them, because they often got loaded during the day. Similarly, things like public bathrooms, parking structures, family members, attractive girls, certain music and particular smells are subtle but powerful triggers. Because they are all around us, *out of our control,* you *must* develop the capacity to recognize, avoid or cope with them.

Triggers always result in consequences, whether you realize it at the time or not. Triggers can lead to **relapse,** if you do not have **a strategy** to manage the cravings that follow. You don't look for triggers. *They come find you.*

Common triggers include the following:
- Advertisements for alcohol.
- Dates of celebrations or events.
- Dishonesty, such as lying.
- Drinking or drug paraphernalia.
- Family members.
- Feeling hungry, angry, lonely or tired.
- Former significant others.
- Money or the anticipation of getting money.
- Moods, such as when you are anxious, happy, confident, frustrated, or negative.
- Music reminding you of partying.
- Nighttime dreams.
- Party friends.
- Places you purchased or used alcohol and drugs.
- Pornography, sex and sexual partners.
- Positive memories of getting loaded.
- Sight or smell of alcohol or drugs.
- Unrealistic expectations.
- Video games.
- Weekends and vacations.

> **Have a strategy to manage cravings or you will find yourself in trouble.**

Crave... The Wave

During recovery - particularly the early months - you will experience strong urges to use drugs and alcohol. These urges are called **cravings.** *Cravings are impulsive, spontaneous urges to use drugs or alcohol.* They can occur any time, *even if you are working a recovery program.*

Cravings are like ocean waves. Sometimes they crash suddenly with extreme power. Other times they gently roll and lap at the shore. Though they differ in frequency and intensity, cravings, like waves, *always retreat* - usually within minutes. As your sobriety progresses, these urges will blend naturally into the background noise of life. Until then, you must prepare, and then act.

Cravings share the following characteristics:
1. Cravings are triggered by people, places and things *(i.e. playmates, playgrounds and playthings!)* They can be triggered by situations and events, too.

2. Cravings are triggered by thoughts and feelings; including thoughts of relapse; and feelings of anxiety, boredom and depression.

3. Cravings can be accompanied by physical symptoms such as heart palpitations, chills and sweating. They can be accompanied by behaviors, such as pacing, as well.

4. Cravings, like waves, are temporary. If you have a plan, then you can resist them.

Recognize, Avoid or Cope Strategies
Triggers and cravings are links in a *chain* of events. Triggers *always* result in **consequences,** whether you realize it at the time or not. That's why it is so important to be aware of triggers, cravings, and healthy strategies for dealing with them.

TRIGGER → CRAVING → ACTION → CONSEQUENCES (Positive or negative)

Healthy strategies for dealing with cravings include all of the following:
- Learn to **recognize** signs of your cravings.
- **Avoid** drugs, alcohol, shot glasses, papers, pipes, needles, mirrors etc.
- You can experience immediate relief simply by talking about your cravings.
- Go to Twelve Step meetings so you can discuss your cravings with others, and learn how others cope with their own cravings.
- Distract yourself with something you like to do. Don't wait till the craving hits you. Make a list of activities to keep with you. Sounds dopey, but better to have it.
- Keep a journal of your cravings, the situations in which they occur, and the coping strategies you used. Review your notes frequently.
- Plan ahead.
- Be vigilant of high-risk people, places, and situations.
- Pray to God or your higher power for help and strength to get through your craving.
- Read recovery literature. Reading educates, motivates and rejuvenates.
- Practice self-affirmations. Tell yourself that you don't have to surrender. Remind yourself that cravings go away quickly. Remember the benefits of sobriety. Repeat Twelve Step slogans.
- **Think it through,** to combat euphoric recall.

EXERCISES
1. I will leave a dangerous situation. Safe places I can go include:

2. I will distract myself with things I like to do. Good distracters are:

3. I will call my list of emergency numbers. People I can call include:

4. **I will challenge my cravings by thinking it through to the pain that will follow. Examples of painful consequences include:**

5. **Triggers can be in the form of a person, place, thing, situation, event, thought or feeling. My triggers include:**

24. Seemingly Irrelevant Decisions

If you are reading this, and have a pulse, then I can pretty much guarantee that most of the decisions you make today will be minor, routine and **seemingly irrelevant.** Turning left instead of right, stopping at a friend's house unannounced or working through lunch instead of eating, are all examples of decisions we make every day without much thought.

Understanding How We Make Decisions

Many of the everyday choices we make have nothing to do with using drugs or alcohol. However, they can move us closer to using or drinking again, *whether we realize it or not.* For the majority of us, making routine decisions carries little **risk.** For years, you arrive at a particular intersection and turn left rather than right. Then, one day, you turn right and are suddenly blindsided by someone blowing through a stop sign. Bad decision making? Absolutely not. Just bad luck.

For the minority of us who struggle with alcohol and drugs, however, the risk of catastrophic consequences resulting from a decision that seems irrelevant is *much* greater. In this case the consequences can include: relapse, jail, DUI, loss of driving privilege, less than honorable discharge from the military, vehicular manslaughter, a mountain of costly fines and more.

Cruising the alcohol aisle at the supermarket is *not* an **irrelevant decision** for a problem drinker, who runs the risk of being triggered, having cravings and relapsing. Similarly, if turning right at the intersection (above) means driving past your old dealer's house, then that choice is *no longer* irrelevant or routine. *If* you turn right, *if* you stop at the dealer's house, *if* you use, and *if* you happen to be randomly drug tested soon thereafter, you will undoubtedly find yourself in a heap of trouble. Here is a tragic **chain of events** starting with a simple right turn!

small decisions, HUGE CONSEQUENCES

We might minimize, deny or rationalize the risk associated with these decisions, but the fact is that the consequences of a decision are the *same,* regardless of whether you thought it through or not. For example, you might find yourself saying: *I have to...* "take this weekend off," "attend a family party," or "spend time with my using friends". ("I have to" is a tip-off to a seemingly irrelevant decision.)

Even *not* making a decision is a seemingly irrelevant decision that can have catastrophic consequences, particularly for those of us with a substance use disorder. A classic example of this is *failing to plan* in advance for transportation home from a bar. It's the sort of poor choice we make all the time, yet don't consider it a *decision* at all.

Catch it Early!
Obviously it is easier to *simply avoid a high risk situation* before you are actually in the situation. One of the things about these *chains of* seemingly minor decisions is that they are *far easier to stop in the beginning* of the chain, than when you are closer to substance use and craving kicks in. So pay closer attention to your decisions, even the small ones. It takes practice to recognize the small, routine

decisions that seem irrelevant. When you do, **weigh** your options first. Then choose the option with the least risk. When making any decision, use common sense:
- Consider all the options you have.
- Think of the consequences for each of the options, both positive and negative.
- Pick a safe decision that minimizes your risk of relapse.
- Watch for thoughts like: "I have to . . .", or "I can handle . . ." or "It really doesn't matter if… ".

EXERCISES
1. Indicate which of the following routine decisions can be trouble for you, and why:
    - ❑ Using drugs other than your drug of choice.
    - ❑ Keeping any type of drug or alcoholic beverage in the home.
    - ❑ Not destroying your drinking or using paraphernalia.
    - ❑ Going to events or parties where alcohol or drugs might be available.
    - ❑ Spending time with using friends.
    - ❑ Keeping past substance abuse a secret from family members.
    - ❑ Not telling using friends, dealers or drinking buddies of your decision to stop.
    - ❑ Having unscheduled time that can lead to boredom, particularly nights and weekends.
    - ❑ Becoming overtired or stressed.

2. Describe the last time you drank or used. What were the smaller decisions led to that choice?

3. Substance abusers often convince themselves a situation is safe when it really is not. What are some of the dangerous situations you have talked yourself into?

3. Describe how the following seemingly irrelevant decisions could lead to relapse:
    A. Stopping at a gas station to "top up with fuel". This is the same gas station at which you used to buy alcohol then drank while sitting in the self-serve car wash. As the gas is pumping, you notice the sign for car wash discounts with each fill-up.

B. Dropping in on an old friend you feel guilty about neglecting. She is someone you used to drink and smoke pot with, and she hasn't changed. Her kitchen cabinet is still stocked with liquor and the upholstery smells of weed. However you just completed treatment and are certain you are "done messing with drugs and alcohol". In fact you believe you could serve as a positive role model for your friend.

C. Becoming over-tired by working really long hours and not going to bed until very late. To make matters worse, you have been living on coffee and cigarettes, eating sparingly, and when you do eat you opt for drive-thru junk food.

D. Getting into a fight with your partner or friend, causing you to storm off.

E. Going to the store for cigarettes, then cruising the alcohol aisle.

F. Going to a *family* reunion.

G. Not depositing your paycheck in the bank immediately.

4. Sometimes *not* planning is a seemingly irrelevant decision, because it leads to idle time which, in turn, can lead to relapse. What plans have you made for this weekend? If none, why? Is this a seemingly irrelevant decision? What could you do this weekend to reduce your chances of winding up in a risky situation?

4. **Following is a story about a person who made *many* seemingly irrelevant decisions that led to high risk situations and, eventually, a relapse. As you read, highlight the decisions she made along the way that, when taken together, made her vulnerable to using:**

JANET RECENTLY COMPLETED A 30-DAY INPATIENT PROGRAM for a serious alcohol and cocaine problem which almost ended her marriage and her life. Upon returning home, she located a nearby Twelve Step meeting with the intention of attending once a week. She also decided she would find a sponsor there once she'd been going long enough to get to know the women.

Although she had already been out of work on medical leave for a month, she felt she needed another week off to settle back in. So, with her husband's blessing, she phoned her office Monday morning and secured the extra week. Janet looked forward to lounging around the house doing nothing. It would be a welcome change from the treatment center, where everything was scheduled from breakfast until late in the evening. In fact, she even decided she would delay her first Twelve Step meeting until her second week home.

By Wednesday, her marriage was beginning to strain. Janet's husband felt she was being lazy, much like when she was drinking and using drugs. On the other hand, Janet - no matter how hard she argued - could not get her husband to understand how tough it was on her to go through recovery, and how much she'd earned this week of: "Me time." Angry and frustrated at his ignorance, the last thing she said to him before he left for work was: "And you wonder why I drank and got high!"

Janet was so mad, she couldn't sit still to enjoy her favorite morning television shows. Rather than waste time showering, she quickly changed clothes, gathered her hair beneath a baseball cap, and set out in her car, driving aimlessly with the sunroof open and radio blaring. However, it wasn't long before she turned off the music and closed the roof. She needed peace and quiet to hear herself think. She began going over and over the things her husband had said, speaking them aloud, and getting angrier with each repetition. When she arrived at the freeway intersection, she instinctively headed North with no particular destination in mind.

Thirty-minutes later, Janet found herself exiting the highway into the same beachfront neighborhood in which she used to buy her drugs. It honestly had not been her plan. In her mind, she was still thinking about the argument, imagining scenarios in which she dazzled her husband with incredible insight and forced him into silent submission with her brilliant debating skills. Nevertheless, the irony of being at that exact place, while sober, made her chuckle. Now that she was here, she was pleasantly surprised (and a bit relieved) to find that the streets, stores and fast food joints she knew so well, weren't triggering an overwhelming urge to use drugs or drink. Ha, she thought. This is the best thing that could have happened to me! Janet felt truly liberated from her addiction.

Rather than get back on the freeway southbound, Janet drove straight towards the beach, enjoying her newfound freedom. She felt so happy she decided to call her husband and share the joyful news. "Are you crazy!", he yelled into the receiver. "What in the world are you thinking?!" His reaction caught her completely off guard. "You'll NEVER understand!" she screamed, before ending the call abruptly and turning off her ringer.

Instead of continuing on towards the beach, she made her way to her dealer's house. Her husband might have thought that to be an unwise decision, but Janet had no intention of using. She just needed to be in the company of someone who wouldn't pick her apart or judge her every move. Her dealer was cool, and they spent many afternoons watching movies, laughing. As she drove down the all-too-familiar street, she could see by the car in the driveway that the dealer was home. Janet pulled to the curb and shut the engine, but she couldn't exit the car. Suddenly, Janet found it difficult to breathe. Her heart was thumping in her ears at the realization that she was craving relief from her feelings. Wiping the sweat from her forehead, Janet spied the front door, knowing with uncomfortable certainty that once inside, she would be lost.

She frantically tried to come up with options which did not include calling her husband or phoning someone from the treatment center, who would undoubtedly spread the word that she was in crisis only days after being released. Somehow, she managed to get herself off of that street and out of the neighborhood, without relapsing. She needed to regroup, badly. Again she headed towards the beach, hoping that some music, sun and cigarettes would set her straight.

Right before the beach turnoff, Janet pulled into the parking lot of a small convenience store which she knew very well. She didn't really need cigarettes, but they were $2.00 cheaper than anywhere else, so it was worth the stop. Once inside, she walked the aisles grabbing a nutrition bar and a bottle of orange juice. While waiting in line to pay, she noticed a neat row of mini vodka bottles next to the register. Quickly, seamlessly, her thoughts moved to a stress-free afternoon sipping screwdrivers at the beach. "Just this once", she promised herself as she scooped up six bottles.

It took Janet less than two-hours to finish her cocktails. With the empty bottles wrapped in the plastic store bag, and the bag stuffed down into a trash bin, she slid back behind the wheel. Besides being unusually drunk and feeling much more guilty then relieved, she was in panic mode. She couldn't risk being caught intoxicated in public, or arrested for driving drunk. It would mean the end of everything. Swallowing hard and gripping the steering wheel tightly, Janet maneuvered her automobile away from the beach and towards the only safe haven she knew. She breathed a sigh of relief upon eyeing the dealer's automobile still in the driveway. This time she couldn't wait to get inside; the cocaine, she knew, would clear her head right up.

A. How many seemingly irrelevant decisions could you identify? _____

B. Why did Janet's trouble begin with her first decision to attend just one A.A. meeting a week?

C. Following are nearly two-dozen seemingly irrelevant decisions Janet made that day. Individually, each of these choices is minor. *None of them was the actual decision to drink or use.* (For example, scooping up six bottles is a major decision, not a minor one.) Yet, when taken together, these small choices had the *same* devastating consequences. Now, recommend a safer alternative decision Janet could have made:
    a. She located a Twelve Step meeting with the intention of attending once a week.

b. She would find a sponsor once she'd been going long enough to know the women.

c. She felt she needed another week off to settle back in.

d. With her husband's blessing, she phoned her office and secured the extra week.

e. Janet looked forward to lounging around the house doing nothing.

f. She postponed her first Twelve Step meeting until her second week home.

g. Janet - no matter how hard she argued - couldn't get her husband to understand.

h. The last thing she said to him was: "And you wonder why I drank and got high!"

i. Rather than waste time showering she quickly changed clothes.

j. Driving aimlessly.

k. Going over the things her husband had said, speaking them aloud and getting angrier.

l. She instinctively headed North, with no destination in particular in mind.

m. Exiting the highway into an unsafe neighborhood, and thinking: "*This is the best thing that could have happened to me!*"

n. Rather than get back on the freeway Southbound, Janet drove towards the beach.

o. She felt so happy she decided to call her husband.

p. Turning off the ringer.

q. Instead of continuing on to the beach, she made her way to her dealer's house.

r. She just needed to be in the company of someone who wouldn't judge her.

s. Janet frantically tried to come up with options which didn't include phoning her husband or someone from the treatment center.

t. Again, heading towards the beach, hoping that music, sun and cigarettes would set her straight.

u. Janet pulled into the parking lot of a small convenience store she knew very well. She didn't really need cigarettes, but they were $2.00 cheaper than anywhere else.

v. Her thoughts moved to a stress-free afternoon sipping screwdrivers at the beach. "Just this once..."

w. Sliding back behind the wheel, drunk.

5. Have some fun. Track the decisions that you face in the course of the next twenty-four hours, both large and small. Consider safe and risky alternatives for each:

MY DECISION	A SAFE ALTERNATIVE	A RISKY ALTERNATIVE

25. Dry Drunk Syndrome

What do you call an alcoholic or addict who is **restless, irritable and discontent**, even though they are *not* drinking or getting high? Mind you, we are not referring to someone who is merely having a bad day. Life is full of those. We're talking about full-blown return to unhealthy, destructive thinking. **Dry Drunk** is an especially popular term used to describe this condition (The Dry Drunk Syndrome by R. J. Solberg).

Originally, when people spoke of someone who was dry drunk, they referred to the actual, physical withdrawal symptoms alcoholics demonstrate when they quit drinking. Nowadays it represents attitudes and behaviors arising *after* treatment.

Dry Drunk Attitudes and Behaviors
Don't be confused. Dry Drunk describes a **problem,** not a person. *Think of Dry Drunk as a **relapse** in every way, minus the actual chemicals*. It is being sober in body but not in mind. Therefore, it is characterized by a **return** to all the wonderful symptoms that go along with addiction: chaos, ego, immaturity, delusions of control etc.

As you would expect, **delusional thinking** and **defense mechanisms** ensure that the dry drunk continues, same as any other addict or alcoholic's thinking. Following are examples of common Dry Drunk attitudes and behaviors:
- Acting indifferent, unresponsive, withdrawn.
- Fantasizing and daydreaming. Slipping farther and farther from reality.
- Difficulty examining thoughts and feelings:
    - Black & White Thinking - Things are all good or all bad with nothing in between.
    - Catastrophizing *("This is the worst day/thing/person ever!")*
    - Magical Thinking - Making assumptions and then acting as if they are reality.
    - ***Musterbating*** - Negative self-talk resulting in feelings of guilt and disappointment.
- Feeling restless, irritable and discontent.
- Being *emotionally constipated* - Being emotionally unavailable. Relying on anger to push people away. Coping with drugs and alcohol.
- Euphoric recall.
- Grandiosity - Exaggerating our own importance.
- Impulsiveness - The inability to delay gratification regardless of the consequences.
- Low self-esteem. The inability to experience joy.
- Indecisiveness - An unhealthy fear of what *might* happen, resulting in nothing getting done.
- Intolerance
- Being judgmental - Criticizing other people as a means of disguising our own defects.
- Moody with mood swings.
- Acting egotistical, pompous, self-absorbed.

Dry Drunks Suffer from Delusional Thinking
Although the person suffering a dry drunk isn't actually using *yet*, they are suffering from delusional thinking. Their unhealthy beliefs and behaviors are protected by defense mechanisms, same as a person who *is* using. Without treatment, they may stay stuck in that sorry state quite a long time before their dry drunk progresses into a full-blown relapse.

Following is part of a text conversation with an alcoholic who just progressed from a dry drunk to full-blown relapse. This person graduated a treatment program one year earlier. He was working a recovery program up until three months ago. Then, things changed.

Unable to find an affordable place to live, he moved between low-priced motels every few days. Recently he started a new job in a completely different industry. Having lost his driver's license, auto insurance and car, he had no other option but to walk the 45-minutes to and from work each day. His parents stopped enabling him by paying his bills and taking over his responsibilities. He stopped going to A.A. meetings, reading, talking to sober friends and exercising. Instead, he isolated in his apartment, playing on the computer. In order to improve his mood, he ate only junk food. He dwelled on resentments against his parents, girlfriend, old rehab and God. He felt betrayed. He deserved better. Everyone was at fault but him. He became fearful of the future and uncomfortable in the present, yet he felt completely in control of his recovery. He ignored his triggers and cravings. For the past three months he was dry drunk. Recently he drank, and then thought of a way around that too. I found him. I couldn't help but admire his delusional thinking. It was flawless. Read the conversation and see for yourself:

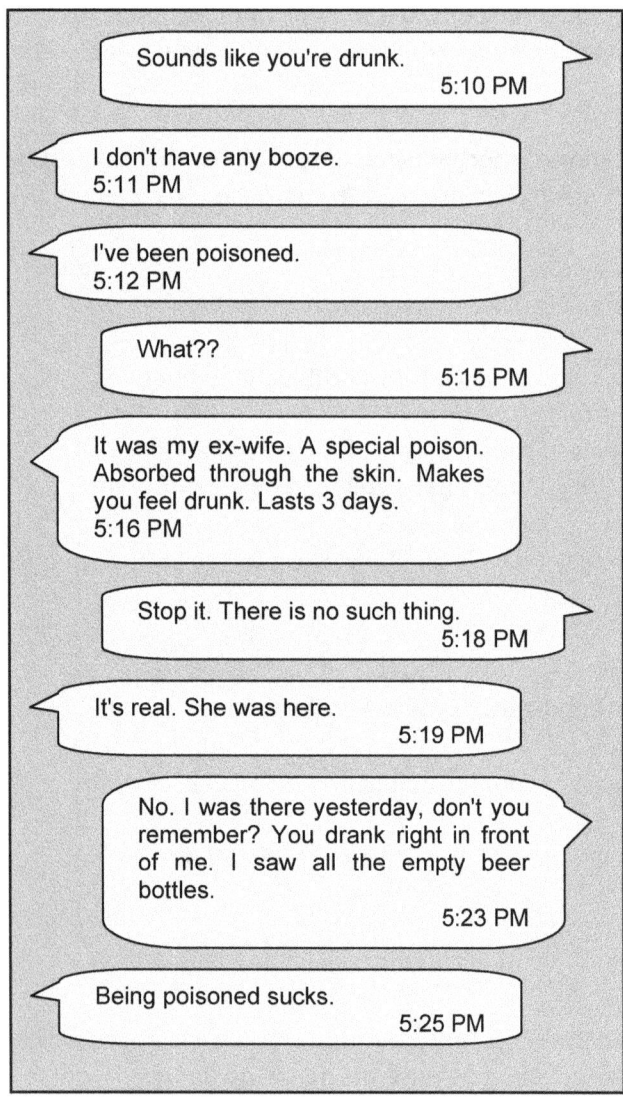

A delusion is a false belief held to be true with absolute certainty, despite overwhelming evidence to the contrary. Or, more simply, *we lie to ourselves and believe that lie.* There is no doubt this person actually believed he was "poisoned" with a substance that made him "feel drunk." He believed every word of the text messages you just read.

Isn't this the perfect delusion for an alcoholic who doesn't want to stop drinking, doesn't want the blame for drinking, and doesn't want any consequences as a result of drinking?! A "3-day poison" gives him a three-day window to binge-drink. Being "poisoned" by someone else absolves him of guilt and consequences. Of course, a poison that makes him "feel drunk" excuses his behavior. Brilliant!

Did you notice that when I reminded him I had been at his house the day before, and observed him drinking, he ignored me? He *had* to. Why? Because he wasn't *lying.* He was deluded. He *believed* what he was saying with all his heart, despite overwhelming evidence to the contrary i.e. I observed him drinking, I found the house littered with empty beer bottles, there is no reason whatsoever for his ex-wife to harm him, and, she has no knowledge of toxicology. (She works as a hair stylist, not a CIA operative.)

Delusional thinking can be based on a few *cherry-picked* facts. In this case, it is true that his ex-wife had stopped at his house - *to drop off their child for a visit.* But that's all. She didn't poison him. In reality, what probably happened is that the sight of her triggered emotional pain, and he drank to cope with that pain. However, good luck getting *him* to realize that. He would rather drink, as would many people with alcohol and drug problems who begin drinking and using drugs following a dry drunk.

Really Dry, Dry Drunks
Be aware that total non-drinkers can exhibit dry drunk behavior too! In fact, **co-dependent behavior** is one of the most common types of Dry Drunk behavior. These folks don't have the alcohol, but they have the "-holic" as in: worryaholic, workaholic, shopaholic, sexaholic, rageaholic etc.

Overcoming Dry Drunk Syndrome
Now that you understand Dry Drunk syndrome, I bet you will begin to notice these symptoms in others. When you do, you will understand that what you are witnessing is a relapse. Try talking sense to that person. Talk till you are blue in the face, if you like. They will tell you life is "good", "fine" and "no problem." They'll make bold pronouncements like: "Don't worry. I'm never going to drink again". When you ask how they are going to accomplish that goal, they will get annoyed and say things like: "I just won't. What, do you think I'm stupid?!" When it comes to their recovery, these people see no reason to turn their lives over to a power greater than themselves. They believe they know what's best. They do not question their sanity and ability to make rational decisions. HALLELUIAH! Of course they are terribly wrong. Perhaps, one day, it will be *you* who is wrong-headed. Then what?

Work your recovery program and you won't have to worry about falling into the dry drunk trap. In particular, be aware of mental stressors, work the Twelve Steps, get a sponsor, make new friends at meetings, volunteer for service work, pray and get used to talking things out *even* when it feels as uncomfortable as yanking out your own teeth. **Recovery is like walking up a down escalator. If you're not moving forward then you're falling backward.**

EXERCISES
1. How can a dry drunk lead to relapse?

2. **Pick two *attitudes* and two *behaviors* from the list above, and give an example of each.**

3. Please describe what *a relapse in every way, minus the actual chemicals* might look like if it happened to you.

4. Have you ever experienced Dry Drunk symptoms? If so, how long were you sober for? What attitudes and behaviors (from the list above) did you display?

5. What other kind(s) of "-holic" are you now, or could you easily see yourself becoming?

6. Think back. Describe the most ridiculous "3-day poison" delusion you used to explain your substance use. Who did you tell, and how did they respond?

26. Toxic Thinking

Substance Use Disorder is a disease that is characterized by relapse. It is often the pattern, because it takes time to **accept** that intelligence, Hollywood good looks, or mental might isn't enough to keep us sober. It also takes time to develop and implement the new **beliefs and behaviors** that will keep us healthy.

It is *so easy* to become **restless, irritable and discontent** during this period of change. In that respect, we are no different from any other human being. But for those of us with a substance use disorder - with so much riding on recovery - a bad attitude can be the short road to ruin. Treatment, is all about changing beliefs and behaviors. But, what brought you to treatment in the first place was a change in **attitude:** from denial to acceptance, helplessness to willingness, uncertainty to determination.

The reverse is true, as well. Your downfall will *also* begin with a change in attitude. Common terms to describe the state of mind leading to relapse, include: **toxic thinking, dry drunk, post acute withdrawal syndrome, white-knuckling it, self-will run riot, throwing a pity-party.**

Stinking Thinking is an expression coined by Gayle Rosellini in **Stinking Thinking. Hazelden; Pamphlet edition.** It is used to describe those times when we revert back to delusional thinking *even though we aren't using or drinking.* It is being negative, frustrated, and prideful in the belief that we are always right and everyone else is wrong.

> "Pride goeth before destruction, and a haughty spirit before a fall." (Proverbs 16:18)

Recognizing Stinking Thinking
We all suffer from toxic thinking at one time or another, and it doesn't automatically go away after twenty-eight days of treatment. Unchecked, stinking thinking can lead to relapse. According to Rosellini, *stinking thinking goes hand-in-hand with chronic relapsing.* In order to recover, we must recognize stinking thinking, and learn how to change our attitudes. If not, then we're sunk. Here are four attitudes that characterize stinking thinking:

1. **Lip Service**
   Lip service is telling other people what they want to hear, in order to make ourselves look good. Lip service is not lying. It is delusional thinking, because we *believe* (on the surface at least) that talking a good game equates to real recovery. We are totally sincere *at that moment*, but are all talk and no action. Why do we sabotage ourselves by being insincere? Because telling people what they want to hear, shuts them the hell up! God knows they give us enough advice over the months and years to choke a mule. That's why recovery isn't about words, it's about action. Following are common examples of lip service:
   - *I promise I will never do it again.*
   - *I have really learned my lesson this time.*
   - *I think A.A. is great, but ...*

- *Getting busted for drunk driving was the best thing that ever happened to me.*
- *I know I will never drink again.*
- *I will quit (smoking, drinking, using, being lazy, losing my temper etc.) as soon as ...*
- *I will do whatever you say, just don't (fire me, divorce me, put me in jail.)*

2. **Grandiosity**

   Grandiosity means believing that we are better than everyone else. You already know this as **ego!** For example, grandiosity is the belief we can continue going to bars without being tempted to drink. Grandiosity is the belief we can continue seeing old drug-using friends without being sucked back into our addiction. Grandiosity is the belief that other people may need the crutch of A.A. or N.A. but we don't need any of that spiritual crap. Grandiosity is the belief that one beer or some spice isn't going to make us lose control. Grandiosity is the belief we can become social drinkers or controlled drug users again. Grandiosity is the belief that rules are for fools. Grandiosity is the belief that somehow, some way, some day, we can magically beat the odds and change our situation without changing ourselves.

3. **Corner-Cutting**

   Corner-cutting is **cheating.** We cut corners when we begin to miss appointments, skip meetings, make excuses and stop taking recovery seriously. According to Rosellini, corner-cutting can be hard to recognize because our first cheats seem small and innocent, and we always have a good excuse. Corner-cutting can be combined with lip service and grandiosity, to sound like this: "Sure A.A. works (lip service), but I have a special relationship with God (grandiosity.) I don't need to pray because He makes sure everything turns out fine (corner-cutting.)"

4. **Defiance**

   How do you feel about the word "No"? As a group, alcoholics and addicts are a defiant lot. We resent being told what to do by anyone, including spouses, kids, parents, bosses, counselors, sponsors, cops, courts and anyone or anything else in authority. Defiance is a sign of **immaturity.** We are children stamping our feet so people pay attention to us and act like we want. We blame others for all our problems. We become fixated on trying to get *them* to change to make us happy. Defiance signals **self-will run riot.** Our ego deceives us into believing that we have all the answers and that everything would be fine if all these stupid people would do things our way. Often we keep our defiant attitude secret, choking on the resentment over and over, day-dreaming of different scenarios where we win and get everything we want.

Challenging the Way You Think

1. **Learn to recognize negative thinking** - You can't change a bad attitude if you're unaware of it. Now that you know what to look for, you will begin to recognize lip service, grandiosity, corner-cutting and defiance the moment you exhibit them. A popular recovery maxim holds that **once a cucumber becomes a pickle, it can never go back to being a cucumber.** As soon as you develop a knack for identifying toxic thoughts, you will feel amazing. (It's amazing to be a pickle!) Identifying these defects of character is required as part of the **"searching and fearless moral inventory"** you will develop, if you choose to work Step Four of the Twelve Steps.

2. **Make a Decision to Act** - Decide that you're sick and tired of your sick and tired old thinking.

Initially your new way of thinking may feel awkward and untrustworthy, because change is frightening. You have undertaken a monumental self-improvement project. Remember the **defense mechanisms** of **rationalizing, justifying, explaining, blaming, lying, minimizing, hiding, manipulating, denying, humor, silence, threatening, isolating, avoiding, intimidating** and **charming.** For years you relied on these tricks to protect you from change and keep you in denial. Now it's time to sweep them away. Be **fearless,** knowing that you are continuing to move closer to reclaiming your life.

3. **Take Action** - *Here's a question for you: Three frogs are sitting on a log. One of them decides to jump off. How many frogs are left on the log?* Think... think... think... The answer is *three.* Why? Just because the frog made a *decision* to jump doesn't mean he actually jumped. *A decision isn't the same as an action.* Without action, your decision is just *wishing.* You've heard the phrase: "The road to hell is paved with good intentions!"

People swear to me all the time that they are going to change. But when I ask for details, oftentimes all I get is wishful thinking. It usually goes something like this:

HIM: "I decided I don't need counseling. I'm going to quit drinking by going to A.A. meetings."

ME: *"But you lost your license and your car. How are you going to get to meetings?"*

HIM: "I'll figure it out."

ME: *"And didn't you tell me that you tried once before to get sober just by attending meetings, but you felt very uncomfortable and stopped going. How will it be different this time around?"*

HIM: "It just will. I really want it this time."

ME: *"What does that mean? Are you going to sit up straighter or hear more words? I'm confused."*

HIM: "Listen, moron. I don't need to explain anything. It *will* be different. I swear."

ME: *"Okay. Calm down. So... what meetings are you hitting this week?"*

HIM: "I don't know. Why?"

ME: *"What do you mean, you don't know?!"*

HIM: "I haven't decided yet."

ME: *"Most evening meetings start at 6PM, 7PM or 8PM. You only have a couple of hours left to find a meeting for tonight."*

HIM: "Oh. Don't worry about that. I've got to go grocery shopping tonight."

ME: *"You mean to tell me that your life is on the line, you're depending on meetings to get sober, and you're not starting tonight?"*

HIM: "I'm gonna ease into it, so I don't get overwhelmed."

ME: *"Overwhelmed?!! Isn't it true that you drink a half-gallon of wine every night? Just how do you plan to not drink later?"*

HIM: "I won't drink."

ME: *"Right. But, how?"*

HIM: "I already told you. I really want it this time. But I promise to look online for meetings when I get back from the store."

ME:	*"So you'll start going to meetings tomorrow. You're committing."*
HIM:	*"Stop pushing me so hard. You're making me not want to go at all."*
ME:	*"I'm simply asking a question."*
HIM:	*"Fine. I'm pretty sure that tomorrow will definitely be my first day going. Okay! But I'm telling you, I already have the mindset that I'm going to stop drinking."*
ME:	*"Do you realize that what you just said makes absolutely no sense? 'Pretty sure' and 'definitely' don't belong in the same sentence. Not that I'm being a nit-picker or anything. Further, whatever 'mindset' you're talking about won't help because alcoholism has nothing to do with willpower. You know this."*
HIM:	*"Then I'll commit right here and now to go to my first meeting tomorrow. Satisfied? Anything to get you off my back."*
ME:	*"That's great news. Good for you for making the commitment to act. How are you going to get there? You lost your license and your car."*
HIM:	*"I'll figure it out."*
ME:	*"AHHHHHHHHHHH."*

Take Action by Choosing Your Attitude
We possess the remarkable ability to change, yet our best intentions often fall flat. Why?

- **Fear can stop us.** Afraid of the unknown or ourselves, we say things like: "It might hurt", and "Change scares me".
- **Laziness can stop us.** "Why bother?" we ask. "I've survived this long without changing".
- **Low self-esteem can stop us.** Afraid to admit our weaknesses, we say things like: "I don't need to change", and "There's nothing wrong with me!"

Take action by asking questions that challenge old beliefs, such as: "Am I being honest?"; "Am I being realistic?"; "Am I being accountable for my actions?"; "Am I being accepting and open?". Let those people who are close to you know that you have decided to change your attitude. *Give them permission* to point out those instances when they notice old thinking. Enlist their support in keeping you **accountable.** Work your program as if you're life depended on it, because it does.

Toxic attitudes suck the joy out of life *even if we're* sober. We become ignorant, selfish, frightened, defensive, egotistical and in denial. We feel victimized, and blame all our problems on everyone else. The opposite of toxic thinking, is **insight.** When you gain insight, you become realistic, honest, humble, sensible and unafraid to act.

The key point to remember about toxic thinking is that *it is unnecessary.* We choose our attitudes in every situation!

EXERCISES

1. Name the four attitudes that signal stinking thinking, and write a short description of each.

2. Give one example, from your own life, for each of these attitudes.

3. Using a dictionary, write out the definition of "insight."

4. Challenging our stinking thinking is a three step process. Name the steps, and write a brief description for each:

   A.

   B.

   C.

5. Take each of the examples in question 2, above, and use the three step process to describe how you might transform stinking thinking into insight.

27. Post Acute Withdrawal Syndrome (PAWS)

You are already familiar with the many varied symptoms of your substance use disorder(s). Those symptoms disappear soon after you become sober. However, once you have been sober for a while, you might notice some uncomfortable feelings returning even though you are working a program. You should be aware that this can happen. Otherwise, you might think you are going crazy.

Post Acute Withdrawal Syndrome (or PAWS) describes symptoms that occur *when you are sober and working a recovery program.* These symptoms result from damage to the nervous system caused by substance abuse, and by the increased stress of recovery. **Symptoms occur 14 days to 6 months into recovery, with the most severe period being 3 to 6 months.** (In general, recovery from substance use disorder takes 6 to 24 months after you stop using.) PAWS is temporary, but you must be patient.

 ***75% TO 95% OF ALL RECOVERING ADDICTS & ALCOHOLICS SUFFER FROM POST ACUTE WITHDRAWAL SYNDROME!***

Common Symptoms of Post Acute Withdrawal
It's common to feel **restless, irritable and discontent**, as they say in A.A. Examples include:
1. **Inability to think clearly** - Intelligence is *not* affected, however you may feel like your head is full of mud at times. For example, you may have a problem concentrating or solving problems, or you may experience the same thoughts going round and round your head.
2. **Memory problems** - Forgetfulness is common. You might read over your grocery list before entering a store, and then completely forget everything on it once inside. Even remembering important events can be difficult. Learning new things becomes difficult, too.
3. **Hyperemotional** - Something calling for two units of reaction gets ten units. You might become enraged over trivial matters, and then regret it later. Likewise, you might react the opposite way and withdraw, unable to feel emotion. Either way, you cannot trust your feelings.
4. **Sleep problems** - Insomnia, unusual or disturbing dreams (like dreams of using drugs and alcohol) or sleeping for unusually long periods of time.
5. **Physical coordination problems** - Dizziness, slow reflexes, stumbling and clumsiness.
6. **Hypersensitivity to stress** - Inability to differentiate between low and high stress leads to overreacting. Sometimes the symptoms go away. As a result, you might feel like you're going crazy, but you are not.

Managing PAWS
Recovery is like walking up a down escalator. It's all about *forward momentum.* You are either strengthening yourself against post acute withdrawal, or you are becoming weaker. There is no middle ground. Since post acute withdrawal is **triggered** by **stress,** *you can control it by managing your stress.* Remember that it isn't the *situation* that stresses you; it is your **reaction** to that situation. The following tools will help you deal with PAWS:
- **Act** immediately to interrupt the symptoms, *before* they get out of control.
- **Talk** about what you're experiencing (even if you don't make sense.)
- **Ask** someone for their opinion on whether you're *perception* of a situation matches reality.
- **Recognize** your stressors, and how you deal with them. Compare your performance to previous episodes and build a mental data base of what works.

- **Learn** and practice stress management techniques such as breathing, meditation, praying, exercise, meetings, reading recovery literature etc.
- Set and enforce **boundaries**, so that you don't take on too much in early recovery.
- Exercise and eat healthy. Avoid caffeine, energy drinks, candy, cakes, junk food, sugary soda etc, because they all produce the same chemical reaction in your body that stress does.
- A relationship with your higher power will reward you with serenity, confidence and hope.
- Everything in moderation, practice patience and do not drink or use no matter what! Drugs and alcohol may temporarily relieve your symptoms, but cause further nerve damage.

Remember that recovery is about *forward momentum*. *If you are not managing your symptoms, then your symptoms will be managing you.* For more information on this important topic, I highly recommend you read **Staying Sober: A Guide for Relapse Prevention by Terence Gorski.**

EXERCISES

1. **PAWS occurs when you are** *sober.* **Identify any uncomfortable physical, mental or emotional feelings you may be experiencing now that you are in early recovery:**
   A. Physical.

   B. Mental.

   C. Emotional.

2. How can these feelings be explained in terms of post acute withdrawal syndrome?

3. What actions from the list above will you implement starting today to manage these *sobriety-based* symptoms?

28. Relapse Prevention Planning

People speak of relapse as if it were *inevitable*. While **relapse** is common, *it is never, ever necessary*. Millions of alcoholics and addicts have gotten sober and stayed that way without a single relapse. So can you.

What Is Relapse?
People mistakenly believe that the *act* of drinking and using again is a relapse when, in fact, it is the *last step in a process* that starts much earlier. Relapse is a **sequence of events**, not *one* particular event.

Relapse doesn't happen suddenly. It is *always* preceded by **warning signs.** Warning signs are the old thoughts, feelings and behaviors you used in the past to cope with emotions. They are red flags, indicating you might be in relapse mode. The Big Book of Narcotics Anonymous puts it this way: **"We begin to slight our program and leave loopholes in our daily lives."**

That's why you need a **relapse prevention plan.** Your relapse prevention plan *prepares* you ahead of time to handle warning signs. It is made up of all the tools and education you already learned, combined with the challenges you are about to face. When you recognize your disease reemerging, you must act *immediately*. Relapse prevention is therefore a *daily effort*. Ignore the warning signs, and you'll face a monumental challenge later when the pull to use is much stronger.

> **FACT: APPROXIMATELY TWO-THIRDS OF PEOPLE CURRENTLY IN RECOVERY WILL RELAPSE WITHIN A YEAR OF LEAVING TREATMENT - 33% WITHIN THE FIRST TWO WEEKS, 60% WITHIN THE FIRST THREE MONTHS, AND 67% WITHIN THE FIRST TWELVE MONTHS.**

Putting Relapse in Perspective
The best insurance policy against relapse is to work your program. As you develop your relapse prevention plan, keep in mind the following key principles:

1. **Relapse Happens**
   Fact is, you will experience the relapse process to a degree at some point during recovery. That's called, *life!* Compulsive substance use alters brain function, resulting in physical, psychological and behavioral changes. *You are not going to feel normal again for six to eighteen months.* Instead, you may feel more anxious, depressed, less focused and motivated, tired, angry, and jumping from one emotional extreme to another. Until your brain chemistry rebalances, you won't feel pleasure like other people. As a result, the **urge** to use can be powerful. The good news is that you are no longer in this battle alone. You have God (or your higher power), your sober fellowship, and a recovery program that *guarantees* success *if you work it*.

2. **Day One, Not Step One**
   While a relapse will reset your sobriety date, it *does not* rob you of all the progress you have made to that point! If you are driving from your house to the store and make an unplanned stop for gas along the way, it doesn't mean you are any farther from the store then where you stopped. You are certainly closer then when you left home, no? Similarly, relapse doesn't wipe away all the knowledge, skills and maturity you've gained in recovery. You simply start again from where you strayed off the path.

3. **Relapse Doesn't Make You a Bad Person**
Relapse doesn't make you anything other than what you already are: a good person with a bad disease; a disease that A.A. calls **"cunning, baffling, and powerful."** But recovery isn't about where you're coming *from*. It's where you are *going* that's important. Regardless of how you manage the ups and downs of sobriety, it is critical to *keep moving forward* knowing setbacks are *temporary*. Embracing shame and guilt will serve no good purpose. In fact, many people have turned relapse to their advantage, reporting that wading back into the muck of their disease only demonstrated how much better it was to be clean and sober.

4. **Relapse Kills**
Relapse doesn't always lead back to compulsive substance use, but it often does, with catastrophic consequences, including overdose and death. Addiction is a **chronic** disease, meaning you have it for life. Addiction is also **progressive.** If left unchecked, it will grow like a tumor. Those who relapse typically return to using their drug of choice at the *same level* at which they left off. Unfortunately, many people fail to realize that their **tolerance** diminishes during recovery. Their usual amount of addictive substance is now *lethal*. If the level of abuse doesn't kill you, then perhaps the *despair* of returning to the same miserable circumstances might. Some people would rather *die* than use again, as evidenced by the *high suicide rate* among recovering addicts and alcoholics. Obviously, getting back involved with the old crowd increases your chances of dying in an accident or drug-related crime, as well.

Recovery Words to Live By
- Act "as if". Think yourself into acting.
- Attitude is a choice.
- Avoid cigarettes, coffee, energy drinks, alcohol-free beer, spice.
- Avoid compulsions like excessive eating, dieting, gambling, working, exercise, sex, thrill seeking and spending. It's easy to switch addictions.
- Avoid the "what if" and "shoulda, coulda, woulda" traps.
- Beware your relapse warning signs and triggers. Keep your Relapse Prevention Plan handy!
- Change old playmates, playgrounds and playthings.
- Courage isn't the absence of fear. It's the belief that something else is more important than fear.
- Develop sober friends or accountability buddies and speak with them regularly.
- Develop spiritual habits like prayer, meditation and reading.
- EGO = Edging God Out. The root cause of this disease is selfishness, or "self-will run riot."
- FEAR = Frustration, Ego, Anxiety, Resentment. FEAR = False Evidence Appearing Real.
- HALT = Avoid making decisions when you are Hungry, Angry, Lonely or Tired.
- I can't (Step One)... He can (Step Two)... I think I'll let Him (Step Three.)
- If nothing changes, nothing changes. Remember the three frogs sitting on a log (or was it two?!)
- It works if you work it. "Success is guaranteed."
- It's not old behavior if you're still doing it.
- It's the effort not the outcome.
- Journaling your thoughts is a good way to dissolve impulsive feelings.
- Keep your side of the street clean. What other people think of you is none of your business.
- KISS = Keep It Simple Stupid.
- Let go and let God. God is God and you aren't.
- Live in the now.
- Once a cucumber becomes a pickle it can never go back to being a cucumber.

- Stay sober one day at a time!
- Practice "rigorous honesty".
- Recovery isn't magic.... It's a miracle.
- Relaxation takes practice.
- Remember the reality of the last drink. "Think it through" to avoid euphoric recall.
- Resentment is looking back, frustration is looking around, anxiety is looking ahead.
- Resentments are the "#1 offender". They cause more relapses than anything else. Holding onto resentments is like drinking poison and expecting someone else to die.
- Serenity Prayer is more than words. It's a code to live by. Reflect upon it daily.
- Shame is the gift that keeps on giving. You can transform shame into guilt.
- Substance Use Disorder is "cunning, baffling, powerful". It's a disease that convinces you that you don't have a disease.
- The "ism" in alcoholism stands for Incredibly Short Memory.
- The good news is you get your emotions back; the bad news is you get your emotions back.
- The man drinks the first drink, the first drink drinks the second, the second drink drinks the man.
- The worst day sober is better than the best day high. A day wasted is a wasted day.
- Triggers → Cravings → Behaviors → Consequences.
- Trying to pray, is praying!
- Twelve Step meetings... 90 meetings in 90 days. Listen for the similarities, not the differences.
- Uncover, discover and discard.
- Use positive affirmations every day to combat toxic thinking.
- When man listens, God speaks; when man obeys, God works miracles.
- You're fighting a disease that never takes a day off. Recovery is like walking up a down escalator.

The Best Offense Is a Good Defense

Realistically facing the possibility of relapse is the only way to remain sober. Invest in your recovery now. Spend time compiling what you know about sobriety into your own relapse prevention plan. Keep it handy to confront relapse at the first step rather than the last, when it is much more difficult. The more thought and effort you put into answering the questions below, the more secure you will feel in your plan. A well constructed plan buys you immediate **peace of mind.**

Every decision to relapse is a sober one! You don't prevent drinking and using by not drinking and using. You do it by working on the thinking and actions that cause you to go there in the first place. Remember this plan may save your life.

Personal Relapse Prevention Plan

1. An effective relapse prevention plan anticipates warning signs and affords you the opportunity to develop healthy solutions in advance. For each of the following warning signs, write one opposite action you can take. Check each box completed as you go:
    - ❑ I find it difficult to focus or concentrate.

    - ❑ I develop aches and pains.

- ❑ I have disturbing, vivid nighttime dreams of using and drinking.

- ❑ I overreact to situations.

- ❑ I have problems getting to sleep and/or staying asleep.

- ❑ I repeatedly set goals that are unrealistically high.

- ❑ I become overconfident about my recovery. I focus on what is wrong with other people.

- ❑ I believe that my disease is unlike anyone else's, and that I am the exception to the rule.

- ❑ I decide that being abstinent is all I need.

- ❑ I do not feel the need to complete all twelve steps.

- ❑ I believe I can stay sober by willpower or intelligence alone.

- ❑ I keep triggers, cravings and other uncomfortable feelings to myself.

- ❑ I start to skip or reduce meetings, therapy appointments, church and sponsor meetings.

- ❑ I convince myself I am cured.

- ❑ I don't have a sponsor, or am not talking to my sponsor on a regular basis.

- ❑ I start isolating myself from others.

- ❑ I think meetings are boring and nothing relates to me. They only make me want to use.

- ❑ I focus on other people's shortcomings instead of my own.

- ❑ I do not share at meetings.

- ❑ I begin lying to people, again. (Little lies count, too.)

- ❑ I think in extremes, viewing my problems as unbearable and unsolvable.

- ❑ I lump all my other problems together and become overwhelmed and unmotivated.

- ❑ I feel ashamed of things I have done.

- ❑ I can't let go of resentment.

- ❑ I construct elaborate schedules for when I'm going to change, but fail to follow through.

- ❑ I focus on things which may or may not happen in the future (i.e. 'Future tripping').

- ❏ I make appointments, only to blow them off.

- ❏ I feel depressed and unmotivated. It's difficult to get out of bed.

- ❏ I have thoughts of ending my life.

- ❏ I behave in an addictive fashion with sex, food, work, gambling, stealing or hurting myself.

- ❏ I choose not to make plans for my free time. I would rather be spontaneous.

- ❏ I suddenly decide to make big changes in other areas of my life, such as changing jobs, relocating, getting divorced, or moving in with a girlfriend/boyfriend.

- ❏ I practice controlled drinking and using.

- ❏ I start using a different chemical than my drug of choice. (This includes addictive drugs that are prescribed to you.)

- ❏ I allow myself to reminisce about getting drunk or high, without also recalling all the negative consequences I experienced as a result.

- ❏ I test my sobriety by going to bars or hanging with my dealer or other unsafe people.

- ❏ I convince myself that relapse is part of recovery, and I just need that one last high or drunk in order to quit with peace of mind.

2. Triggers can be social, mental, emotional, financial, marital or geographical. Identify your triggers, along with a healthy way to cope with each:

TRIGGER	HOW I WILL COPE
1.	1.
2.	2.
3.	3.
4.	4.
5.	5.

3. What benefits will you get from sharing your feelings when you are triggered?

4. Take the four points you learned from Putting Relapse in Perspective, and put them together into one sentence you will be able to reread anytime you think about relapse.

5. Chapter 7 of the N.A. Big Book states, "Our egos tell us that we can do it on our own, but... we find that we cannot really do it alone, when we try, things get worse." Why is that?

6. What will your Twelve Step meeting schedule look like for the next 30 – 90 days:

DAY	TIME	ADDRESS
SUNDAY		
MONDAY		
TUESDAY		
WEDNESDAY		
THURSDAY		
FRIDAY		
SATURDAY		

7. SPONSOR: Name and contact. When/where will you meet? What is the plan to work together?

8. BASIC NEEDS: Plans for housing, sober living, eating, transportation etc.?

9. FAMILY: How to reunite with family. Have you made amends? How will you rebuild trust?

10. **FINANCES:** Employment, job search, retraining, education, child support etc.?

11. **HEALTH:** Medical or dental issues? Plans for after-care or counseling? Exercise, sleep, nutrition?

12. **LEGAL OBLIGATIONS:** Outstanding legal issues that must be addressed?

13. **LEISURE TIME:** How will you occupy your spare time? Animals, family, exercise, hobbies, reading or music? Will you go to the beach, bike ride, hike, undertake household projects, participate in sports, travel, write etc?

14. SOCIAL LIFE: Who can you trust to not drink or use? Which of your friends are dependable?

NAME	PHONE
1.	
2.	
3.	
4.	
5.	

15. SPIRITUALITY: How to stay in constant contact with your Higher Power i.e. read, pray, worship, serve and meditate?

16. OTHER.

29. Bonus 1: Eating Your Way to Recovery
A Customized Diet for Your Body and Goals!

It is a fact that alcohol affects every cell in the body. You know what else affects every cell in the body? *FOOD!* So what better way to repair the damage caused by alcohol and drug abuse, then to eat your way back to health.

The substances you ingested have taken a toll on your body. But, how much of a toll? That's a question most of us would rather not think about. As compulsive substance users, we are victims of our own **neglect.** We skip meals. We do not hydrate properly. We eat low quality, high calorie foods. As a result, we find ourselves malnourished; underweight or overweight; with bad skin, hair and teeth. Even worse, what you see on the outside only *hints* at the internal damage. When we begin recovery, we quickly become disheartened to find our **metabolism** is not functioning nearly the way it did before our disease.

Substance abuse exacts a profound toll on our health; affecting the brain, heart, kidneys, liver, lungs, circulatory system, endocrine system (particularly the adrenal glands), gastrointestinal tract, immune system, nervous system and more. Here, we begin at the beginning. We focus on the metabolism, or, more precisely, the **macro and micro nutrients** supplied by the foods we eat. Once you understand the link between the foods you eat and how your body processes those foods, you can turn the tables and control your body, rather than being its victim. You will be able to use food - with precision - to burn fat, add quality muscle and restore your health.

Turn the tragedy of alcohol and drug abuse into a physiological *triumph.* Follow the step-by-step directions to jolt your body back into prime working order, and do it in much less time than it took you to get to fall apart! The whole process is so simple, you can start with *your next meal* and see results in the way you look and feel in only a few days. Read this worksheet to the end, then make your decision. Whether you are experienced with nutrition, or don't have a clue where to start, the next fifteen minutes can change your life.

Beware of Extreme Diet Behavior
Most people are perplexed when it comes to proper nutrition. We have followed all sorts of diets, but experienced little in the way of *lasting* results. Thankfully, this is not going to be one of those times!

It is no surprise that addicts and alcoholics in early recovery tend to go overboard on carbohydrates like fruit, bread, pasta, potatoes, sugared cereal, cake, candy, cookies, soda and basically anything sweet and easy to grab. We eat for *quick energy.* We eat to *cope with emotions* like anger and remorse. We eat to feel just a little bit of *joy.* We eat because we are *lonely.* We eat because we are *bored.*

Carbohydrates are the body's preferred source of immediate energy. But, there is a problem. *Carbohydrates themselves act like a drug*, causing a cascade of unwanted physiological reactions. For example, going overboard on carbohydrates can trigger an increase in **insulin,** a hormone that can throw your body out of balance with disastrous consequences. An article from the *American Journal of Clinical Nutrition* confirms that a diet rich in carbohydrates, but low in protein, increases blood fat. Bingeing on carbohydrates also makes you tired, and increases your appetite later. As you will soon see, your health can suffer big time.

Going to the other extreme - by slashing carbohydrates from your diet - can also lead to disastrous consequences by creating a condition called **ketosis.** Normally, carbohydrates are the preferred fuel source for the body, including the brain, heart and organs. Starving the body of carbohydrates forces a switch to fat as the primary fuel source. This can be useful for very short periods, such as to jump start an Atkins® style (high protein) diet. However, the risks associated with ketosis are many, including an increased risk of bad cholesterol, cancer, bone calcium loss, and kidney and blood pressure problems.

Looking at Carbohydrates a Whole New Way with the Glycemic Index
Carbohydrates make eating fun and healthy. Your body depends on carbohydrates for everything from walking to talking to thinking. Switching to any other energy source is like putting diesel fuel in a high performance car. Carbohydrates like fruits and vegetables provide fiber, vitamins, minerals and phytonutrients which you cannot get elsewhere. Research shows that carbohydrates are needed to maintain adequate levels of the feel-good brain chemicals **serotonin** and **dopamine,** which compulsive substance users have depleted so repeatedly (i.e. brain drain!) The problem isn't carbohydrates. Rather, it is how to enjoy all the benefits of carbohydrates without any of the unintended consequences. The answer can be found in the **Glycemic Index.**

The Glycemic Index **(GI)** *is a numerical system of measuring how fast a carbohydrate is digested, triggering a rise in blood sugar;* the higher the number, the more rapid the response. A low GI food causes a small rise. A high GI food triggers a spike. A food with a GI of **less than 55 is considered a low** glycemic food, while **56 to 69 is moderate** and **over 70 is considered high.** *The key is that all carbohydrates are not alike.*

Understanding the Glycemic Index allows you to control insulin, lose fat, and still enjoy carbohydrates. Dr. Andrew Weil agrees: "We should pay attention to the Glycemic Index of carbohydrate foods - that is, the ease with which the body converts them to blood sugar. High glycemic foods like rice cakes, bread, and potatoes stress the body's insulin system and probably are chief culprits in obesity."

You should have a list of foods with their GI value in your kitchen and on your phone for reference. A list of low glycemic foods is included with this worksheet, or search for one online. For the moment, look at the following abbreviated list of carbohydrates along with their glycemic values.

GLYCEMIC INDEX OF COMMON FOODS
www.diabetes-guide.org

Glucose	100	Oranges	44	Black beans	30
Potato (baked)	98	Spaghetti	41	Lentils	29
Honey	75	Milk (whole)	40	Grapefruit	25
Potato (boiled)	70	Apples	39	Cherries	22
Bread (white)	70	Ice cream	36	Soybeans	25
Sweet potato	61	Milk (skim)	32	Soy beans	18
Orange juice	46	Carrot (raw)	31		

Notice that this index uses **glucose as the baseline** with its index set as being equal to **100.** Also high on the scale are **highly processed, starchy foods** like potatoes and bread. Foods below 55 are considered low glycemic, and include beans, apples and vegetables.

Blood Sugar's Wild Ride
Normal blood sugar - called **glucose** - ranges in the 60 to 100 mg/dl blood. *High glycemic carbohydrates act like high octane fuel.* Once ingested, they quickly convert to glucose and shoot into the bloodstream. The result is a rapid rise in blood sugar, which we call a **sugar rush.**

The pancreas responds by flooding your system with the hormone insulin. Insulin drives glucose out of the bloodstream and into tissues, where it can be used as energy. Unfortunately, what goes up *rapidly* must also come down *rapidly*. Here, the fast and furious release of insulin plunges blood sugar levels well below normal, creating a hormonal imbalance known as **hypoglycemia,** or simply, low blood sugar.

Once blood sugar drops below 50 mg/dl, your body goes into *panic mode.* The adrenal glands produce **adrenaline** to stabilize blood sugar, but only at the expense of other organs and tissues which are robbed of fuel. It is important to note that a drop in blood sugar, signaling the release of adrenaline, can *also* occur when you *skip meals or take too much time between meals.* It is *also* responsible for the uncomfortable feeling you get when undergoing extreme *stress*; as in **fight, flight or fright.** *Perhaps these are the best reasons for working your recovery program and taking charge of your nutrition.*

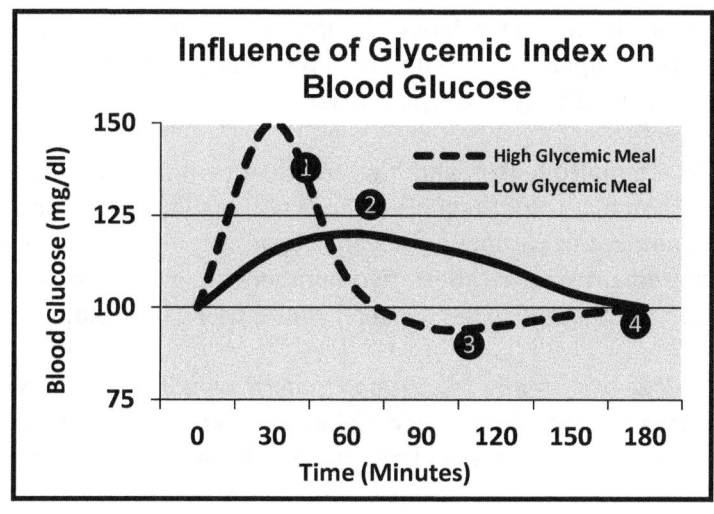

The cycle of highs and lows just described are represented in the adjacent diagram. Notice the sharp rise in blood sugar produced by high GI foods ❶, compared to low GI foods ❷. The spike signals the overproduction of insulin and release of triglycerides, while adrenaline is released at the low point. *Notice how long the low point lasts* ❸. *High glycemic, sugary foods actually result in a longer period of low energy.*

Extreme highs and lows set the stage for poor health and performance.

There are a host of risks and unwanted side-effects associated with the hormonal imbalance caused by improper eating. You won't believe how bad they are, particularly for those of us in recovery. Which of the following side-effects can you identify with?

- ❑ **Weight Gain.** Insulin is the key regulator of the enzyme LPL (Lipoprotein Lipase), the "gatekeeper" of fat storage. An increase of LPL causes the storage of excess calories in fat cells. At the same time, it prevents the release of stored fat for energy. *In other words, when you over stimulate insulin by overeating high glycemic carbohydrate, you also over stimulate the enzyme that controls fat storage.*

- ❑ **Increased Appetite and Cravings for Sweets.** Low blood sugar causes you to be hungrier sooner than normal. It also causes you to crave sweets in order to relieve irritability, shakes, weakness and panic.

- ❑ **Loss of Lean Muscle Tissue.** Depriving the body of carbohydrate fuel diverts glucose from muscle, liver, kidney and brain tissue.

- ❑ **Ineffective Use of Natural Human Growth Hormone (Hgh).** Are you downing a sugary drink before exercising, or eating sweets before bedtime? Better rethink that strategy. One of the most important anti-aging, muscle building hormones in the world, **human growth hormone,** *cannot be utilized in a high glycemic environment.* Hgh is released in small "spurts" throughout the day, with the largest occurring during exercise, and approximately one-hour after you fall asleep. In order to get the most benefit from your natural supply, it is crucial to eat properly.

- ❑ **Adrenal Exhaustion.** The process of releasing adrenaline, is part of the well-known "fight or flight" response. It is an important defensive system, but *it can be overused to the point of exhaustion.* Compounded by caffeine, alcohol, smoking and stress, adrenaline slowly loses its effectiveness. In fact, constant attack on the adrenals could lead to chronic fatigue.

- ❑ **Insulin Resistance.** Receptor cells slowly become immune to insulin and starved of nourishment. This can lead to diabetes.

- ❑ **Increased Risk of Heart Disease.** The body responds to high glycemic carbohydrates by releasing insulin. The liver also responds by releasing blood lipids. Once in the bloodstream, these sticky, gooey fats can bind to the arterial walls, causing the heart to work harder, and increasing the risk of heart disease. Just how serious a health risk? According to Harvard Medical School, if smoking increases the risk of heart disease by a factor of 4, a high triglyceride/HDL ratio increases the likelihood of a heart attack by a factor of 16!!

- ❑ **Syndrome X.** Syndrome X (also known as Metabolic Syndrome) is thought to be caused by insensitivity to insulin, resulting in too much insulin in the blood. Symptoms include one or more of the following: high blood sugar, high blood lipids, obesity and high blood pressure. Syndrome X increases the risk for coronary artery disease, stroke and type-2 diabetes.

High glycemic carbohydrates to especially avoid are **maltodextrin** and **high fructose corn syrup.** If these appear high on the ingredient list of a product, then buy something else. The first thing you should look at on a label is the list of ingredients. Check the amount of carbohydrates and sugar per serving. If a high glycemic carbohydrate is near the top of the ingredient list, and these two numbers are close, then you can be reasonably sure that the product will promote the rapid rise in insulin you're trying to avoid.

Remember, when it comes to carbohydrates, slow and steady (digestion, that is) wins the race. Low glycemic carbohydrates provide the *exact same 4 calories* as the high glycemic variety. They are just metabolized at a slower rate. You get all the energy, performance and health benefits, while your caloric intake remains exactly the same.

A word of caution about basing your diet *solely* on the Glycemic Index... The glycemic value of a *meal* will be affected by the other foods you eat *along with* your carbohydrates. *Mixing protein and fat into the meal slows digestion, lowering the overall glycemic value.* That's why ice cream is considered low glycemic. But, is it really a healthy choice? Therefore, don't use the glycemic index in a vacuum. *If you have to eat high glycemic carbohydrates, be sure your meal also includes other foods and they are healthy choices.*

Creating Your Customized Program
Congratulations on making it this far! A program for eating that is customized to your body and recovery goals begins by recalibrating your diet. From now on: 50% of your calories will come from carbohydrates, 25% from protein, and 25% from fat. We refer to this more as simply, **50/25/25**:

1. **25% PROTEIN.** Begin by determining your daily protein needs. On this one, simple but critical calculation will turn the entire success or failure of your effort. Here's why. Protein is the most important and *easiest to determine* variable of a nutrition plan for anyone interested in recovering their health and replacing body fat with muscle. Consumption is based on the time-honored principle that a successful anabolic state requires 1.0 grams of protein per pound of bodyweight.

   Listen carefully. This does *not* mean you should eat more protein than anything else! Eating too much protein can be harmful to the body for all the reasons mentioned earlier. You do, however, need to eat *enough* protein and then build the rest of your nutrition program on that foundation. Your recovery diet is **protein balanced,** not protein based.

   In addition to rearranging your intake of carbohydrates, protein and fat, there is one more variable to consider, and that is **calories.** To effectively stoke the metabolism furnace, you need to consume enough fuel. So it makes sense to adjust your *total calorie intake* according to the amount of calories you *expend*. Which of the following best represents the amount of exercise you will invest to reach your goal?

   - ❏ 0.4   *Minimal activity.*
   - ❏ 0.6 – 0.7   *3 – 4 times per week for 45 minutes each day.*
   - ❏ 0.9   *5 – 6 times per week for at least 1 hour each day.*

   It is time to weigh yourself and create your recovery diet, as follows:

ACTIVITY LEVEL	
x **BODY WEIGHT**	
= **GRAMS OF PROTEIN PER DAY**	

2. **50% CARBOHYDRATES**. As we discussed, eat **low glycemic carbohydrates** whenever possible. Low glycemic foods are premium fuel for recovering alcoholics and addicts. Since they move slow and steady through your system, low glycemic carbohydrates provide a longer-lasting source of energy. *A study conducted at San Jose State University found that low glycemic carbohydrates can increase endurance and stamina by as much as 60%.* Refer back to the

diagram. Observe how low GI foods cause a more reasonable rise in blood sugar, while *never* dropping your energy level below 100 ❹.

Not only will low glycemic carbohydrates provide you with steady energy and important nutrients, but they are the ultimate **appetite suppressant.** Since they are digested more slowly, you can't help but feel satisfied longer.

All these benefits, just by changing the foods you eat! *When it comes to carbohydrates, slow and steady wins the race.* According to the 50/25/25 formula, your daily carbohydrate intake is double that of protein:

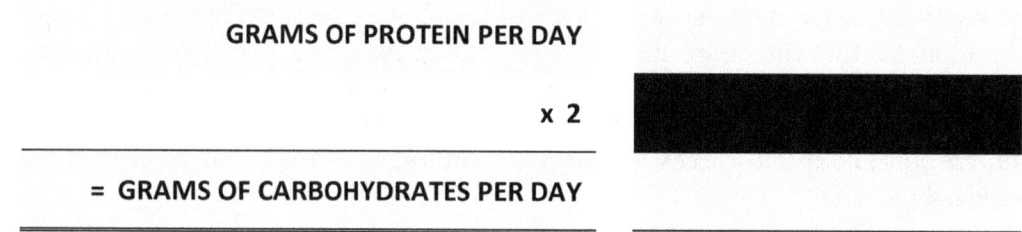

3. **25% FAT.** At **9** calories per gram of fat (versus **4** calories per gram of protein or carbohydrate), this macronutrient is the body's source of **sustained energy.** One-quarter of your calories should come from *healthy fats.* Choose foods that are high in essential fatty acids (EFA's), especially Omega-3. Cold-water fish like salmon are a great source healthy fats and protein. Other sources include avocados, almonds, flaxseed and olive oil. To determine the amount of fat you need to eat every day, you must account for the caloric differential as follows:

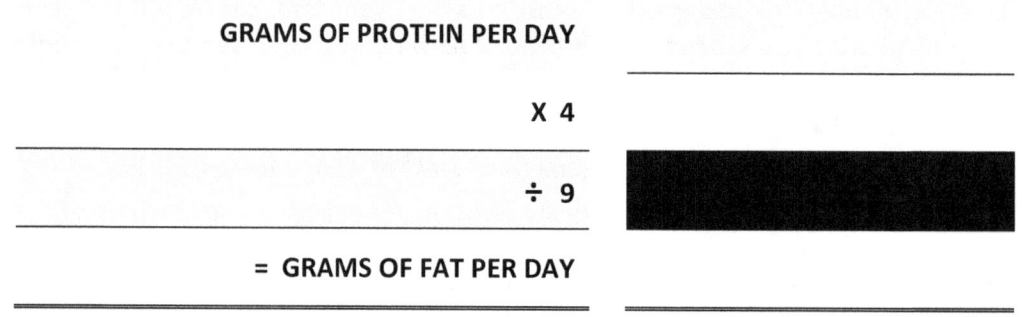

4. **TOTALS.** All that's left to creating your customized diet based on your recovery goals is to divide each total into five meals/snacks spread equally throughout the day. It is a good idea to have at least three solid meals a day, and a combination of two meal replacement drinks or bars. Good sources of protein include turkey, chicken, fish and egg whites.

If you elect to use nutritional supplements, select a protein-only supplement and combine carbohydrates and fat to meet your goal for that meal. A great tip is to finish your day with a shake before bedtime, because it enables your body to maintain a **positive nitrogen balance** throughout the night. Simply put, that means you're not losing muscle during those eight hours of sleep (and starvation!) Pick a good quality protein supplement consisting of whey *and* casein, guaranteeing *immediate* absorption and *long-term* bioavailability. With so many selections, and the superior processing technologies used today, you can't really make a mistake. Try to buy a single serving before purchasing the entire container, in order to experience the taste and digestibility. Remember, if you don't like it, you won't use it.

Determine your totals as follows:

	PER DAY (From above)	PER MEAL (Divided by 5 meals)
CARBOHYDRATES (50%)		÷ 5 =
PROTEIN (25%)		÷ 5 =
FAT (25%)		÷ 5 =

Start Today!
Whether you are a couch potato or professional athlete, a customized diet consisting of 50% low glycemic carbohydrates/25% protein/25% healthy fats is ideal for anyone recovering from substance abuse. The benefits cannot be ignored: enhanced appetite control; increased fat oxidation; reduced fat storage; and significantly improved energy, mood and health. Simply determine your ideal intake of carbohydrates, protein and fat based on the 50/25/25 model, read food labels and make low glycemic carbohydrate selections. Record your progress using the attached Progress Report.

Work on cutting low glycemic carbohydrates, and watch your body shift into high gear. When it comes to carbohydrates, slow and steady wins the race! Eating a protein balanced, low glycemic diet, will reward you with the long-term health and fitness results you're after. It's the plan that will fuel your recovery, and it's a plan you can live with.

LOW GLYCEMIC FOODS LIST (Low < 55, & Med 55 - 69)

Based on the average GI derived from multiple studies by different laboratories

BEANS
Baked
Black
Garbanzo
Hummus
Kidney
Lentils
Navy
Pinto
Soybeans

BREAD
Ezekiel
Mixed grain
Oat bran
Pita (white, wheat)
Pumpernickel
Rye kernel
Sourdough (rye, wheat)
Whole grain
Whole wheat tortillas

CEREAL
All bran
High fiber
Hot cereal (steel cut oats, slow cooking)
Oat bran
Rolled oats
Special K

DIARY
Cheese
Cottage cheese
Ice Cream, vanilla
Milk (almond, chocolate, low fat, rice, soy)
Yogurt (low fat)

FAT/OIL/BUTTER
Canola
Coconut oil
Light mayonnaise
Margarine
Olive oil
Safflower oil

FRUIT *(Raw is best)*
Apple
Apricot (dried)
Banana (less ripe)
Berries (blueberries, strawberries, raspberries, blackberries, boysenberries)
Cherries
Grapefruit
Grapes
Guava
Juice (apple, grapefruit, orange, pineapple carrot)
Kiwi
Lemon
Mango
Melon (cantaloupe, honeydew)
Nectarine
Orange
Papaya
Peach
Pear
Pineapple (canned)
Plum
Pomegranate
Raisins
Watermelon

GRAINS
Brown rice
Converted rice
Couscous
Quinoa
Semolina
Vermicelli

JAMS/JELLIES
(With low GI fruits and without sugars)

NUTS
Almond butter
Almonds
Peanut butter (natural)

Peanuts
Cashews
Pistachios
Sunflower seeds

OTHER
Healthy Choice
Steamers
Kashi Steamers

PASTA
Capellini
Fettuccine
Linguini
Macaroni
Pierogies
Ravioli and Tortellini (cheese, meat)
Spaghetti (5 min boil)

PROTEIN
Canadian bacon
Eggs
Meat (beef, pork, lamb, buffalo, venison, veal)
Poultry (chicken, turkey)
Seafood (shrimp, scallops, lobster, calamari, mussels, salmon, tuna, fish)
Soy
Tofu

SALAD
Green (Caesar, Chefs, Cobb, Spinach)
Egg
Fruit (made with acceptable fruits)
Pasta (fresh)
Shrimp/Seafood
Vegetable (made with acceptable veggies)

SNACKS
Nuts
Pound cake

Pudding
Sponge cake

SOUPS
Black bean
Chili
Gumbo
Jambalaya
Lentil
Minestrone
Onion
Tomato

VEGETABLES *(Fresh or frozen)*
Artichoke
Arugula
Asparagus
Avocado
Broccoli
Brussels sprouts
Cabbage
Carrots
Cauliflower
Celery
Cucumbers
Eggplant
Jicama
Kale
Lettuce (all types)
Mushroom
Olives
Onions
Peppers (all)
Pickles
Radishes
Sauerkraut
Snow peas
Spinach
Squash (acorn, butternut, winter, yellow)
Sweet potatoes
Tomatoes
Water chestnuts
Watercress
Yams

Progress Record

WEEK ____	MON	TUE	WED	THUR	FRI	SAT	SUN
WEIGHT							
BODY FAT %							
BREAKFAST							
SNACK							
LUNCH							
SNACK							
DINNER							
SNACK							
TOTAL CALORIES							
EXERCISE TIME							
WEEK ____	MON	TUE	WED	THUR	FRI	SAT	SUN
WEIGHT							
BODY FAT %							
BREAKFAST							
SNACK							
LUNCH							
SNACK							
DINNER							
SNACK							
TOTAL CALORIES							
EXERCISE TIME							
WEEK ____	MON	TUE	WED	THUR	FRI	SAT	SUN
WEIGHT							
BODY FAT %							
BREAKFAST							
SNACK							
LUNCH							
SNACK							
DINNER							
SNACK							
TOTAL CALORIES							
EXERCISE TIME							

Progress Record

WEEK ____	MON	TUE	WED	THUR	FRI	SAT	SUN
WEIGHT							
BODY FAT %							
BREAKFAST							
SNACK							
LUNCH							
SNACK							
DINNER							
SNACK							
TOTAL CALORIES							
EXERCISE TIME							
WEEK ____	**MON**	**TUE**	**WED**	**THUR**	**FRI**	**SAT**	**SUN**
WEIGHT							
BODY FAT %							
BREAKFAST							
SNACK							
LUNCH							
SNACK							
DINNER							
SNACK							
TOTAL CALORIES							
EXERCISE TIME							
WEEK ____	**MON**	**TUE**	**WED**	**THUR**	**FRI**	**SAT**	**SUN**
WEIGHT							
BODY FAT %							
BREAKFAST							
SNACK							
LUNCH							
SNACK							
DINNER							
SNACK							
TOTAL CALORIES							
EXERCISE TIME							

Progress Record

WEEK ____	MON	TUE	WED	THUR	FRI	SAT	SUN
WEIGHT							
BODY FAT %							
BREAKFAST							
SNACK							
LUNCH							
SNACK							
DINNER							
SNACK							
TOTAL CALORIES							
EXERCISE TIME							
WEEK ____	MON	TUE	WED	THUR	FRI	SAT	SUN
WEIGHT							
BODY FAT %							
BREAKFAST							
SNACK							
LUNCH							
SNACK							
DINNER							
SNACK							
TOTAL CALORIES							
EXERCISE TIME							
WEEK ____	MON	TUE	WED	THUR	FRI	SAT	SUN
WEIGHT							
BODY FAT %							
BREAKFAST							
SNACK							
LUNCH							
SNACK							
DINNER							
SNACK							
TOTAL CALORIES							
EXERCISE TIME							

Progress Record

WEEK ___	MON	TUE	WED	THUR	FRI	SAT	SUN
WEIGHT							
BODY FAT %							
BREAKFAST							
SNACK							
LUNCH							
SNACK							
DINNER							
SNACK							
TOTAL CALORIES							
EXERCISE TIME							
WEEK ___	MON	TUE	WED	THUR	FRI	SAT	SUN
WEIGHT							
BODY FAT %							
BREAKFAST							
SNACK							
LUNCH							
SNACK							
DINNER							
SNACK							
TOTAL CALORIES							
EXERCISE TIME							
WEEK ___	MON	TUE	WED	THUR	FRI	SAT	SUN
WEIGHT							
BODY FAT %							
BREAKFAST							
SNACK							
LUNCH							
SNACK							
DINNER							
SNACK							
TOTAL CALORIES							
EXERCISE TIME							

Notes:

30. Bonus 2: Finding Your Dream Job

It is not the intention of this exercise to lock you into any particular job or career. It is to get you thinking about finding employment in a new way: a way that is convenient and highly efficient. With the internet, you can research in minutes what used to take days or even weeks. By making smart use of it, you could be on your way to an exciting, profitable future *today* if you really wanted.

Many people are overwhelmed by the vast resources available, or are underwhelmed by what they perceive to be the obstacles blocking their dream. Both of these matters can be overcome with proper planning. This exercise is the first step in formulating that plan.

What Is It You Want, Really?
Work is not a one-size-fits-all proposition. What is it you really want? If you want **employment**, then your satisfaction will be in the form of *wages*. Pursue a **career,** and benefit from *advancement*. Follow a **calling** and your investment in *time and effort* becomes your satisfaction (in which case you need not even get paid to enjoy yourself.) Find an opportunity that offers all these things, and you've got a dream job as well as an amazing life ahead of you.

If you don't already have a job, then it is advisable in early recovery to find *employment*. This is often called a "get well job". It is a job that is comfortable, low stress, and occupies your time while putting cash in your pocket. Employment, however, can also bring joy as well as serve as a rung on your career ladder. The key isn't starting out with postings on Careerbuilder or Craigslist. Instead, it starts with you.

Ever meet someone who is wildly successful, yet feels unfulfilled and empty? Maybe that someone is you? Many who strive and sacrifice for big paychecks, fancy titles or celebrity, and get them, find the *American dream* to be shallow. Big paychecks can easily lead to bigger addicts and alcoholics. I, as well as anyone, personally know this to be true. Just prior to my own recovery, I founded and ran a multi-million dollar business which sold products worldwide. What I found was that the more money I made, the harder I worked. The harder I worked the more anxious and unhappy I became. The worse I felt, the more I spent on drugs and alcohol to cope with those feelings. For me, as for many of us, money and drugs grew in proportion to my success. Honestly, if money bought happiness, then Hollywood would be the happiest place on earth!

Those of us in recovery have to be purposeful in *everything* we do. We can't afford to make a mistake, like being miserable while sitting atop a pile of cash! Be happy in what you do... *and you will be happy, regardless.* Strive to find a job in line with who you are, accounting for your core **values, talents** and **abilities.** This is often referred to as your **life's purpose.** Working a *job, career* or *calling* that is in line with your life's purpose will strongly support your recovery. It will build self-worth and dignity. It will keep you genuine. It will energize you and connect you to others.

> **"Whatever you do, do well. For when you go to the grave, there will be no work or planning or knowledge or wisdom."** (Ecclesiastes, 9:10)

Getting Started

Following are simple questions designed to walk you through the process of identifying interesting employment opportunities. (Use the internet to locate key information on careers, education and training resources):

- **My interests include:**

- **My talents include:**

- **If I had the chance to become anything in the world, I might like to be a:**

- **What are the kinds of things a person working in this field does?**

- **What skills are required?**

- **Visiting a job board like Craigslist, Monster or Careerbuilder, search for any three openings in this field. Generally, what education and training is required?**

- What is the average salary range you could expect?

- Is the outlook for jobs in this field rising or falling (specify your source of information)?

- Identify one or more *related* professions?

- List three schools or training programs that could launch your career in this field. What do you like about each?

- List the websites for three companies currently employing professionals in that field.

- Do you know anybody - or do you know someone *who knows someone* - that might be willing to help you secure a job in this profession? If so, list their contact information.

- What businesses, enterprises, agencies, groups or people could you contact for the purpose of arranging a brief, informal meeting to discuss the opportunities in this field?

Is it becoming clear? If not, play 20-questions. Go quickly through the following list, answering as many as you can:

1. **What are your aspirations?**

2. **What do you daydream about for the years ahead?**

3. **Five years from now, what do you think you will wish you had done?**

4. **What would you do if you knew you could not fail at it?**

5. **What could you do that would make you proud of yourself?**

6. **What could you do that would show that you were living a life in line with your core values?**

7. **What are you never too tired to do?**

8. **What excites you?**

9. **In what area of life are you most organized?**

10. **When are you most self-disciplined?**

11. **What activities do you do well and which ones can you just barely get done?**

12. Do you like to be in groups, or do you prefer individual pursuits?

13. What do you think about?

14. What do you visualize?

15. What do you talk to yourself about?

16. How would your life be different if you had the education or training you desired?

17. What about you inspires others?

18. If you had one day to live, what would you do?

19. What do you want your obituary to say about you?

20. Right now, how would you answer; "What is my purpose in life?"

Where to Go From Here
This exercise is only meant to serve as an introduction to the research *process*. A job should be highly individual. Yes, a job is a means to live. However, the *best* jobs offer something infinitely more valuable: *fulfillment and satisfaction*. You deserve a job you *love*.

You owe it to yourself to explore every area in which you might be interested. One of the best books available is: *What Color Is Your Parachute? 2012: A Practical Manual for Job-Hunters and Career-Changers* by Richard N. Bolles. Additionally, if you are currently attending college, the Career Center may offer a variety of assessment tools designed to identify your aptitudes and narrow your search.

Attached are samples of two popular résumé formats: *Chronological* and *functional*. A chronological format works well if you already have a strong work history. On the other hand, a functional format focuses on your skills and achievements rather than your chronological work history. A functional format is useful if you are changing careers or have gaps in your employment history. To call attention to your background, you will want to make good use of action words. A list of action verbs is also included. Once a job interview is secured, you can prepare yourself by using the interview preparation worksheet.

As the saying goes; "If you do what you love, you'll never work a day in your life."

> **"The biggest mistake people make is not making a living at doing what they most enjoy."** (Malcom Forbes)

Reverse Chronological Format

YOUR NAME
Home Address
City, State, Zip Code
Home and Cell Phones
E-mail

Objective:
A position that uses your skills.

SUMMARY

- Years of work experience, paid and unpaid, relevant to target position's requirements
- Achievement that proves you can handle the target
- Another achievement that proves you can handle the target
- Skills, competencies, characteristics — facts that further your ability to handle target job
- Education and training relating to the target (if unrelated, bury in resume body)

PROFESSIONAL EXPERIENCE AND ACCOMPLISHMENTS

[dates]   **Job Title**   Employer, Employer's Location
A brief synopsis of your purpose in the company, detailing essential functions, products and customer base you managed.
- An achievement in this position relevant to objective (do not repeat summary)
- A second achievement in this position relevant to current objective
- More accomplishments, i.e., awards, recognition, promotion, raise, praise, training

[dates]   **Job Title**   Employer, Employer's Location
Detailed as above.

[dates]   **Job Title**   Employer, Employer's Location
A briefer synopsis of your purpose in the company, overviewing functions, products, customer base.
- An achievement made during this position relevant to current objective
- More accomplishments, i.e., awards, recognition, promotion, raise, praise, training

[dates]   **Job Title**   Employer, Employer's Location
An even briefer synopsis of your purpose in the company, overviewing functions, products, customer base.
- An achievement made during this position that's relevant to current objective

EDUCATION AND PROFESSIONAL TRAINING

Degree(s), classes, seminars, educational awards and honors
Credentials, clearances, licenses

> **Functional Format**

YOUR NAME
Address, City, State, Zip Code
Home and Cell Phones
E-mail

Job Title You Desire

More than (# years paid and unpaid) work experience, in target area, contributing to an (achievement/result/high ranking in industry/top 5% of performance reviews). Add accomplishments, strengths, proficiencies, characteristics, education, brief testimonial — anything that supports your target job title.

PROFESSIONAL EXPERIENCE AND ACCOMPLISHMENTS

A TOP SKILL (Pertinent to objective and job requirements)
- An achievement illustrating this skill, and the location/employer of this skill*
- A second achievement illustrating this skill, and the location/employer of this skill*

A SECOND TOP SKILL (Pertinent to objective and job requirements)
- An achievement illustrating this skill, and the location/employer of this skill*
- A second achievement illustrating this skill, and the location/employer of this skill*

A THIRD TOP SKILL (Pertinent to objective and job requirements)
- An achievement illustrating this skill, and the location/employer of this skill*
- A second achievement illustrating this skill, and the location/employer of this skill*

A FOURTH SKILL (Optional — must relate to objective and job requirements)
- Detailed as above

A UNIQUE AREA OF PROFICIENCY (Pertinent to objective and job requirements)
- An achievement testifying to this proficiency, including the location/employer*
- A list of equipment, processes, software, or terms you know that reflect your familiarity with this area of proficiency
- A list of training experiences that document your qualifications and proficiency

EMPLOYMENT HISTORY

[dates]	**Job Title**	Employer, Location
[dates]	**Job Title**	Employer, Location
[dates]	**Job Title**	Employer, Location
[dates]	**Job Title**	Employer, Location

PROFESSIONAL TRAINING AND EDUCATION
Degrees, credentials, clearances, licenses, classes, seminars, training

* Omit locations/employers if your work history is obviously lacking in lockstep upward mobility

Putting Your Resume in MOTION with Action Verbs

Action verbs get a prospective employer's attention. They add dimension to your qualifications, and strengthen and enhance your accomplishments. Action verbs make your resume more professional. Here are more than 350 action verbs to show prospective employers just how capable and qualified you are.

ACTION VERBS

Accelerated, Accomplished, Achieved, Acquired, Acted, Activated, Adapted, Addressed, Adjusted, Administered, Advanced, Advertised, Advised, Advocated, Aided, Allocated, Analyzed, Answered, Anticipated, Applied, Appraised, Approved, Arbitrated, Arranged, Ascertained, Aspired, Assembled, Assessed, Assigned, Assisted, Attained, Audited, Authored, Automated, Awarded

Balanced, Boosted, Briefed, Budgeted, Built

Calculated, Catalogued, Centralized, Changed, Chaired, Charted, Checked, Clarified, Classified, Coached, Collaborated, Collected, Combined, Commanded, Communicated, Compared, Compiled, Completed, Composed, Computed, Conceptualized, Condensed, Conducted, Conferred, Conserved, Consolidated, Constructed, Consulted, Contacted, Contained, Contracted, Contributed, Controlled, Converted, Coordinated, Correlated, Corresponded, Counseled, Created, Critiqued, Cultivated, Customized,

Decided, Decreased, Defined, Delegated, Delivered, Demonstrated, Designated, Designed, Detected, Determined, Developed, Devised, Diagnosed, Directed, Discovered, Dispatched, Dispensed, Displayed, Dissected, Distinguished, Distributed, Documented, Doubled, Drafted

Earned, Edited, Educated, Eliminated, Emphasized, Employed, Enabled, Enacted, Encouraged, Enforced, Engineered, Enhanced, Enlarged, Enlisted, Ensured, Entertained, Established, Estimated, Evaluated, Examined, Executed, Expanded, Expedited, Experimented, Explained, Explored, Expressed, Extended, Extracted

Fabricated, Facilitated, Familiarized, Fashioned, Finalized, Fixed, Focused, Forecasted, Formed, Formulated, Fostered, Found, Founded, Fulfilled, Furnished

Gained, Gathered, Generated, Guided

Handled, Headed, Helped, Hired, Hypothesized

Identified, Illustrated, Imagined, Implemented, Improved, Improvised, Incorporated, Increased, Indexed, Indoctrinated, Influenced, Informed, Initiated, Innovated, Inspected, Inspired, Installed, Instituted, Instructed, Insured, Integrated, Interpreted, Interviewed, Introduced, Invented, Investigated, Inventoried, Issued

Joined, Judged, Justified

Launched, Learned, Lectured, Led, Located, Logged

Maintained, Managed, Marketed, Maximized, Measured, Mediated, Merged, Minimized, Mobilized, Moderated, Modified, Monitored, Motivated

Navigated, Negotiated, Netted

Observed, Obtained, Opened, Operated, Ordered, Orchestrated, Organized, Originated, Outlined, Overhauled, Oversaw

Participated, Performed, Persuaded, Photographed, Pinpointed, Piloted, Pioneered, Placed, Planned, Predicted, Prepared, Presented, Presided, Prevented, Printed, Prioritized, Processed, Produced, Programmed, Projected, Promoted, Proofread, Proposed, Protected, Proved, Provided, Publicized, Published, Purchased

Qualified, Queried

Raised, Ran, Rated, Reached, Realized, Reasoned, Received, Recommended, Reconciled, Recorded, Recruited, Reduced, Regulated, Rehabilitated, Related, Remodeled, Rendered, Repaired, Replaced, Reported, Represented, Researched, Resolved, Responded, Restored, Restructured, Retrieved, Reversed, Reviewed, Revised, Revitalized, Routed

Saved, Scheduled, Screened, Searched, Secured, Selected, Separated, Served, Shaped, Shared, Simplified, Simulated, Sketched, Sold, Solved, Sorted, Spearheaded, Specialized, Sponsored, Staffed, Standardized, Started, Stimulated, Stored, Streamlined, Strengthened, Structured, Studied, Summarized, Supervised, Supplied, Supplemented, Supported, Surpassed, Surveyed

Tabulated,, Targeted, Taught, Terminated, Tested, Tightened, Totaled, Tracked, Traded, Trained, Transcribed, Transferred, Transformed, Translated, Transmitted, Traveled, Treated, Trimmed, Tutored, Typed

Uncovered, Undertook, Unified, United, Updated, Upgraded, Used, Utilized

Validated, Verified, Vitalized, Volunteered

Weighed, Widened, Won, Worked, Wrote

How to Interview for a Job

Before the Interview
Answer the following questions as part of your research and preparation for the interview:
- What you want in an opportunity that you don't have now.
- What you don't want, that you have experienced in the past.
- What role will provide the kind of gratification you find motivating.
- What your lifestyle requirements are.

During the Interview
Early in the interview you need to ascertain the company's expectations:
- What skills are they hoping you will bring to their company?
- What is the most immediate problem they have for you to solve?
- What challenges are they anticipating for the position, as they look into the future?
- How do they measure performance?
- What is the reporting structure?
- What can exceptional performance lead to in the way of career path opportunity?

1. Early in the interview, ask: "What skills and background do you want to attract to your company?"

2. Follow up with:
   A. "What do you need a person to accomplish in the first 6 months and first 12 months?"
   B. "What challenges (PROBLEMS) do you have, (or) do you need this person to solve, (or) that will make the position interesting and bring a person gratification?"
   C. "How do you judge *above average* performance for this position?"

3. Briefly, share your past successes. Relate them to what you just learned. Use the following format:
   A. FEATURE: Successes that you have on your resume. What the problem or objective was and what strategies you came up with.
   B. ACCOMPLISHMENT: What was the specific result?
   C. BENEFITS: How will these accomplishments benefit them?

Key Points to Remember
- The interview is all about *them*, not you. It is about their **pain**, and what they believe is the way that it will get corrected. Once you can *feel* their pain, share with them your experiences and accomplishments in such a way that see you as the solution to their pain.
- Prepare to ask questions that show interest in their cause/need. *Bring your notes in with you.* It is perfectly appropriate to refer to them during the interview. In fact, it shows you prepared.
- *Do not* ask questions about **compensation**, benefits, vacation or work hours.
- If asked what you are looking for in the way of compensation, *do not* give a number. Respond with something like: "I'm confident that you know the value of the position to the organization, and off appropriate compensation."
- You can, when asked, answer the question regarding your current earnings, by responding: "My decision will not be based on money, but on what I can offer your organization in leveraging

your successes. That is how we all win." If *pressed* for a number, respond: "Are you asking because you want to make me an offer?" That will normally back them off, or, give you the opportunity to add: "I have enough information to make a decision. Is there anything else you need to know to extend me an offer?"

The Question of Inexperience
If presented with a question regarding a lack of specific **experience,** acknowledge the fact, then present a compensating fact about yourself that minimizes the void. For example:

Question: This position has managerial responsibility and we see that you do not have this in your experiences.

Answer: "That is correct however I feel I am prepared to take on that role. Supervision is about leadership. In my current/previous job I was chosen to lead a particular project/target goal. I believe this happened as a result of my ability to encourage/motivate/stimulate/guide members of a group to work well together."

The Subject of Drugs and Alcohol
It is inappropriate to be asked if you smoke, drink or take drugs. Your height, weight, use of sick days, presence of disabilities or past medical procedures/sicknesses is similarly *off limits*. Interviewers *do* have the right to ask if you've violated company policies regarding alcohol, or whether you use *illegal* drugs (as opposed to simply "drugs".) In general, there is no reason for you to ever *offer* information about your past substance use or recovery. Should you be asked an inappropriate question, you can redirect it back at the interviewer by saying something like: "That's a strange question to ask. Have you had problems with that before?"

Most Asked Interview Questions
Write the answers out beforehand and role-play them if you can:
- **What accomplishments are you most proud of?** This is why you were asked to prepare the Feature/Accomplishment/Benefit section above.
- **What failures or mistakes have you learned from?**
- **What motivates you?** This is where you show them your passion!
- **Tell me about yourself?** Don't drift off into a personal history. Relate comments back to career growth steps.
- **Why would/did you leave your last position?** *Stay positive!*
- **What do you see in our company that attracts you?** This is your opportunity to show that you researched the company, and give complimentary feedback.
- **Where do you see yourself in five years?** Include in your answer the success you foresee for the company as well.
- **"Do you have any questions for me?"** Have these questions pre-planned.

How to Dress
Prior to your interview, call and ask the receptionist about typical office dress. You can also visit the company, a similar company or their website in advance. Dress the same or one level up. For example, if employees wear slacks and open long sleeve shirt, add a tie. If they wear shirt and tie, add a jacket (you can always take it off.)

Closing the Interview
1. "I have had my questions all answered, do you feel I have the qualifications required to be considered for the position?" This will allow you to find any holes that might exist, and to do one more Feature/Accomplishment/Benefit sell to overcome the objection.

2. Save these three very important questions for the end of the interview:
    A. "What do you need a person to accomplish in the first 6 months and first 12 months?"
    B. "What is the next step?"
    C. "Would you like me to call you, or will you be getting back to me?"

After the Interview
Send a thank you e-mail immediately after the interview. In as few words as possible, summarize how your unique qualifications are the solution to their pain.

Notes:

I. Quiz: Do I Have a Substance Use Disorder?
DSM-5 Diagnostic Criteria for Substance-Related Disorders

People may say you are an alcoholic, or you might suspect you are addicted, but how do you really know? If I asked would you say things like; "I drink too much", "All my friends say I am", "I love to party" or "I got a DUI"? You might be surprised to learn that none of these things defines the disease we now call Substance Use Disorder.

You certainly wouldn't walk into a job interview unprepared, would you? Heck... most people wouldn't go to the grocery store without a list! So, before someone slaps a label on you, or you label yourself, you should be armed with the facts as to what defines addiction. It is important information. Being able to recognize when the good times are over may save your life.

What Defines Addiction?
Alcoholism was officially recognized as a *disease* by the medical community as far back as 1956. Just like other diseases, Substance Use Disorder: Never goes away, will continue to get worse, has well defined symptoms, and is predictable (often fatal). According to the American Psychiatric Association, addiction is characterized by the following eleven traits. As you read, check off those that apply to you:

- ❑ **Compulsion.** Do you sometimes use more of the substance or for a longer time than you would like? Do you sometimes drink to get drunk? Do you stop after a few, or does one lead to more?

- ❑ **Persistent desire to quit or unsuccessful efforts to quit or control substance use.** Have you wanted to quit? Have you tried and failed to quit or cut down?

- ❑ **Much time/activity to obtain, use, recover.** Have you spent excessive amounts of time planning to use, obtaining, using, concealing and recovering from drugs and alcohol? Do you daydream about getting drunk or high? Have you spent time scheming of ways to avoid getting caught?

- ❑ **Craving.** Do you experience an overwhelming desire or urge to use? When you think of using alcohol or drugs, do you experience a physical reaction like a dog seeing his food bowl? Examples include increased heart rate, sweaty palms, a burst of pleasurable feelings etc.

- ❑ **Failure to fulfill major role obligations.** Has substance use interfered with your responsibilities at work, school or home? Do you blow off events or call in sick in order to use or recover from using?

- ❑ **Use despite recurrent social or interpersonal problems.** Have you continued to use chemicals even though they interfere with your ability to interact with others?

- ❑ **Isolation.** Has substance use caused you to withdraw from participating in social, occupational or recreational activities?

- ❑ **Use in physically hazardous situations.** Have you continued to drink or use even though that behavior places you in physically dangerous situations? Have you gotten a DUI?

- ❑ **Use despite recurrent physical or psychological problems.** Do you continue to use even though you have a physical or psychological ailment that is likely to have been caused or worsened by the substance?

- ❑ **Tolerance.** Do you continue to need more of the substance to get the same high?

- ❑ **Withdrawal.** When you stop using, do experience physical or emotional withdrawal, including irritability, anxiety, shakes, sweats, nausea, or vomiting?

Scoring:
Mild Substance Use Disorder = 2 - 3
Moderate Substance Use Disorder = 3 - 4
Severe Substance Use Disorder = 6+

When It's Over IT'S OVER!
To meet the medical definition of an addict or alcoholic, you need answer yes to only two (2) of these questions. If you did, I want you to stop for a moment and think about how that makes you feel. Before today you may have gone quite a long time abusing drugs and alcohol. In fact you might not even remember just how long other than knowing those substances have always been there for you. All the while you suffered under the misconception that it was under control,

The truth is, if you have a substance use disorder then you probably waved *adios* to the good times long ago. Guess what... they are not coming back no matter how much you try. Take it from me. I tried so hard to keep the party going that I lost my job, career, house, marriage, health, friends and finances. Don't let *ego* get in your way. Accept reality and get started on your recovery today, because you do not have to live like this any longer. I am a recovering addict and alcoholic who found that life is so much better without chemicals. There are millions more like me. If we can do it, so can you.

> **"People are not apt to consider being an addict highly desirable. But if we realize that the gains from recovery in a Twelve Step program *may not be easily found in other ways*, being addicted may not be the curse that we thought it to be."** (Addictive Thinking, page 85)

II. Alcoholics Anonymous Handy Reference
Copyright A.A. World Services, Inc.

TWELVE STEPS

(Known as the surrender steps)
1. We admitted we were powerless over alcohol - that our lives had become unmanageable.

2. Came to believe that a Power greater than ourselves could restore us to sanity.

3. Made a decision to turn our will and our lives over to the care of God *as we understood Him.*

(Known as the self-examination steps)
4. Made a searching and fearless moral inventory of ourselves.

5. Admitted to God, to ourselves, and to another human being the exact nature of our wrongs.

(Known as the working steps)
6. Were entirely ready to have God remove all these defects of character.

7. Humbly asked Him to remove our shortcomings.

8. Made a list of all persons we had harmed, and became willing to make amends to them all.

9. Made direct amends to such people wherever possible, except when to do so would injure them or others.

(Known as the maintenance steps)
10. Continued to take personal inventory and when we were wrong promptly admitted it.

11. Sought through prayer and meditation to improve our conscious contact with God, *as we understood Him*, praying only for knowledge of His will for us and the power to carry that out.

12. Having had a spiritual awakening as the result of these Steps, we tried to carry this message to alcoholics, and to practice these principles in all our affairs.

PRAYERS AND PROMISES

The Promises (A.A. Big Book, pages 83-84)
If we are painstaking about this phase of our development, we will be amazed before we are half way through. We are going to know a new freedom and a new happiness. We will not regret the past nor wish to shut the door on it. We will comprehend the word serenity and we will know peace. No matter how far down the scale we have gone, we will see how our experience can benefit others. That feeling of uselessness and self-pity will disappear. We will lose interest in selfish things and gain interest in our fellows. Self-seeking will slip away. Our whole attitude and outlook upon life will change. Fear of people and of economic insecurity will leave us. We will intuitively know how to handle situations which

used to baffle us. We will suddenly realize that God is doing for us what we could not do for ourselves. Are these extravagant promises? We think not. They are being fulfilled among us - sometimes quickly, sometimes slowly. They will always materialize if we work for them.

Third-Step Prayer (Page 63 A.A. Big Book)
God, I offer myself to Thee - to build with me and to do with me as Thou wilt. Relieve me of the bondage of self, that I may better do Thy will. Take away my difficulties, that victory over them may bear witness to those I would help of Thy Power, Thy Love, and Thy Way of life. May I do Thy will always!

Seventh-Step Prayer (Page 76 A.A. Big Book)
My Creator, I am now willing that you should have all of me, good & bad. I pray that you now remove from me every single defect of character which stands in the way of my usefulness to you and my fellows. Grant me strength, as I go out from here to do Your bidding.

Eleventh-Step Prayer (Page 99 A.A. Big Book)
Lord, make me a channel of thy peace - that where there is hatred, I may bring love - that where there is wrong, I may bring the spirit of forgiveness - that where there is discord, I may bring harmony - that where there is error, I may bring truth - that where there is doubt, I may bring faith - that where there is despair, I may bring hope - that where there are shadows, I may bring light - that where there is sadness, I may bring joy. Lord, grant that I may seek rather to comfort than to be comforted - to understand, than to be understood - to love, than to be loved. For it is by self-forgetting that one finds. It is by forgiving that one is forgiven. It is by dying that one awakens to eternal life.

Serenity Prayer (Page 41 A.A. Big Book)
God, grant me the serenity to accept the things I cannot change, courage to change the things I can, and the wisdom to know the difference. Living one day at a time; enjoying one moment at a time; accepting hardships as the pathway to peace; taking, as He did, this sinful world as it is, not as I would have it; trusting that He will make all things right if I surrender to his will; that I may be reasonably happy in this life and supremely happy with Him forever in the next.

St. Francis Prayer
Lord, make me a channel of thy peace, that where there is hatred, I may bring love; that where there is wrong, I may bring the spirit of forgiveness; that where there is discord, I may bring harmony; that where there is error, I may bring truth; that where there is doubt, I may bring faith; that where there is despair, I may bring hope; that where there are shadows, I may bring light that where there is sadness, I may bring joy. Lord, grant that I may seek rather to comfort than to be comforted; to understand, than to be understood; to love, than to be loved. For it is by self-forgetting that one finds. It is by forgiving that one is forgiven. It is by dying that one awakens to Eternal Life.

III. Attendance Form for Support Group Meetings
(To use, cut and remove or photocopy)

NAME OF ATTENDEE: _____

The above individual is required to attend support group meetings. It would be greatly appreciated if the Secretary or other leading member of the group signs this record of attendance at the END of the meeting. The attendee is expected to complete all of the columns except for the SIGNATURE column. Thank you.

NAME OF MEETING	TIME	DATE	SECRETARY SIGNATURE

NAME OF ATTENDEE:

The above individual is required to attend support group meetings. It would be greatly appreciated if the Secretary or other leading member of the group signs this record of attendance at the END of the meeting. The attendee is expected to complete all of the columns except for the SIGNATURE column. Thank you.

NAME OF MEETING	TIME	DATE	SECRETARY SIGNATURE

IV. Key Statistics on Alcohol and Drug Use

Fortunately there is a tremendous amount of accurate information available on the topic of substance use disorder and recovery; so much so that it may feel overwhelming. This section serves as a good starting point. Here you will find key statistical findings culled from the most important and timely resources available, including: ***Key substance use and mental health indicators in the United States: Results from the 2015 National Survey on Drug Use and Health***; and, ***Facing Addiction in America: The 2016 Surgeon General's Report on Alcohol, Drugs, and Health***. They are included so that you might better understand substance use disorder. For more information about the National Survey on Drug Use and Health, or to download the full publication, visit http://store.samhsa.gov. For more information about the Surgeon General's report or to download the full publication, visit http://Addiction.SurgeonGeneral.gov.

Definitions
- A **Substance Use Disorder** *is a medical illness that impairs health and function. Prolonged, repeated misuse of a substance can lead to a substance use disorder,. Substance use disorders range from mild to severe. Severe and chronic substance use disorders are commonly referred to as 'addiction'.*
- **Current** *use is defined as within the past 30 days.*
- **Substance misuse** *is the use of any substance in a manner, situation, amount, or frequency that can cause harm to users or those around them.*
- **Prescription drug misuse** *is the use of any prescribed drug in any way not directed by a doctor, including use without a prescription of one's own; use in greater amounts, more often, or longer than told to take a drug; or use in any other way not directed by a doctor.*
- **The Ten Illicit Drug categories** *are cocaine/crack, hallucinogens, heroin, inhalants, marijuana and methamphetamine; as well as the misuse of prescription pain relievers, sedatives, stimulants and tranquilizers.*
- A **drink** *is defined as anything that contains approximately 0.6 ounces (14 gm) of alcohol, such as 12 oz of most beer brands, 5 oz of most table wine or one shot (1.5 oz) of 80 proof spirits.*
- *SAMHSA defines* **Binge drinking** *for men, as having 5 or more standard drinks and, for women, 4 or more drinks on the same occasion on at least 1 day in the past 30 days.*
- **Heavy drinking** *is defined by the Centers for Disease Control (CDC) as consuming 8 or more drinks per week for women, and 15 or more drinks per week for men, and by the Substance Abuse and Mental Health Services Administration (SAMHSA), for research purposes, as binge drinking on 5 or more days in the past 30 days.*

GENERAL

- In 2015, 20.8 million people aged 12 or older had a substance use disorder. That is equivalent to the number of people who suffer from diabetes and more than 1.5 times the annual prevalence of all cancers combined (14 million).
- Of the 20.8 million people aged 12 or older who have a substance use disorder, 15.7 million people had an alcohol use disorder, 7.7 million people had and illicit drug use disorder, and 2.7 million (13 percent) had *both* an alcohol use and an illicit drug use disorder.

- Substance misuse and substance use disorders cost the U.S. more than $442 billion annually in lost productivity, health care expenses, crime, law enforcement and other criminal justice costs. These costs are almost twice as high as the costs associated with diabetes, which is estimated to cost $245 billion each year.

ALCOHOL

- In 2015, 138.3 million people aged 12 or older reported current alcohol use.
- In 2015, 66.7 million people aged 12 or older (51.7 percent) reported binge alcohol use in the past month, which corresponds to about half of all current alcohol users (48.2 percent).
- In 2015, 17.3 million people aged 12 or older (6.5 percent) reported heavy alcohol use in the past month.
- Among people aged 12 to 20, 13.4 percent are binge drinkers, and 3.3 percent are heavy drinkers.
- In 2015, 2 out of 5 young adults aged 18 to 25 reported binge alcohol use in the past 30 days, and 1 out of 10 young adults reported heavy alcohol use in the past 30 days.
- All 50 states and the District of Columbia currently prohibit possession of alcoholic beverages by individuals younger than 21

DRUGS

All Illicit Drugs
- 27.1 million people aged 12 or older were current illicit drug users in 2015, representing 1 in 10 people aged 12 or older (10.1 percent).
- 8.2 percent of adults aged 26 or older (of 17.1 million in this age group) were current users of illicit drugs in 2015.
- Approximately 1 in 5 young adults age 18 to 25 (22.3 percent) were current users of illicit drugs in 2015, corresponding to about 7.8 million young adults.
- 2.2 million adolescents aged 12 to 17 (8.8 percent) were current users of illicit drugs in 2015.

Marijuana
- Marijuana is by far the most commonly used illicit drug.
- In 2015, 22.2 million people aged 12 or older (8.3 percent) were current users of marijuana. This was similar to 2014, but higher than 2002 to 2013.
- In 2015, 6.5 percent of adults aged 26 or older (13.6 million) were current users of marijuana.
- In 2015, about 1 in 5 young adults aged 18 to 25 were current users of marijuana, corresponding to 6.9 million young adults (19.8 percent).
- In 2015, 7.0 percent of adolescents aged 12 to 17 (1.8 million) were current users of marijuana.

Prescription Drugs (Pain Relievers, Tranquilizers, Stimulants or Sedatives)
- In 2015, 119.0 million Americans aged 12 or older (44.5 percent) used prescription drugs in the past year.
- In 2015, 6.4 million people aged 12 or older (2.4 percent) were current misusers of prescription drugs. This includes 4.1 million adults aged 26 or older, 1.8 million young adults aged 18 to 25, and 1 in 50 adolescents (2.0 percent) aged 12 to 17.
- Prescription pain relievers are the second most commonly used illicit drug,

- Of the 6.4 million people aged 12 or older who were current misusers of prescription drugs, 3 of 5 reported misusing pain relievers.
- 3.8 million people aged 12 or older (1.4 percent) were current misusers of pain relievers in 2015.
- In 2015, people aged 12 to 49 who misused prescription drugs for the first time were typically in their early to late 20s.
- Among people aged 12 or older who misused pain relievers in the past year, the most common source for the last pain reliever that was misused was from a friend or relative (53.7 percent), and about one third misused a prescription from one doctor. About 1 in 20 people who misused pain relievers bought the last pain reliever they misused from a drug dealer or stranger.

SUBSTANCE USE DISORDER AND MENTAL HEALTH

- In 2015, an estimated 43.4 million adults aged 18 or older (17.9 percent) had a mental illness.
- About a third of all people experiencing mental illnesses and about half of people living with severe mental illnesses also experience substance abuse. These statistics are mirrored in the substance abuse community, where about a third of all alcohol abusers and more than half of all drug abusers report experiencing a mental illness.
- Many individuals with a substance use disorder *also* have a mental disorder, and some have *multiple* substance use disorders. Men are more likely to develop a co-occurring disorder than women.
- In 2015, approximately 8.1 million adults aged 18 or older (3.3 percent) had both a mental illness *and* substance use disorder in the past year. Fewer than half (48.0 percent) received treatment for either disorder.
- Over 40 percent of people aged 12 or older who had a substance use disorder also had a mental illness.
- It is estimated that 30 to 60 percent of patients seeking treatment for alcohol use disorder meet criteria for Post Traumatic Stress Disorder (PTSD), and approximately one-third of individuals who have experienced PTSD have also experienced alcohol use disorder.

DIRE CONSEQUENCES

- Behavioral health problems such as substance use, violence, impaired driving, mental health problems, and risky sexual activity are now the leading causes of death for those aged 15 to 24.
- Alcohol misuse contributes to 88,000 deaths in the U.S. each year; 1 in 10 deaths among working adults is due to alcohol misuse.
- There are more than 2,200 alcohol overdose deaths in the U.S. each year – an average of six deaths every day. More than three quarters of alcohol overdose deaths occur among adults between the ages of 35 and 64, and 76 percent of those who die from alcohol overdose are men.
- In 2014, 9,967 people were killed in car crashes while driving under the influence of alcohol, representing nearly one-third (31 percent) of all traffic-related fatalities in the U.S.
- Alcohol is involved in about 20 percent of the overdose deaths related to prescription opioid pain relievers.
- In 2014, more than 47,000 people died from a drug overdose. Included in this number are nearly 30,000 people who died from an overdose involving prescription drugs. This is more than in any previous year on record.

- In 2014, 61 percent of drug overdose deaths involved prescription opioids and heroin. Heroin overdoses more than tripled between 2010 and 2014.
- Deaths from cocaine overdose were higher in 2014 (5,415 deaths) than in the previous six years.

TREATMENT AND RECOVERY

- As with other chronic, relapsing medical conditions, treatment can manage the symptoms of substance use disorders and prevent relapse.
- In 2015 an estimated 21.7 million people aged 12 or older needed substance use treatment (ie. People who had an SUD in the past year or received substance use treatment at a specialty facility in the past year). That corresponds to about 1 in 12 people aged 12 or older (8.1 percent).
- In 2015 only 10.8 percent of people aged 12 or older (2.3 million people) who needed substance use treatment received treatment at a specialty facility in the past year.
- In 2015 15.7 million people were in need of treatment for an alcohol use disorder (7.8 percent for men and 4.1 percent for women) and nearly 7.7 million people needed treatment for an illicit drug use disorder (3.8 percent for men and 2.0 percent for women).
- About 40 percent of people who know they have an alcohol or drug problem feel they are *not ready* to stop using, and others simply feel they do not have a problem or a need for treatment.
- Research shows that treatment for substance use disorders – including inpatient, residential, and outpatient – *is cost-effective* compared with no treatment. Every dollar spent on substance use disorder treatment saves $4.00 in health care costs and $7.00 in criminal justice costs.
- The number of people who are in 'remission' from a substance use disorder is approximately 10.3 percent and is greater than the number of people who define themselves as being in 'recovery'.
- Approximately 50 percent of adults aged 18 or older (25 million) who once met diagnostic criteria for a substance use disorder are currently in stable remission (1 year or longer).

"I did then what I knew how to do. Now that I know better, I do better." (Maya Angelou)

V. The Big Book and The Good Book

You may be surprised at how *interwoven* the big book is with Twelve Step recovery programs. No, we're not talking about the Big Book of Alcoholics Anonymous. We're speaking of the *original big book*: The Bible. How can a holy text written millennia ago, have any relation whatsoever to an instruction manual written barely seventy-years ago (by a washed-out stockbroker, no less?)

Both books promote the concept of a higher power. But simply knowing *of* Him doesn't explain the miraculous change experienced by those that choose to follow the teachings in these texts. More likely, the key lies in our **submitting** to Him. In fact, whether your big book is the Bible, Alcoholics Anonymous, or both, the act of turning your life and will over to God will lead to serenity.

I am fascinated by the story described in Matthew 14:28-30, of the apostle Peter walking on water:

^{28} "Lord, if it's you," Peter replied, "tell me to come to you on the water." ^{29} "Come," he said. Then Peter got down out of the boat, walked on the water and came toward Jesus. ^{30} But when he saw the wind, he was afraid and, beginning to sink, cried out, "Lord, save me!"

Like many stories in the Bible, it is difficult to empathize completely with a situation that occurred over two thousand years ago. This story refers to the body of water known as the Sea of Galilee, located in Israel. Most people have not personally visited the area, so let's try something different that may help you better appreciate what is going on. Let's change the setting to something that is a bit more relevant. Bear with me. I assure you... though only four-sentences in length, this tale is as dense with meaning as a diamond.

Pretend for a moment that Jesus has appeared in New York City and has been performing all sorts of miracles. Of course his presence has electrified the world. Every move he makes is streamed live around the planet.

You decide to journey to the Big Apple to see for yourself. From news accounts you are aware that many others are flocking to Manhattan Island, making it practically impossible to get around by automobile. But you know this city pretty well. So you opt to catch a train to Pennsylvania Station. You take the escalator to street level and find yourself in the middle of the city.

Streets are choked with people searching for Jesus. Clueless as to where he might be, you shuffle East, pressed shoulder-to-shoulder with the pack. At Fifth Avenue you join another pack migrating North. It seems like New Year's Eve everywhere. Difficult to see and impossible to hear above the roar, you can barely breathe. But you soldier on a few blocks more.

Then, it happens. At Rockefeller Center, directly in front of the famous Empire State Building. Suddenly the masses part and, there, before you, is Jesus.

You are caught off guard. Jesus is looking at you. Everyone else, too. Mustering all your courage, you ask rock-star Jesus if he could perform a miracle for you. You tell him it doesn't matter if the miracle is big or small, but this is your *one* chance to have a personal connection with God, and you couldn't live with yourself later if you didn't ask now. He replies; "Of course. I know the perfect thing."

He tells you to enter the building in front of you and take the elevator to the observation deck on top. You do. Once the elevator doors open, rock-star Jesus is magically there waiting. Except for Him, you are all alone. He points to the iron fence ringing the entire observation deck, instructs you to scale the fence and, once on top, *step off into the air*. "Have faith, keep your arms at your sides at all times and enjoy the miracle" He says. (Want to get real? Go to the Empire State Building website and view actual photos from the observation deck at www.esbnyc.com.)

You clamber up the fence hand over hand. It's difficult because the tips of the bars bend inwards to prevent people from doing exactly what you're attempting. You make it, and are surprised at how silent and peaceful it is. To the west you can see beyond the Hudson River to New Jersey. To the northeast is the Long Island Sound; beyond are Connecticut and Rhode Island. And to the east lies Long Island. Barges crawl along the East River, beneath the famous suspension bridges connecting Manhattan Island to these other lands. Forty blocks downtown, the new World Trade Center building rises majestically from lower Manhattan, and the Statue of Liberty holds her lamp high in the harbor beyond. Rooftops gleam shiny new. It is early. Your breath hangs in the crisp air. So much chaos 103-stories below... Yet, from your exceptional perch, everything is so clear, so organized. You are privy to the pattern of life. You feel equally awed, powerful and terrified.

Jesus appears in front of you. Not with flowing robes or floating like a ghost. He is flesh and bone. And he is standing, rock solid, as if on a sky blue catwalk. With a lazy flexing of His fingers He calls you forward. "Come, experience your miracle."

You cast your eyes down... down... and still further down. Now the ground is all you can see. Suddenly you no longer see Jesus as a rock-star. He is more like *ATM-machine* Jesus and, unfortunately, you have no idea whether there is enough faith in your account to cover the heavy withdrawal you are about to make.

Reality has slammed into you like a tsunami. Instantaneously you turn white with fear. Your hands run frigid while beads of sweat pour over your head and face like fat Florida rain. You shrink. Afraid to move. Afraid to breathe. You raise your eyes to meet His.

My question is, *what would you do??*

The Sea of Galilee is especially known for the ferocity of its weather. Ships sunk and people died all the time. You can understand why when you look at the geography of that area. The Sea of Galilee spans 64 square miles (nearly the size of Washington, D.C.) and reaches a depth of 200 feet. It lies 680 feet below sea level, where the air is warm and moist. Perfect for growing dates and bananas. It is surrounded by mountains topping 2,000 feet where the air is cool and dry. The great difference in height and climate results in violent, unpredictable weather. Whipping winds funnel through the mountains and across the relatively small and shallow body of water. When the warm, moist air collides with the cool, dry air, storms strike without warning, putting small boats like Peter's in *immediate* peril.

As a fisherman who made his living on the Sea of Galilee, the apostle Peter was acutely aware of the danger. Being in a small fishing boat was dangerous enough. But being *without* one would have meant certain death. In Peter's world, stepping *out* of a boat when the winds were blowing on the Sea of Galilee was the equivalent of stepping *off* the top of the Empire State Building to you and me.

Yet Peter stepped out anyway, and for a short time he did the impossible. He walked on water; something no other person has done in the entire history of water. But what does any of this have to do with recovery from substance abuse?

First of all, none of this really surprises me. Reading up on Peter I find he demonstrated many of the same character traits I see in alcoholics and addicts. He was a Type-A personality, a leader, someone who didn't take *No* for an answer. He had poor impulse control. He could be fearless. Although he did some shameful things which he deeply regretted, he was a good man.

Second, recovery is about *perspective.* Peter saw *opportunity.* He observed Jesus and thought; "Cool!" None of the other fellows in the boat wanted to take their chances on the water. As the saying goes: "What doesn't kill you makes you stronger." Or: "Ex infirmitas adveho vires", Latin for "from weakness comes strength." Earnest Hemingway writes: "The world breaks everyone and afterward many are strong at the broken places." In 2 Corinthians 12:9-10 Paul writes: "...power is perfected in weakness... for when I am weak I am strong." There appears to be a universal consensus that disappointment is fertile ground for success. So if weakness is a *prerequisite* to strength, then is weakness *really* weakness or is it the first step to strength? You tell me. Depends on *your* perspective.

Finally, recovery requires you to *step out in faith*, whether it's out of a boat on rough seas, off a tall building *or simply by accepting that you cannot control your drinking and drug use.*

Would *I* step off the roof of a terrifyingly tall building if asked by God? Absolutely. I'd be wetting my pants; but sure. *Though it wouldn't require much faith when I'm looking God straight in the eyes*! (Nothing against Peter. I'm just saying...) It's when you *don't* see God, when you *don't* see hope, when you *don't* see a way out of the darkness... *that's* when stepping out in faith *really* matters. That's also when faith is *rewarded*. Strength is forged in the furnace of weakness. The stronger your feelings of hopelessness, shame, fear and resentment; the better your fuel, the hotter your flame, the more valuable your reward.

Make a decision. Step out of the boat, off the building and from the mouth of the furnace. Have faith. Your pain and problems can mark the beginning of *the opportunity of a lifetime.* Recovery is measured in feet; as in *one foot in front of the other.*

EXERCISES

If you draw strength for your recovery from The Bible then it's important to know exactly where to look to find those words of comfort when they're needed most. A number of scripture verses are listed below. Refer to your Bible, and answer the questions.

1. Nothing in life comes easy. Bill W said; "Thus was I convinced that God is concerned with us humans when we want Him enough" (A.A. Big Book page 33.) The Big Book also says; "Half measures availed us nothing" (page 59.) Read Deuteronomy 4:29. How much effort does it take to find God and recover?

2. Read Psalm 103:12, Hebrews 9:14, 1 John 1:7 and Romans 8:1. You might be feeling shame or guilt over your past behavior. Are these feelings from God?

3. Feeling low? Stop looking down instead of up. Read Psalm 139. How much does God love you?

4. Read John 13:12-17. What does Jesus say is the main characteristic of an effective leader?

5. Read Hebrews 11:32-35, Philippians 4:13 and 2 Corinthians 12:10. What are these verses communicating about recovery?

6. Read Ecclesiastes 4:9-12 and finish the following sentence. *It important to go to meetings and connect with other addicts and a sponsor because...*

7. Read Philippians 2:4-16. Do resentments serve a purpose?

8. Philippians 4:6-9 commands you to do what when feeling restless, irritable and discontent?

9. Read James 1:2-8. How does this passage relate to your recovery?

10. Read James 1:12-15 and answer the following questions:
    A. Describe the four steps to relapse?

    B. What do you gain from the pain of recovery?

11. Read James 4:13-16. Why is it so important not to procrastinate in your recovery?

12. Read 1 Peter 4:12-13. Are painful experiences like your recovery out of the ordinary?

13. For each of the Twelve Steps, find supporting scripture verses by referring to the concordance at the back of your Bible. Use the next page for your answers. It is much easier than you think.

For Family and Friends Part 1 of 5

VI. Signs and Symptoms of Substance Use Disorder

In 1956, the American Medical Association recognized alcoholism as a physiological disease. Substance use disorder is as much a disease as schizophrenia and diabetes. Accepting this concept is key to understanding the insanity behind drug and alcohol abuse. Why? Because being stricken with a disease takes away completely the ability to *choose*.

No one *chooses* to have cancer. Likewise, addicts often *don't want* to use alcohol and drugs. Without help, addicts cannot stop using chemicals completely. **Chemicals** *become as indispensible as air or water.* The person is **compelled** to continue even when they *despise* the drugs, and know there will be catastrophic consequences as a result. What would examples of that be? They might leave the hospital after a near death experience, and buy liquor on the way home. Or, they might experience chest pains, yet continue using cocaine. When it comes to drugs and alcohol, *they have lost their* **ability** *to choose.*

Before today, you may have labored under the misconception that the person you love lacked the **willpower** to change. Over and over in your mind, you may have thought that while some people possess the strength, smarts, courage, fortitude, character, self-control and common sense to manage their drug and alcohol use; others were born weak-willed, defective, dummies or hopeless losers. You openly blamed him or her for lacking the ability to *just be normal*. Perhaps it is a relief for you to learn that none of these labels apply, *because substance use disorder has nothing to do with willpower or any other personal quality.* The person you love is a *good* person with a *bad* **disease.**

What follows, is intended to introduce you to substance use disorders: why they are classified as a disease, what drives them, how to recognize them, why they are deadly and what to do about them.

Substance Use Disorder is a D-I-S-E-A-S-E
Chances are, a whirlwind of anger, pain and suffering brought you here. You have watched someone you care about kill themselves a little every day. At this point you might be wondering: if substance use disorder is truly a disease – a disease that robs a person of the ability to **choose** whether or not to drink or use – then what in the world is it that drives this **insane** behavior?

Substance use disorders share the same **characteristics** as other diseases. They are:
- **Symptomatic.** The symptoms are not a mystery. They have been well defined.
- **Primary.** The disorder is the *cause* of other diseases or makes existing illnesses worse.
- **Predictable and progressive.** The disorder *always* gets worse if left untreated, even when the addict is not actually using or drinking. *Temporary periods of abstinence are not progress.*
- **Chronic.** Some diseases go away. Not this one.
- **Fatal if left untreated.** At present there is no known cure.
- **Treatable with 100% success.** You can put this disease into remission for life!

Yet unlike other diseases, substance use disorders do not *just* attack the *physical body*. More than the liver, kidneys and heart are in jeopardy. This is a disease which Alcoholics Anonymous (page 58) calls "**cunning, baffling, powerful**" for good reason. Why is this disease so devastating? Because it is a **bio-psycho-social** disease, meaning it attacks the user physically, mentally, emotionally and spiritually. It radically alters their behavior, ravages their families, and keeps them shielded from reality. For this reason, any successful recovery program must address *each* of these components.

What Triggers the Disease in the First Place?
You've probably asked yourself this question countless times. Obviously no one *suddenly* becomes an addict or alcoholic. Rather, it is the result of a gradual **progression** of increased drinking and drug use.

It starts innocently enough with **experimentation:** perhaps sneaking a beer from the refrigerator, trying a joint with friends or popping a pain killer when absolutely nothing hurt. If the experience is positive, then using becomes **recreational:** or every so often. This leads to **habituation,** which is using the substance on a regular basis. Notice the person has, thus far, been drinking and drugging free of any problems. Using chemicals has been a matter of **euphoria** or **relief.** In other words, they have been using to 1.) Feel good, or 2.) Relieve emotional pain.

Habituation can lead to **abuse,** and abuse leads to **consequences.** For instance, the person might get caught driving drunk, or fail a random drug test at work. *Most* substance abusers learn from their mistakes. They see the **correlation** between their drinking or drugging and the negative consequences experienced. This **insight** leads them to change their behavior. For them, it's just not worth it.

Not everyone can stop. Call it genetics, a brain condition, a disease, an **allergy and obsession**, or being spanked as a child. It doesn't matter. Once past a certain point, there is no turning back. They are **dependent:** abusing mind-altering substances pathologically, unreasonably and uncontrollably.

Angry
Anxious
Ashamed
Confused
Depressed
Desperate
Disappointed
Discouraged
Disgusted
Embarrassed
EMOTIONAL PAIN
Exhausted
Frustrated
Guilty
Hopeless
Lonely
Powerless
Resentful
Scared
Worthless

Most people can associate chemical abuse with the problems it creates, and then change their behaviors.

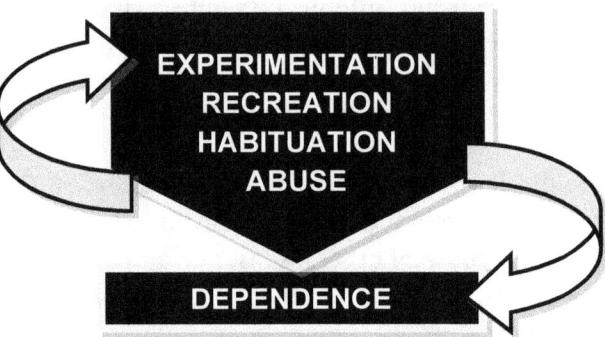

Unfortunately, having a disease means that some of us lack that ability.

**The Disease of Substance Use Disorder:
Progression from Experimentation to Dependence**

Symptoms of Substance Use Disorder
If you suspect someone you care about has a substance use disorder, there is probably good reason. According to the Diagnostic and Statistical Manual of Mental Disorders (DSM-5) published by the American Psychiatric Association, substance use disorder is characterized by the following eleven traits:

- ❑ **Compulsion.** The inability to control the amount used.
- ❑ **Unsuccessful efforts to quit or control substance use.**
- ❑ **Considerable time is spent using, concealing, planning or recovering from using.**
- ❑ **Craving.** An *overwhelming* urge to use.
- ❑ **Failure to fulfill major role obligations at work, school or home.**
- ❑ **Use despite recurrent social or interpersonal problems.**
- ❑ **Isolation.**
- ❑ **Use in physically hazardous situations.** Using even in physically dangerous situations.
- ❑ **Use despite recurrent physical or psychological problems.**
- ❑ **Tolerance.** Needing more and more of the substance to get the same high.
- ❑ **Withdrawal.** Cessation causes symptoms such as irritability, anxiety, shakes, sweats, nausea.

(Scoring is as follows: 2 - 3 = Mild substance use disorder. 4 - 5 = Moderate substance use disorder. 6+ = Severe substance use disorder.)

Delusional Thinking
One of the worst symptoms of the disease originates in the user's own brain. It is their utter reliance on **delusional thinking.** Delusional thinking is what allows all the other symptoms to go unchallenged.

Why is it, do you suppose, that such obvious symptoms as: drinking and using every day throughout the day just to function, severe mood swings, run-ins with the law, and multiple emergency room visits; aren't *recognized immediately* by the addict and alcoholic as serious warning signs? How can an addict, whose physical and mental health is falling to pieces, *not* see what he's doing to himself? How can an alcoholic who secrets bottles throughout the house and amongst the outside bushes, not track with her bizarre behavior? After all, these are *gigantic red flags* to others. And, as time passes, the symptoms *get worse* and repeat themselves over and over again, yet they don't comprehend it. The frustration for those around the user is unbearable, as they desperately hold a mirror up to the addict or alcoholic hoping they will see what is clearly reflected back to them, without luck. How do you fight that?!

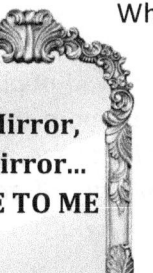

What is a **delusion,** anyway? A delusion is a *false* belief held with *absolute conviction*. For your loved one to maintain his or her disease, they must **lie** to themselves, and *believe* that lie. That's why people with this disease usually don't seek treatment on their own. *They simply aren't aware.* In other words, they don't see an addict or alcoholic staring back at them in the mirror. Instead they see someone who is: tired, overworked, hurting, stressed, unemployed, discovering themselves, in control, the life of the party, blowing off steam, victimized, losing weight, creative, successful, a failure, no different than anyone else, etc. They see everything but the truth, and actually believe these lies.

The book: *Intervention*, written by Vern Johnson, calls this delusional state; "pathological mental mismanagement", and this mismanagement is accomplished through the use of **unconscious** lies, called **defense mechanisms.** Think of each defense mechanism as a block in a wall that separates your loved one from the **truth** of their condition. Undoubtedly these defense mechanisms are painfully familiar, because you've dealt with this illogical, unreasonable crazy-talk for way too long. Defense mechanisms include: **agreeing, anger, arguing, avoiding, awfulizing, blaming, charming, controlling, denying, euphoric recall, explaining, humor, intellectualizing, intimidating, judging, justifying, lying, manipulating, minimizing, naive, personalizing, pouting, rationalizing, shaming** and **withdrawing.**

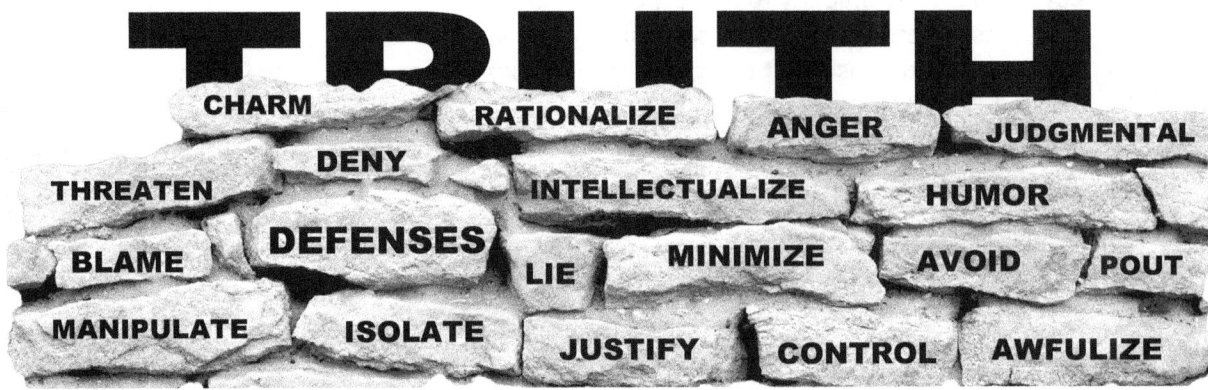

The Heart of the Disease
Once a person uses chemicals compulsively, their **tolerance** to that chemical increases until something happens that is as unexpected as it is unwelcome. *Every alcoholic and addict will eventually find that those substances which initially brought them relief or euphoria, stop working.* These same substances now have the *opposite* effect. This is the heart of the disease.

To understand, you first need to know a bit about how the brain works. When certain regions of the brain are stimulated, they produce pleasurable feelings. These feelings result from naturally occurring chemical messengers called **neurotransmitters,** which are released between nerve cells. **Dopamine** is one example of a neurotransmitter associated with pleasure. For example, the good feeling associated with earning a promotion, having sex, eating chocolate or receiving some other kind of reward, is related to the release of dopamine in the brain. This process is part of the brain's **reward system.**

Dopamine is *also* stimulated by alcohol and drugs, *except those substances produce a much more intense and longer lasting surge of dopamine than natural stimuli.* The behavior is **self-reinforcing,** meaning it feels so good that it reinforces the need to experience it again and again. By **conditioning** the brain to **crave** substances, *brain chemistry is altered.* The reward system is **hijacked!** Dopamine helps explain why people *cannot stop,* despite knowing how destructive it is.

Of course there is a price to be paid. Eventually, brain cells become **desensitized** to, and **depleted** of, dopamine. The user experiences less and less *euphoria* even though they are using more than ever. Instead of their mood returning to normal, it falls short: they **crash.** Now, the need to feel better is greater than ever: they **crave.** *The cycle of euphoria, crash and craving is the hallmark of addiction.* Inevitably, they depend on chemicals *just to feel normal.* The booze and drugs are now producing the *opposite* effect, called the **Paradoxical Effect.** Yet, they are compelled to continue on.

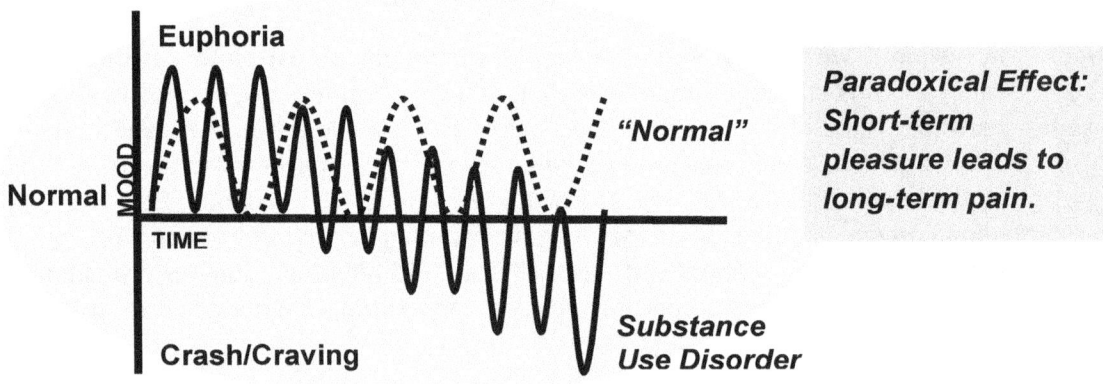

Paradoxical Effect: Short-term pleasure leads to long-term pain.

The Paradoxical Effect is illustrated on the chart above. Brain scans show that these brain alterations persist *long after* the user stops. That's why substance use disorder is a *brain disease,* of which drugs and alcohol are only *symptoms.*

What may have previously seemed incredible to you perhaps makes a bit more sense now? You can see this effect at work in alcoholics who need an *eye-opener* to stop shaking in the morning. You see it in the opiate dependent person who swallows many times the recommended dosage and, rather than being knocked out, becomes clear-headed and energetic. And, you see it in the heroin user who must shoot-up every few hours like clockwork just to feel "well" in his or her skin. In each case, the substance has the opposite effect. *Chasing the high* is what makes substance abuse so deadly.

Co-occurring Disorders
Oftentimes the addict or alcoholic is experiencing a mental illness *in addition to* a substance use disorder, and some people have multiple substance use disorders. This dual diagnosis is referred to as 'co-occurring disorders'. The existence of co-occurring disorders will make it more difficult to assess the type and severity of either illness. It will also require the family to have more patience in dealing with the situation.

Either substance abuse or mental illness can develop first. There are a number of reasons why substance use disorders and mental disorders occur together. The most obvious reason is that certain substances can, at least temporarily, reduce the symptoms of mental illness, thus making the person feel more "normal". Secondly, a person might be predisposed to a mental disorder which is then triggered by chronic substance abuse. For example, research suggests that alcohol use increases the risk of post traumatic stress disorder (PTSD), and marijuana may contribute to schizophrenia. In this case it is particularly horrifying to know that the emergence of a potentially life-long mental disorder was prompted by the abuser's own hand. Finally, the presence of co-occurring disorders may be due to a combination of factors, including genetics, brain injury, and exposure to stressful life experiences.

Raising Bottom
What does it take to break through delusional thinking? Does the abuser have to even *want* help to benefit from it? Many people believe the addict or alcoholic must hit **bottom** before they accept help, with bottom being the point at which it is more uncomfortable to use then it is to not use. Does that thought scare you? It should. No doubt you are aware of one or more incidents that *should have* been bottom, but were not. Where exactly *is* bottom, anyway?! For many, bottom is the bottom bunk of a prison cell, the concrete of skid row, or the dirt of a cemetery plot.

Stop and think about the part others may be playing in this tragedy. *Most addicts and alcoholics could never support their lifestyle without help.* Husbands, wives, children, family, friends, employers, co-workers, maybe even you unwittingly contribute to the problem by giving a few dollars, paying bills, providing a place to sleep, buying booze, making excuses, taking on extra responsibility, looking the other way, etc. These things are all done out of love, because watching this horrible situation progress is killing everyone. **Enabling** by family members is a *primary* reason abusers don't get sober! Believe me. To everyone who has enabled the situation to continue: *PLEASE STOP!*

Instead of hoping they find their own bottom, the best way to help save your loved one's life is to *raise their bottom for them.* A proven method of doing this is through the process of **intervention.** An intervention is anything that breaks a pattern of behavior. Intervention is a **team** effort. While you can't control the abuser, you certainly *do* control your own actions, and can influence others. In the past you held up a mirror to the addict or alcoholic, but their delusional thinking prevented them from seeing the truth. Intervention gathers together all the significant people in the abuser's life: all of them holding up the same mirror. Intervention drags all the dirty secrets into the light of reality.

Success!
Intervention is a unique opportunity to redirect your love *away* from the disease and onto the *person* who is suffering. It takes **courage.** The participants will risk their relationship in order to save a life. Intervention is the power of the group saying to the one in pain, *we will no longer love you to death!* **Love** and **truth** are what finally break through delusional thinking.

In Alcoholics Anonymous the saying is; **"If nothing changes, nothing changes!"** You can't possibly *hope* a disease away. But, you can help treat it if you take proper action.

SOBERING FACTS...

- In 2015, 20.8 million people aged 12 or older had a substance use disorder. That is equivalent to the number of people who suffer from diabetes and more than 1.5 times the annual prevalence of all cancers combined (14 million).
- In 2015 an estimated 21.7 million people aged 12 or older needed substance use treatment while only 10.8 percent received it.
- Of the 20.8 million people aged 12 or older who have a substance use disorder, 2.7 million (13 percent) have *both* an alcohol use and an illicit drug use disorder.
- In 2015, 66.7 million people aged 12 or older (51.7 percent) reported binge alcohol use in the past month, which corresponds to about half of all current alcohol users (48.2 percent).
- In 2015, 2 out of 5 young adults aged 18 to 25 reported binge alcohol use in the past 30 days.
- According to the University of Michigan's 2014 Monitoring The Future study, one in five (19 percent) 12th graders reported binge drinking at least once in the prior two weeks.
- All 50 states and the District of Columbia currently prohibit possession of alcoholic beverages by individuals younger than 21
- Alcohol misuse contributes to 88,000 deaths in the U.S. each year; 1 in 10 deaths among working adults is due to alcohol misuse.
- Marijuana is by far the most commonly used illicit drug.
- In 2015, 22.2 million people aged 12 or older (8.3 percent) were current users of marijuana. This was similar to 2014, but higher than 2002 to 2013.
- In 2013, the American Medical Association (AMA) declared that cannabis is a dangerous drug and is a public health concern, and the sale of cannabis should not be legalized.
- The American Society of Addiction Medicine's (ASAM) public policy statement on "Medical Marijuana" clearly rejects smoking as a means of drug delivery.
- Individuals entering treatment under pressure are just as successful as those who volunteer.
- According to NIDA, drug addiction relapse rates are similar to other diseases such as diabetes, hypertension and asthma. Relapse isn't failure. It signals a need to adjust treatment.
- According to research that tracks individuals in treatment over extended periods, most people who get into, and remain in, treatment stop using drugs, decrease their criminal activity, and improve their occupational, social, and psychological functioning.

VII. Codependency and Enabling

The American Medical Association recognized alcoholism as a physiological disease in 1956. Whether the problem is alcohol, illegal or prescription drugs, substance use disorder is a disease as much as schizophrenia and diabetes. Without help, compulsive substance users cannot stop using drugs completely. They are **compelled** to continue using, even when they are *certain* there will be catastrophic consequences as a result. When it comes to chemicals, *they have lost the ability to choose.*

If someone you love develops diabetes, that person usually changes their behavior to stay well. For example, they might cut sugar from their diet or begin taking insulin. The behaviors of others around them, however, remain pretty much the same. On the other hand, substance use disorder is recognized as a **family** disease because, in a family, each member affects - and is affected by - every other member, causing them to react and sacrifice in ways they would otherwise see as extremely unhealthy.

What is Enabling
It's crazy for parents to pay their kid's bills because that kid smokes so much dope he can't hold a job. It's insane for a husband to find a partially-filled bottle of vodka floating in the toilet tank, and not broach the subject later for fear he's going to embarrass his wife. How foolish to watch your buddy black out weekend after weekend, without stepping up and declaring that there is something wrong. *The addict and alcoholic could never continue without this help!*

When someone is **codependent,** they act in ways that **enable** the compulsive substance user to *continue* abusing substances. Other terms for "enable" are: to allow, facilitate, permit and make possible. Usually, where there is an addict or alcoholic *there is also an enabler.* Enablers feel like they are on a sacred mission to *save* the life of the person in trouble. They are driven by feelings of *love, guilt and anger*. They **cope** with these feelings by **obsessively** trying to *control the uncontrollable*: their loved one's behavior. For example, if we are talking about a loved one with diabetes, the enabler will take charge of monitoring that person's blood sugar level, remind them to take their medication, cook all healthy meals, stock the pantry with low sugar products etc. The problem is that the abuser *doesn't care one lick* about their disease. Whenever they are away from home, they eat mountains of sugary foods and never check their blood. The enabler *is not* saving the abuser. They are only *prolonging* their agony.

There *always* comes a point at which alcoholics and addicts *cannot continue* abusing substances without the *assistance* of those close to them. Yes, it is offered out of love. But this kind of *help* is misguided, because it *does not* move the person in trouble towards a healthy lifestyle. Instead, each enabling behavior pushes the person you are trying to *save,* closer and closer to death or jail. Take it from somebody who was in the exact same position as your loved one. The alcoholic and addict will always pervert your help to further their habit, and actually take *pride* in being so damn clever. *Enabling by family members is a primary reason those of us with a substance use disorder do not get sober.*

> **"Worrying, obsessing, and controlling are illusions. They are tricks we play on ourselves. We feel like we are doing something to solve our problems but we're not."** (Codependent No More by Melody Beattie, page 58)

> ### The Insanity of Enabling Someone Who is Sick
>
> Someone you love has just been diagnosed with throat cancer. The doctor says they must stop smoking immediately or they will die a quick and brutal death. Despite the warnings, they just can't quit. What are some of the ways in which you might help them? Chances are you would do everything *within your power*. You might buy them nicotine patches, an electronic cigarette, chewing gum or lollipops. You might transport them to a psychologist, addiction specialist, lay or faith-based support group, or investigate hypnosis therapy. You might provide them with encouraging books or literature. You might destroy packs of cigarettes lying around the house. Certainly, you would strive to be straight-forward with them about the danger of their behavior and how it affects others.
>
> *Now, let's talk about what you would NOT do.* You wouldn't smoke around them. You wouldn't give them money or the car to buy cigarettes, even if they were climbing the walls from nicotine withdrawal. You wouldn't offer them a safe place to smoke because you'd rather they smoked under your supervision. You wouldn't suggest they switch to chewing tobacco, alcohol or illegal drugs. You wouldn't ignore obvious warning signs such as the odor of tobacco on their clothes or breath, a dirty ashtray on the backyard picnic table, or an unusual abundance of air fresheners. You wouldn't cover for the smoker by lying to others. You wouldn't hold your tongue whenever they announced they were going to visit their smoking buddies. You wouldn't take over the burden of their responsibilities if you suspected they were leaving to smoke elsewhere. You wouldn't lie to their doctor. You wouldn't be so ready to believe they were getting up from bed to run out to the convenience store in the middle of the night because they had a hankering for a Diet Coke® with Lime. You wouldn't rifle through their pockets for cigarettes only to find some, and then keep the secret to yourself. You certainly wouldn't walk around on eggshells in your own home all the time, acutely suspicious something was wrong but afraid to say anything.
>
> A **reasonable** person would understand that none of these behaviors help. Yet the enabler is not reasonable. They do all of these things and more, because they are addicted to trying to control - *and thereby save* - the addict whom they love dearly.

What Does it Mean to be Addicted to a Person with an Addiction?
Basically, it means that your mood is a function of their mood. For example, have you ever caught yourself staring at your loved one's eyes, smelling their breath, hugging them with one hand while patting their pockets with the other, or checking their Facebook account to see where they've been? How did you feel when their eyes were clear; breath minty fresh; and they were exactly where they said they would be? Relieved, right? Damn relieved!! That's called **mood-altering up.** You felt relief, *because they were okay.*

But when their eyes were glassy or blinking wildly, their jaw grinding, they reeked of alcohol or marijuana, or their time-table didn't make sense, then the alarms went off in your head and you became wracked with anxiety. That's called **mood-altering down.** *You hit an emotional low because they drank or used, and you couldn't control it.*

The question then becomes: *what is and is not help?* Adding the alcoholic's responsibilities to your own is not helping them hit bottom and face the reality of their disease. Nor is refusing to set boundaries because you are ashamed or afraid. Nor is setting boundaries but not **enforcing** the consequences when you are tested. (And you *will* be tested!) Either is lying, making excuses for them or looking the other way. Nor is providing them with a place to sleep, money, a phone, insurance, food or transportation. *It is all a misguided attempt to control something which is not within the realm of your control.*

It is this **illusion of control** that results in your *high*. That's why codependency is so powerful. Although it is done out of loving desperation, enabling behavior is *selfish, selfish, selfish*, because it is you alone who benefits. The hard truth is that when the nightmare is finally over; when the person you love finally receives proper treatment and recovers (God willing); they may end up *hating you* for *nursing* their disease along, when they could have faced their bottom sooner. I know I did.

> **The Serenity prayer is as much for the codependent as it is for the addict: "God, grant me the serenity to accept the things I cannot change; The courage to change the things I can; And the wisdom to know the difference. Amen"**

Which of the following signs of codependency can you relate to?
- ❑ When you like me, then I feel good about who I am.
- ❑ When you approve of me, then I feel good about who I am.
- ❑ When you're struggling, it is impossible for me to find peace and fulfillment.
- ❑ My mood depends on your mood.
- ❑ I am constantly focused on solving your problems.
- ❑ I am constantly focused on making you happy.
- ❑ I am constantly focused on protecting you.
- ❑ I am constantly focused on trying to get you to do things my way.
- ❑ I feel important when I "save" you from pain.
- ❑ I make your interests and hobbies my Interests and hobbies.
- ❑ I control how you dress and look because I feel you are a reflection of me.
- ❑ I unaware of how I feel because your feelings come first.
- ❑ I don't know what I want because your wants come first.
- ❑ If I don't know what you feel or want, then I assume.
- ❑ The dreams I have for my future are linked to you.
- ❑ My fear of rejection determines what I say and do.
- ❑ I use giving as a way of feeling safe in our relationship.
- ❑ The more I am involved in your world, the more isolated I become from mine.
- ❑ I value your opinion and way of doing things more than my own.
- ❑ The quality of my life is in relation to the quality of your life.

> **"Anxiety is the endless rehashing of the same useless thoughts."** (Codependent No More by Melody Beattie, page 58)

Going Against Your Best Instincts

IT is painful for me to come clean about this, but I've finally accepted the reality that my eldest boy is an addict. Even worse, I'm his dealer and chief enabler.

I've been feeding his terrible addiction for the past seven years. Every day, like clockwork, I drive him down to the local park where he meets up with his buddies who are also addicts and dealers. Then, it's a free-for-all where they all party right out in the open. Within the last month, things at the park have gotten pretty bad. His body is starting to give out. To be honest with you, I'm scared.

You would think that, of all people, a substance abuse counselor like me would know better! And I do, *believe me.* Intellectually I understand that the problem isn't *just* him. It's me. He has reached the point all addicts inevitably reach where he can't possibly continue his habit without help: *my* help. Armed with this knowledge, the sane person would stop. No more paying doctor's bills. No more transportation. No more enabling. No more hurting him.

I haven't been able to stop. Lately, he binges until he literally cannot walk. So I hold him in my arms, carry him home and put him to bed, only to repeat the same sick cycle all over again the next day.

Is any of this making sense, or am I talking in circles? Circles probably, because intelligence has nothing to do with addiction regardless of whether you are the addict or the enabler. Rather, I'm acting out of **emotion.** *I love my boy.* I'm happiest when he's happy. (That's my high.) I am afraid he will hate me if I stop. I can't bear the pain evident on his face each time the craving takes hold of him. My brain makes use of these excuses. Twists them around. Fools me into believing that things will be different *tomorrow,* magically, and without me having to change in any way.

Enabling is pure insanity. It's an addiction itself. I am addicted to how Buster feels. Looking back on my confession I notice a lot of "I, I, I..." That makes sense. Enabling, like other addictions, is a **selfish** disease. There's a fine line between loving someone, and loving them to death. In order to stop, you must first accept that there *is* a difference. Only then can enablers, like me, address the selfishness underlying their actions. Selfishness is part of **ego**. Another way to think of ego is *Edging God Out*.

In order for my boy to get healthy, *I* must get healthy. Forget about going cold turkey. That doesn't work. I'd be jumping out of my skin. Instead, I'll do what I counsel other enablers and codependents to do to get healthy. First, accept that I'm behaving selfishly; then attend Al-Anon or CoDA meetings and make friends there; read books like Co-Dependent No More: *How to Stop Controlling Others and Start Caring for Yourself,* by Melody Beattie; and give the rest up to God.

If Buster was my son rather than my eight year old Yorkie-Poodle, and we were talking about booze or narcotics instead of a fanatical obsession with tennis balls, I hope I'd be strong enough to take my own advice. Like I said, Buster has been limping off the field at the dog park after our daily marathon sessions of fetch. I've finally decided to listen to my higher power at the Veterinary Hospital, and rest him a few weeks, regardless of the soulful looks he gives me. Unfortunately, the prognosis for chemically dependent people enabled by loved ones is usually far more ominous. That's why I continue to be inspired by families who find the courage to defy their best instincts, and let go.

Overcoming Codependent and Enabling Behavior
Believe it or not, as an interventionist and counselor who has worked with hundreds of addicts and their families, I have found it *infinitely more difficult* to convince a codependent they have a problem then to convince the alcoholic and addict! This is echoed universally among my peers. Even in the face of *overwhelming evidence,* it is difficult to convince a codependent that their behavior is allowing the situation to worsen for both the addict and themselves.

To overcome enabling behavior, the codependent must work a program of **recovery** same as the chemically dependent person. They must go to meetings, read, get a sponsor and cultivate friendships within the fellowship. These behaviors must be adopted *without delay.* Why? Consider what is at stake: The very life of the addict, family finances, the marriage, the sanity and happiness of everyone, careers, children, the future…

When a codependent person works a program of recovery, they learn how to detach with love, how to set and enforce healthy boundaries, and how to speak truthfully without judgment or fear. In doing so, they can reclaim a life centered on their *own* identity and values. Often they can repair relationships with others close to them. They dump the eggshells and gain serenity.

Support is available for codependent family members. One of the most popular programs is Al-Anon, which is the counterpart to the Twelve Step program of Alcoholics Anonymous. It was founded by Lois Wilson, wife of Alcoholics Anonymous co-founder Bill Wilson, which in itself should tell you a lot about the symbiotic relationship between substance abusers and codependents! Similar programs include Alateen, Adult Children of Alcoholics, and Codependents Anonymous. Of course, the codependent can also work with mental health professionals.

I strongly recommend you read more on the subject. A suggested reading list is included in the appendix. In particular, one of the most popular books ever written on the subject is Codependent No More: *How to Stop Controlling Others and Start Caring for Yourself*, by Melody Beattie (Hazelden.) It has sold over five million copies during the past twenty-five years. On page 34, the author very concisely explains the challenge of recovery, stating: **"…the heart of the definition of recovery lies not in the *other person* - no matter how much we believe it does. It lies in *ourselves*, in the ways we have let other people's behavior affect us and in the ways we try to affect them: the obsessing, the controlling, the obsessive "helping," the caretaking, low self-worth bordering on self-hatred, self-repression, abundance of anger and guilt, peculiar dependency on peculiar people, attraction to and tolerance for the bizarre, other centeredness that results in abandonment of self, communication problems, intimacy problems, and an ongoing whirlwind trip through the five-stage grief process."**

Now is the Time to Start
Don't make the common mistake of short-changing *your own* recovery. Remember, those people with a substance use disorder, who embrace treatment, will be directed by experts and immersed in meetings and materials for the first twenty-eight days, followed by months and years of relapse prevention. What are *you* willing to do to support them and you? Is it enough to read one book? Will one Al-Anon or CoDA meeting cut it? Can you manage without friends in recovery, too? Use the back of the page to make a list of the changes you will make in your own behaviors.

Perhaps the more pertinent question is: how much longer do you want to tip-toe on eggshells?

> "The beginning of love is to let those we love be perfectly themselves, and not to twist them to fit our own image. Otherwise we love only the reflection of ourselves we find in them." (Thomas Merton: *No Man Is an Island*)

MORE SOBERING FACTS...

- In 2015 an estimated 21.7 million people aged 12 or older needed substance use treatment while only 10.8 percent received it.
- About 40 percent of people who know they have an alcohol or drug problem feel they are *not ready* to stop using, and others simply feel they do not have a problem or a need for treatment.
- In 2015, 6.4 million people aged 12 or older (2.4 percent) were current misusers of prescription drugs. This includes 4.1 million adults aged 26 or older, 1.8 million young adults aged 18 to 25, and 1 in 50 adolescents (2.0 percent) aged 12 to 17.
- According to the CDC, drugs exceeded motor vehicle accidents as a cause of death in 2009, killing at least 37,485 people nationwide - one life every fourteen minutes.
- Prescription pain relievers are the second most commonly used illicit drug. 3.8 million Americans misused prescription pain relievers in the past month, which represent 1.4 percent of the population aged 12 or older.
- According to the CDC, overdoses involving prescription painkillers now kill more Americans than heroin and cocaine combined.
- Among persons aged 12 and older who misused pain relievers, 53.7% obtained the drug from a friend or relative, and about one third misused a prescription from one doctor.
- Cocaine and amphetamines may cause psychosis that can last long after the drug is stopped.
- Euphoria, crash and craving results from a drug's rapid onset and short duration in the brain. In contrast, Methadone and Buprenorphine result in gradual onset and stable levels in the brain.
- About a third of all people experiencing mental illnesses and about half of people living with severe mental illnesses also experience substance abuse. These statistics are mirrored in the substance abuse community, where about a third of all alcohol abusers and more than half of all drug abusers report experiencing a mental illness. Men are more likely to develop a co-occurring disorder.
- Suicide is a leading cause of death among alcohol and drug abusers.
- Panic attacks and psychotic reactions are being seen with increasing frequency as the potency of cannabis increases. Acute psychotic events are even more common in smokers of Spice.
- In 2014, 61 percent of drug overdose deaths involved prescription opioids and heroin. Heroin overdoses more than tripled between 2010 and 2014.
- Deaths from cocaine overdose were higher in 2014 (5,415 deaths) than in the previous six years.
- Individuals entering treatment under pressure are just as successful as those who volunteer.
- According to NIDA, drug addiction relapse rates are similar to other diseases such as diabetes, hypertension and asthma. Relapse isn't failure. It signals a need to adjust treatment.
- According to research that tracks individuals in treatment over extended periods, most people who get into, and remain in, treatment stop using drugs, decrease their criminal activity, and improve their occupational, social, and psychological functioning.

For Family and Friends Part 3 of 5

VIII. Implementing Boundaries

If someone you love is chemically dependent, then the rules of the household are probably all shot to hell. A good way to improve the situation is to redefine your relationship on paper in the form of an agreement. A good "boundaries agreement" will benefit *you* as much as them. It takes the responsibility for recovery off your shoulders and puts it all on theirs, where it belongs. That way, if they don't stay sober, they will be punishing themselves.

Those of us who are chemically dependent do not like reality... not one bit. In fact, we do whatever it takes to avoid it completely. However, our freedom to avoid reality *depends* on your *unwillingness* to enforce the rules. Of course, we are very skilled at manipulating you into being this way. Our bag of tricks includes fits of rage, blaming, guilting, lying, withdrawing and sarcasm. Over time, we wear you down so the rules apply to everyone but us. You become so intimidated that you will do anything to avoid upsetting us. On the rare occasion we do stick to our word - however insignificant the incident, we make you feel like we are doing you the biggest favor in the world. The patients are running the asylum! Sound familiar?

Boundaries are like rules, but they are from *your* perspective, not the perspective of the chemically dependent person. Is there a difference? Yes... a big one. You cannot force the addict to stick to your rules. That is their decision. However, you *can* specify where their behavior crosses the boundary marking where your responsibilities begin. For example, you cannot control whether someone uses illegal drugs away from the home. However, using those drugs on *your* property puts *you* at risk. A boundaries agreement protects you from becoming responsible for *their* problems.

Many families are unsuccessful at implementing rules. Typically they run into one of two difficulties. Either they issue rules without any consequences, or, the consequences are never enforced. Unlike the past, the new agreement will have clear consequences for unacceptable behavior. Equally important, it will be made clear that the consequences are to be enforced swiftly and without exception. Anything less will send the abuser mixed messages, causing you to lose all credibility while giving them more reasons to use.

Implementing boundaries is an act of love. Ideally a boundaries agreement is created with input from all parties, because when everyone has a say in what affects them, they are more likely to support it. It should be written as a contract, read and signed by all and posted on the refrigerator. In a co-parenting situation, it should be posted on both refrigerators. The first boundary should always be that they stay "clean and sober". There is no "grace period". Beginning with the *very first time* a boundary is violated, you need only point to the agreement. Consequences become the *automatic* result of unacceptable behavior. You can tell the abuser that you sympathize with their situation. You can tell the abuser that you love them and wish it hadn't come to this. You can tell the abuser that it just plain sucks. But, you *cannot* change the consequences *they* have brought on by *their* actions.

Chronic substance abusers desperately need structure. So, you aren't doing us any favors by not enforcing boundaries. You are simply "enabling" us to avoid reality, walk all over you and kill ourselves with chemicals. Think about *that* the next time you consider whether to let us get away with breaking the rules. We might not appreciate your efforts at this moment, but we will thank you later, I promise.

Following is a sample boundaries agreement you can use as the basis for creating yours:

Boundaries Agreement

Following are simple and reasonable boundaries that give us all structure and allow you to heal and grow. I/we love you and want you to succeed in everything you do. I/we will support your efforts so long as you respect the following:

1. You remain clean and sober.
2. No alcohol or other drugs in your possession, at home, on property or in car.
3. So long as you test dirty for drugs, you cannot use the car/phone/etc.
4. You submit to weekly testing on a random basis to stay accountable and rebuild trust.
5. In order to support your efforts, you will receive weekly chemical dependency counseling starting today. You agree to follow the treatment plan developed by the therapist.
6. To ensure you are in good health, you must be accessed by a psychiatrist and a medical doctor. The assessments must take place within two weeks, and you must follow the recommendations.
7. (Note: Other boundaries might involve homework, grades, employment, curfew, chores, allowance, and relationship with friends etc.)

These boundaries are all or nothing. Choosing to ignore any one of these boundaries - <u>even once</u> - is to choose drugs over sanity. There are consequences for choosing *insanity*. Consequences for violating <u>any</u> of the boundaries are as follows:

- Inpatient rehab for a minimum of 30-days, or moving out of the house immediately and assuming all your own expenses. If you choose to move, all the locks on the doors will be changed and all your personal possessions will be placed in bags on the driveway for you to retrieve. If they remain unclaimed in one week, they will be donated.
- Absolutely no monetary or other help from any family member. That includes no bail or attorney, should you be arrested.
- No phone, car, auto insurance, Xbox etc.
- If you come to the house, I/we will call the police immediately. I/we will no longer accept your phone calls or respond to your texts or emails. The only exception will be if you call to say you choose inpatient rehab. Then I/we will get you to treatment.
- If you give the impression you might harm yourself, I/we will call 9-1-1 immediately.

Should you choose *insanity*, I/we suggest you call the local Health and Human Services Crisis Line at _____ for information on free County resources, including motel vouchers, shelters, detox, counseling, food banks, clothing, medical care and suicide prevention.

I/we realize I/we have an issue with "enabling" unhealthy behavior. As a result I/we commit to working a program of Al-Anon by going to meetings, reading, getting a sponsor and affording you the dignity of resolving your own messes in the future.

It is my/our hope that you use this opportunity to get sober, grow, find your passion in life and get back on your feet financially.

_____   _____
Signature/Date   Signature/Date

IX. Intervention

in·ter·ven·tion (noun) Action affecting another's affairs. The deliberate entry into a situation in order to prevent undesirable consequences.

Intervention is used for one purpose: to get your loved one into **treatment** *today.* People are called together to participate in an **intervention,** when the addict or alcoholic faces dire consequences and there is really no other choice. Frequently, this means death, divorce, jail, hospitalization, loss of parental rights etc. The process of intervention is used to prevent all these other potential outcomes. It is an act of *love*, used as a last resort. *For this reason, there must be no anger, blame or guilt expressed by participants.* Remember, the goal is to get the person into treatment.

That's not to say you don't have a right to your feelings. You do... in spades! Feelings of anger, guilt, trauma and disgust are all legitimate and common. But, at *this* point in time you would only be *wasting your breathe.* Why? The alcoholic and addict you are talking to, suffers from **delusional thinking.** They don't agree with the *basic premise* that their life is out of control. So express your feelings later, after your loved one is **sane,** understands what you are saying, and has acquired healthy coping skills. If you think you are going to have a difficult time putting aside your own feelings, please do not attend the intervention.

Since you will likely have only one chance at this, I highly recommend you retain a **certified intervention specialist.** They can help you with further education on substance use disorders, organizing the intervention, selecting the treatment center, transportation and more.

Intervention Basics
Planning an intervention begins with selecting a **treatment facility.** Start with the resources listed in the appendix. Review your selections online. Read the reviews, if any. Call and speak with the person in charge of **intake.** Explain your situation and, together, determine if that program is a good fit. Each place has its own requirements dealing with gender, presence of co-occurring illnesses, medications, whether or not the person requires detox, bed availability, packing list, and form of payment. If your loved one has medical insurance, have the information handy when you call.

Once the plans are completed, it is time to gather together of all the people who play a significant role in the abuser's life. Hold a rehearsal, or a **pre-intervention meeting**. Include immediate family, relatives, friends, co-workers, spiritual leaders etc. Even pets can make an impact. Include children only if they comprehend what's taking place, can make an impact and will not be harmed.

Make copies of the worksheets For Family and Friends Part 1, Part 2 and Part 3, and read them *aloud together.* Decide on a date, time and place for the intervention that is convenient for all participants. It should also be a date and time when you *know* the abuser is available. Do *not* choose the abuser's home, because they can legally order everyone to leave. Select one of the participants to transport the person to the intervention. Do not let them drive themselves, since they can leave too easily.

The Love Letter

Each participant must write an **Intervention letter** to be read aloud, one at a time, during the intervention. This is the *heart* of the intervention. *Your feelings of love and hope are what will break through the loved one's delusional thinking and motivate them to seek help.* Here are some guidelines:

- Be 100% honest with love

- Don't ask questions. Avoid name-calling

- Use "I" instead of "You" sentences. For example: "I worry when you are home all day alone drinking", instead of: "You stay at home all day drinking."

- Always use specific examples, such as: "On Monday you drank till you blacked out"; and, "I am angry that you missed Dad's party to stay home and drink."

- Watching your loved one kill themselves is traumatic. Now is your opportunity to convey your pain by using specific feeling words. For example: "I'm *afraid* every time I come home from work that you will be lying dead on the floor"; "I felt *betrayed* when I found out you took money from our savings to buy drugs"; and, "I *love* you so much that I can't stand by while you do this to yourself".

Your letter should be formatted into sections. Use the following template:

1. Opening statement: **"Dear (name), I am here because I love and care about you."**

2. Why you love them and why they're such a great person: **"I remember when…"**; or, **"It seems like just yesterday when…"** Recount happy memories you have of them, specific examples of fun things you did together, and things they accomplished

3. Ways in which their life has been affected by drinking and using drugs: **"I have seen (drinking and/or drug abuse) affect your life in the following ways…"** *Specific* examples of consequences they have suffered. (Things they often don't think anyone else notices!) This includes hospital visits, medical diagnoses, quantity of drugs used, obligations missed, withdrawal symptoms, inappropriate behavior, lifestyle choices, discarded paraphernalia found, legal and financial issues, their treatment of others, intimacy issues etc.

4. Ways in which *your* life has been affected i.e. physical, mental, emotional, financial etc: **"Your (drinking and/or drug abuse) has affected my life in the following ways…"** The more raw, specific and honest you are, the more impactful your admission will be.

5. Your concerns if they refuse to leave for treatment today: **"If you do not stop and get help now I am afraid…"**

6. Close your letter with a plea to enter treatment *today:* **" I want you in my life. My greatest wish is that you accept this gift and go to treatment today!"**

   Stop here for now. There is no need for a bottom line if they agree to treatment. If not…

7. Consequences if they refuse treatment today. This is your bottom line: **"There is nothing I won't do to help you get well, but nothing I <u>will</u> do to help you kill yourself any further. So from now on…"** You must *prove* you are ready to stop enabling. **Consequences** are actions you are

prepared to *enforce immediately, no matter what! All* participants must agree to strictly enforce their bottom lines. No exceptions. No compromises. No weakness.

A bottom line is *not* a punishment. In fact it is not even about your loved one. It is about *you*: how *you* will move forward and how your behavior will *change* to become more healthy, *whether or not they choose treatment*. Examples include: "If you do not agree to treatment, I/you will move out today"; "If you don't agree to treatment, I will no longer lie/clean/buy alcohol/make excuses/pay bills for you"; "If you do not agree to treatment today, I will contact child protective services so at least your children will be safe"; and, "If you do not agree to treatment today, you cannot return to work."

Ignore the Noise, Remember the Goal
Let me reassure you that the majority of people *accept* the offer of treatment *without* any mention of bottom lines. They are tired of being sick and tired. Others relent after hearing the consequences of not going, and realizing that they will no longer receive the help they count on to maintain their lifestyle.

For others, intervention is not a **single day** process. Their disease is going to stamp its feet, scream, sulk, threaten, promise and try to barter its way out of treatment. It can be a hell of a show. But that's all it is: a Broadway production... empty words... **noise!** Do *not* get sucked in. Remember that you are dealing with someone *who does not grasp reality*. Your *only* goal is to get that person to treatment. You want to hear the word "Yes". Everything else is noise. Bottom lines are implemented immediately upon the conclusion of the intervention. Then, it's just a matter of time before that person finally feels enough pain that they begin to view rehab as a *relief*. Good Luck!

Use the following section for planning, and to write your intervention letter.

For Family and Friends Part 5 of 5

X. Forcing Someone To Get Help:
"5150" 72-Hour Involuntary Mental Health Hold, Adult Protective Services, Child Protective Services

Intervention is defined as: "The deliberate entry into a situation in order to prevent undesirable consequences." It is often initiated by a family member with the help of a professional intervention specialist. However, there are other types of interventions which can be used in specific situations. if someone you love needs immediate help, but doesn't want it, you *may* be able to intervene on him or her using the **5150, seventy-two hour involuntary mental health hold; Adult Protective Services;** or, **Child Protective Services.**

"5150" 72-Hour Involuntary Mental Health Hold

A **seventy-two hour mental health hold:** also known as **Welfare and Institutions Code 5150 (5150** for short), is a process initiated by you, in which designated personnel such as police officers and mental health professionals can admit a person to the hospital on an **involuntary** basis.

Code 5150 can be used when a person is in **acute** crisis. So, not only is that person suffering from a substance use disorder, but **compulsive abuse** of those chemicals has placed him or her in such a dark place, that they become an immediate danger to themselves or others. For someone to qualify for a 5150 involuntary hold, they must meet one of the following criteria: *they are a danger to themselves, they are a danger to others, or they are unable to provide for themselves.*

Examples of an acute crisis that meet one of these criteria include:

- Your loved one may feel so hopeless that he tells you he wants to commit suicide. Since suicide is the leading cause of death among people who abuse alcohol and drugs, *his claim represents an immediate danger to himself*.

- Your loved one may be using such high quantities of chemicals, that he becomes sleep-deprived, slips into a psychotic state and hallucinates This is often a result of cocaine or methamphetamine abuse. Since he is clearly not in his right mind, *he represents an immediate danger to himself and others.*

- Your loved one may become so obsessed with drinking and using drugs that *she can no longer care for herself properly:* she neglects her hygiene. she doesn't eat or hydrate, she ignores the bills, she doesn't take out the trash and lives in filth etc. When children are involved, they are chronically neglected as well.

To initiate the 5150 process, you simply pick up the telephone and dial **9-1-1.** Make sure you describe the person's chronic substance abuse history to the emergency operator and the emergency personnel that arrive on scene. If you can, videotape your loved one's actions and statements beforehand. *Nothing* is off limits when it comes to intervening on someone in crisis.

Once a person is detained, the hospital is required to do an evaluation, including a blood test to determine what chemicals are present in the patient's body. Ask them for the results. The law allows for the person in crisis to be held *up to seventy-two hours.* If the hospital feels it is not warranted, the person may be released earlier. On the other hand, the person also be put on a **fourteen-day** involuntary mental health hold, if necessary.

The 5150 is a lifesaver in more ways than one. Most important, it keeps someone in crisis from harming themselves or others. Second, it gives you a *window of opportunity* to arrange a formal **intervention** and/or secure proper substance abuse treatment, knowing your loved one is temporarily in a safe environment. Third, while someone is detained, they are in fact **detoxing under medical supervision.** the first step in the process of recovery. After a few days clean, they may even become rational enough to agree to treatment voluntarily.

Adult Protective Services (APS) and Child Protective Services (CPS)
Adult Protective Services can intervene on adults *(65-years and older)* and dependent adults *(18-64 who are disabled),* when these adults are unable to meet their own needs, or are victims of abuse, neglect or exploitation. Therefore, APS can intervene on the person with the substance use disorder, or, on behalf of those negatively affected by that person's behavior. Child Protective Services intervenes on abused and neglected children and their families. You can find the APS and CPS agency telephone numbers in your area by calling **4-1-1,** or searching online.

Identifying the Crisis
Code 5150, APS and CPS can be a Godsend. Use them wisely. You must be specific when speaking with officials. Describe how this crisis meets one or more of the following criteria. A space is provided after each for you to use to organize the key facts of the situation.

1. **Danger to Self:** Has the person stated their intention to harm themselves? Do they have a plan? Do they have lethal means?

2. **Danger to Others:** Is their behavior a danger to others?

3. **Neglect of Self:** Does acute addiction/alcoholism, depression or another mental condition render them unable to provide for their own basic needs?

4. **Abuse or Neglect of Others:** In what way have the person's dependents been abused or neglected?

XI. Crisis and Treatment Resources

Following is a Partial List of Southern California and National Resources:

ORGANIZATION	WEBSITE	PHONE
211 San Diego Info Line: Shelters, meals, clothing, clinics, other services	www.211sandiego.org	211
Adult Children of Alcoholics (ACA)	www.adultchildren.org	(562) 595-7831
Al-Anon/Alateen: For families and friends	www.al-anon.alateen.org	(800) 344-2666
Alcohol and Drug Helpline: Provides referrals to local facilities		(800) 821-4357
Alcoholics Anonymous (A.A.)	www.aa.org	(212) 870-3400
American Association of Poison Control Centers	www.aapcc.org	(800) 222-1222
Anorexia and Bulimia Crisis Line		(800) 227-4785
Aviation Medicine Advisory Service	www.aviationmedicine.com	(866) 237-6633
Centers for Disease Control & Prevention (CDC)	www.cdc.gov	(800) 232-4636
Celebrate Recovery: Christian based Step recovery program	www.celebraterecovery.com	(949) 609-8305
Cocaine Anonymous (C.A.)	www.ca.org	(310) 559-5833
Codependents Anonymous (CoDA): For families and friends	www.coda.org	(888) 444-2359
Crystal Meth Anonymous (CMA)	www.crystalmeth.org	(213) 488-4455
Drug Abuse Information and Referral Line		(800) 662-4356
Drug Enforcement Agency (DEA): Free Fact Sheets on every drug of abuse	dea.gov/druginfo/factsheets.shtml	
Dual Recovery Anonymous (DRA): For anyone who is both chemically dependent and affected by mental illness	www.draonline.org	(913) 991-2703
Gamblers Anonymous (GA)	www.gamblersanonymous.org	(888) 424-3577
Human Intervention Motivation Study (HIMS): Coordinates the identification, treatment and return to the cockpit of impaired aviators.	www.himsprogram.com	
Kleptomaniacs, Shoplifters, Hoarders Anonymous	www.shopaholicsanonymous.org	
Legal Aid Society of San Diego	www.lassd.org	(877) 534-2524
Marijuana Anonymous (MA)	www.marijuana-anonymous.org	(800) 766-6779
Narcotics Anonymous (NA)	www.na.org	(818) 773-9999
National Cocaine Hotline		(800) 262-2463

National Council on Alcoholism and Drug Dependence (NCADD)	www.ncadd.org	(800) 622-2255
National Helpline for Substance Abuse		(800) 262-2463
National Institute on Alcohol Abuse and Alcoholism (NIAAA)	www.niaaa.nih.gov	
NIAAA Rethinking Drinking	RethinkingDrinking.niaaa.nih.gov	
National Institute on Drug Abuse (NIDA)	www.drugabuse.gov	(800) 662-4357
National Institute on Drug Abuse for Teens	teens.drugabuse.gov	
National Institutes of Health (NIH)	www.nih.gov	
NIH Medline: Directory of diseases, conditions, medications	www.nlm.nih.gov/medlineplus/	
National Alliance on Mental Illness (NAMI): For persons with mental illness and their families	www.nami.org	(800) 950-6264
Nicotine Anonymous	www.nicotine-anonymous.org	
Orange County CA Alcohol & Drug Abuse Services: Directory of residential and non-residential mental health and alcohol and drug services	ochealthinfo.com/bhs/about/adas	
Overeaters Anonymous (OA)	www.oa.org	
Psychology Today Magazine: Directory of therapists and programs	www.psychologytoday.com	
Rational Recovery: Non-Twelve Step. Addiction is a choice	www.rational.org	
SAFE Alternatives (Self Abuse Finally Ends)	www.selfinjury.com	(800) 366-8288
San Diego CA Crisis Services Line: Directory of residential and non-residential mental health and alcohol and drug services, detoxification, justice, and DUI programs	www.sdads.org	(800) 479-3339
Sex and Love Addicts Anonymous (SLAA)	www.slaafws.org	(210) 828-7900
Sexaholics Anonymous (SA)	www.sa.org	
Sober Living Network: Search for a sober living home in California	www.soberhousing.net	
Suicide Hotline		(800) 784-2433
US Dept of Health & Human Services (HHS): Agency for protecting the health of Americans and providing essential human services to those least able to help themselves. Locate your local HHS to find information on alcohol and drug services. (Website for San Diego County is ww.sdcounty.ca.gov/hhsa/programs/bhs/alcohol_drug_services/index.html.)	www.hhs.gov	

XII. Suggested Reading and More

Here is a list of informative and motivational books and movies which I can personally recommend.

BOOKS

1. **Addict in The Family: Stories of Loss, Hope, and Recovery** by Beverly Conyers
2. **Addictive Thinking: Understanding Self-Deception** by Abraham J. Twerskl, M.D.
3. **Alcoholics Anonymous 12 Steps And 12 Traditions**
4. **Another Chance: Hope and Health for the Alcoholic Family** by Sharon Wegscheider-Cruse
5. **Beyond Codependency** by Melody Beattie (Follow-up book to Codependent No More)
6. **Big Book of Alcoholics Anonymous**
7. **Big Book of Cocaine Anonymous (Volumes I & II)**
8. **Big Book of Narcotics Anonymous**
9. **Boundaries: When to Say Yes, How to Say No to Take Control of Your Life** by Henry Cloud and John Townsend
10. **Celebrate Recovery Updated Participant's Guide Set, Volumes 1-4: A Recovery Program Based on Eight Principles from the Beatitudes** by John Baker (Christian)
11. **CoDependent No More: How to Stop Controlling Others and Start Caring for Yourself** by Melody Beattie
12. **Courage to Change: One Day at a Time in Al-Anon II** (Daily readings)
13. **Daily Bread** (FREE Christian daily devotional)
14. **Feel the Fear... and Do It Anyway** by Susan Jeffers
15. **Healing the Shame That Binds You** by John Bradshaw
16. **If You Want to Walk on Water, You've Got to Get out of the Boat** by John Ortberg (Christian/Motivational) "Fear is not an event, but rather a *judgment* about an event. Failure is not something that happens to us or a label we attach to things. It is a way we think about outcomes."
17. **Just For Today Daily Devotional** by Alcoholics Anonymous
18. **Living Sober** by A.A. World Services
19. **Love First: A Family's Guide to Intervention** by Jeff Jay and Debra Jay
20. **Man's Search for Meaning** by Viktor Frankl (Motivational) "That which does not kill me makes me stronger"; and, "Life can only be discovered, not dictated."
21. **Purpose Driven Life** by Pastor Rick Warren (Christian/Motivational) "You Were Made for a Purpose."
22. **Rational Recovery: The New Cure for Substance Addiction** by Jack Trimpey (A.A. alternative)
23. **Recovery Bible**
24. **Staying Sober: A Guide for Relapse Prevention** by Terence Gorski
25. **The Four Agreements: A Practical Guide to Personal Freedom** by Don Miguel Ruiz (Motivational) "Be impeccable with your word. Don't take anything personally. Don't make assumptions. Always do your best."
26. **The Language of Letting Go** by Melody Beattie

27. **The Lucado Life Lessons Study Bible, NKJV: Inspirational Applications for Living Your Faith** by Max Lucado
28. **The Places that Scare You: A Guide to Fearlessness in Difficult Times** by Pema Chodron
29. **The Power of Now: A Guide to Spiritual Enlightenment** by Eckhart Tolle (Spiritual/Motivational) "You are carrying in your mind the insane burden of a hundred things that you will or may have to do in the future instead of focusing your attention on the one thing that you *can* do now."
30. **The Tao of Natural Breathing: For Health, Well-Being, and Inner Growth** by Dennis Lewis
31. **Waking The Dead: The Glory of a Heart Fully Alive** by John Eldredge (Christian/Motivational for guys)
32. **Where Is God When It Hurts?** by Philip Yancey (Christian/Healing) "Cultivate a proper fear of the Lord, for that fear can supplant all others."
33. **Wild At Heart: Discovering the Secret of a Man's Soul** by John Eldredge (Christian/Motivational for guys)

MOVIES & TELEVISION

1. **28 Days** (Staring Sandra Bullock)
2. **Bill W.** (2012 Documentary)
3. **Clean and Sober** (Staring Michael Keaton)
4. **Days of Wine and Roses** (Starring Jack Lemmon and Lee Remick)
5. **Everything Must Go** (Starring Will Ferrell)
6. **Intervention** (Television series on A&E)
7. **My Name is Bill W.** (Starring James Woods and James Garner)
8. **Once Were Warriors** (Starring Rena Owen and Temuera Morrison)
9. **Peaceful Warrior** (Starring Nick Nolte and Scott Mechlowitz)
10. **Pleasure Unwoven: An Explanation of the Brain Disease of Addiction** (Documentary)
11. **The Lost Weekend** (Staring Ray Milland and Jane Wyman)
12. **When a Man Loves a Woman** (Starring Andy Garcia and Meg Ryan)
13. **When Love is Not Enough: The Lois Wilson Story** (Starring Winona Ryder and Barry Pepper)

XIII. Reference Sources

Chapter 1. Getting Started
- Anonymous, A. (2002.) The Big Book of Alcoholics Anonymous, 4th Edition. A.A. World Services.
- Anonymous, A. (2002.) Twelve Steps and Twelve Traditions. A.A. World Services.

Chapter 2. How the Program Works
- Substance Abuse and Mental Health Services Administration. (2004.) Clinical Guidelines for the Use of Buprenorphine in the Treatment of Opioid Addiction: Treatment Improvement Protocol (TIP) 40. U.S. Department of Health and Human Services, Maryland.
- Substance Abuse and Mental Health Services Administration. (2008.) Detoxification and Substance Abuse Treatment Training Manual: Treatment Improvement Protocol (TIP) 45. U.S. Department of Health and Human Services, Maryland.

Chapter 3. Autobiography of Substance Abuse
- Anonymous, A. (2002.) Twelve Steps and Twelve Traditions. A.A. World Services.

Chapter 4. Substance Use Disorder and Brain Drain
- American Psychiatric Association. (2013.) Diagnostic and Statistical Manual of Mental Disorders, 5th Edition, Text Revision (DSM-5.) American Psychiatric Association; 5th edition.
- Anonymous, A. (2002.) The Big Book of Alcoholics Anonymous, 4th Edition. A.A. World Services.
- Anonymous, A. (2002.) Twelve Steps and Twelve Traditions. A.A. World Services.
- Butler Center For Research (October 2012.) Drug Abuse, Dopamine, and the Brain's Reward System, Hazelden Research Update.
- Cocaine Anonymous World Services. (1993.) Hope, Faith & Courage: Stories from the Fellowship of Cocaine Anonymous. Cocaine Anoymous World Services.
- Gorski, T.M. (1986.) Staying Sober: A Guide for Relapse Prevention- Based Upon the CENAPS Model of Treatment. Independence Press; First edition.
- Johnson, V.E. (1986.) Intervention: How to Help Someone Who Doesn't Want Help. Hazelden.
- National Institute on Drug Abuse (www.NIDA.org).
- Perkinson, R.R. (2011.) Chemical Dependency Counseling: A Practical Guide. SAGE Publications, Inc; Fourth edition.
- Samantha Smithstein, P.D. (2010, August 19.) Dopamine: Why It's So Hard to "Just Say No". Psychology Today Magazine.
- Substance Abuse and Mental Health Services Administration. (2007.) Enhancing Motivation for Change: Treatment Improvement Protocol (TIP) 35. U.S. Department of Health and Human Services, Maryland.
- Twerski, A.J. (1997.) Addictive Thinking: Understanding Self Deception. Hazelden; Second edition.

Chapter 5. Delusional Thinking and Defense Mechanisms
- Anonymous, A. (2002.) The Big Book of Alcoholics Anonymous, 4th Edition. A.A. World Services.
- Perkinson, R.R. (2011.) Chemical Dependency Counseling: A Practical Guide. SAGE Publications, Inc; Fourth edition.
- Substance Abuse and Mental Health Services Administration (www.SAMSHA.org).

- Twerski, A.J. (1997.) Addictive Thinking: Understanding Self Deception. Hazelden; Second edition.

Chapter 6. Sick and Tired of Being Sick and Tired!
- Anonymous, A. (2002.) Twelve Steps and Twelve Traditions. A.A. World Services.

Chapter 8. Substance Use Disorder Kills
- Alliance for Consumer Education (www.inhalant.org).
- American Society of Addiction Medicine (www.ASAM.org).
- Centers for Disease Control and Prevention (www.CDC.gov).
- Kershaw, C.D. & Guidot, D.M. Alcoholic Lung Disease. Alcohol Research & Health. 2008; 31(1):66-75.
- Mayo Clinic (www.mayoclinic.org).
- National Institute on Alcohol Abuse and Alcoholism (www.NIAAA.NIH.gov)
- National Institute on Drug Abuse (www.NIDA.org and www.drugabuse.gov).
- National Stroke Association (www.stroke.org).
- Retrieved from www.collegedrinkingprevention.gov.
- Retrieved from www.HepCHope.com.
- Retrieved from www.webmd.com.
- Substance Abuse and Mental Health Services Administration (www.SAMHSA.gov).
- U.S. National Library of Medicine (www.nlm.nih.gov/medlineplus/drugabuse.html).

Chapter 9. Do Twelve Step Programs Work?
- A.A. General Service Office (GSO) of the United States and Canada. A.A. 1989 Triennial Membership Survey.
- A.A. General Service Office (GSO) of the United States and Canada. A.A. 1996 Membership Survey.
- Alexander, J. (1941, March 1). Alcoholics Anonymous: Freed Slaves of Drink, Now They Free Others. Saturday Evening Post.
- Arthur, S.; Tom, E.; & Glenn, C. (2008). Alcoholics Anonymous recovery outcome rates: Contemporary myth and misinterpretation.
- Betty Ford Institute Consensus Panel. What is recovery? A working definition from the Betty Ford Institute. J. Subst Abuse Treatment 2007:33(2)39-47.
- C., Bill. The Growth and Effectiveness of Alcoholics Anonymous in a Southwestern City, 1945 - 1962. Quarterly Journal of Studies on Alcohol. June, 1965; 26(2):279-284.
- Halverson, R. (1957). Perspective: Devotional Thoughts for Men. Zondervan Publishing House.
- Hunt, W.A., Barnett W. & Branch, L.G. (1971). Relapse Rates in Addiction Programs. Journal of Clinical Psychology. 27:455-456.
- Koerner, B.I. (2010, June 23). Secret of AA: After 75 Years, We Don't Know How It Works. Wired Magazine.
- National Institute on Alcohol Abuse and Alcoholism (1989, October). Relapse and Craving. Alcohol Alert.
- Project MATCH Research Group. Matching alcoholism treatments to client heterogeneity: Project MATCH three-year drinking outcomes. Alcoholism: Clinical and Experimental Research. 1998; 22:1300-1311.
- Room, R., & Greenfield, T. (2006, April). Alcoholics Anonymous, other 12-step movements and psychotherapy in the US population, 1990. Addiction. 88(4):555-562.

- Tonigan, J. S., & Rice, S. L. Is it beneficial to have an Alcoholics Anonymous sponsor? Psychology of Addictive Behaviors. 2010; 24(3):397-403.

Chapter 10. Principles of Recovery
- Anonymous, A. (2002.) The Big Book of Alcoholics Anonymous, 4th Edition. AA World Services.
- Stevenson, Robert Louis. (1886.) The Strange Case of Dr. Jekyll and Mr. Hyde. New York: Scribner.

Chapter 11. Is My Life Really Out of Control?
- Anonymous, A. (2002.) The Big Book of Alcoholics Anonymous, 4th Edition. A.A. World Services.
- Anonymous, A. (2003.) Experience, Strength and Hope: Stories from the First Three Editions of Alcoholics Anonymous. Alcoholics Anonymous; 1st edition.
- Perkinson, R.R. (2011.) Chemical Dependency Counseling: A Practical Guide. SAGE Publications, Inc; Fourth edition.
- Twerski, A.J. (1997.) Addictive Thinking: Understanding Self Deception. Hazelden; Second edition.

Chapter 12. Why is Spirituality So Important to Recovery?
- Anonymous, A. (2002.) The Big Book of Alcoholics Anonymous, 4th Edition. A.A. World Services.
- Anonymous, A. (2003.) Experience, Strength and Hope: Stories from the First Three Editions of Alcoholics Anonymous. Alcoholics Anonymous; 1st edition.
- Frankl, V. (1993.) Man's Search for Meaning. Buccaneer Books.
- Gorski, T. M. (1986.) Staying Sober: A Guide for Relapse Prevention- Based Upon the CENAPS Model of Treatment. Independence Press; First edition.
- Perkinson, R.R. (2011.) Chemical Dependency Counseling: A Practical Guide. SAGE Publications, Inc; Fourth edition.
- World Service Office. (2008.) Narcotics Anonymous. World Service Office; 6 edition.

Chapter 14. The Meaning of Recovery
- Substance Abuse and Mental Health Services Administration. (2011.) Strategic Initiative #4: Recovery Support. U.S. Department of Health and Human Services, Maryland.

Chapter 15. Finding and Working with a Twelve Step Sponsor
- Anonymous, A. (2002.) Twelve Steps and Twelve Traditions. A.A. World Services.
- Anonymous, A. (2002.) The Big Book of Alcoholics Anonymous, 4th Edition. A.A. World Services.

Chapter 18. Managing Stress
- Tighe, Allen A. (1998.) Stop the Chaos. Hazelden.
- Lewis, D. (2006.) The Tao of Natural Breathing: For Health, Well-Being, and Inner Growth. Rodmell Press; Revised edition.
- NIKE (www.livestrong.com).

Chapter 19. Anger and Substance Abuse
- Anonymous, A. (2002.) Twelve Steps and Twelve Traditions. A.A. World Services.
- Anonymous, A. (2002.) The Big Book of Alcoholics Anonymous, 4th Edition. A.A. World Services.
- Substance Abuse and Mental Health Services Administration. (2012.) Anger Management for Substance Abuse and Mental Health Clients: A Cognitive Behavioral Therapy Manual. U.S.

Department of Health and Human Services, Maryland.

Chapter 20. STOP to Communicate
- UNICEF. (2001.) Life Skills-Based Education Drug Use Prevention Training Manual.

Chapter 21. Guilt and Shame Are Not the Same
- Bradshaw, J. (2005.) Healing the Shame That Binds You. HCI; Revised edition.
- Substance Abuse and Mental Health Services Administration. (2002.) Building Self-Esteem: A Self-Help Guide (SMA-3715.) U.S. Department of Health and Human Services, Maryland.
- Substance Abuse and Mental Health Services Administration. (2011.) Strategic Initiative #4: Recovery Support. U.S. Department of Health and Human Services, Maryland.

Chapter 22. Boosting Your Self-Esteem
- Bradshaw, J. (2005.) Healing the Shame That Binds You. HCI; Revised edition.
- Ruiz, D.M. (1997.) The Four Agreements: A Practical Guide to Personal Freedom (A Toltec Wisdom Book.) Amber-Allen Publishing.
- Substance Abuse and Mental Health Services Administration. (2002.) Building Self-Esteem: A Self-Help Guide (SMA-3715.) U.S. Department of Health and Human Services, Maryland.

Chapter 23. Triggers and Cravings
- Budney, A. (1998.) NIDA Therapy Manuals for Drug Abuse - Manual 2 (NIH Publication Number 98-4309.) U.S. Department of Health and Human Services, National Institutes of Health.
- Daley, D.M. (1999.) NIDA Therapy Manuals for Drug Abuse - Manual 4 (NIH Publication Number 99-4380.) U.S. Department of Health and Human Services, National Institutes of Health.

Chapter 24. Seemingly Irrelevant Decisions
- Budney, A.A. (1998.) NIDA Therapy Manuals for Drug Abuse - Manual 2 (NIH Publication Number 98-4309.) U.S. Department of Health and Human Services, National Institutes of Health.
- Kadden, R.C. (2003.) Project MATCH Cognitive Behavioral Coping Skills Therapy Manual (NIH Publication No. 94-3724.) Monti, P.M., Abram, D.B., Kadden, R.M. and Cooney, N.: National Institute on Alcohol Abuse and Alcoholism, Maryland.
- Monti, P.A. (1989.) Treating Alcohol Dependence. Guilford Press, New York.

Chapter 25. Dry Drunk
- Solberg, R. (1983.) The Dry Drunk Syndrome. Hazelden; Pamphlet edition.

Chapter 26. Toxic Thinking
- Rosellini, G. (1985.) Stinking Thinking. Hazelden; Pamphlet edition.

Chapter 27. Post Acute Withdrawal Syndrome (PAWS)
- Gorski, T.M. (1986.) Staying Sober: A Guide for Relapse Prevention - Based Upon the CENAPS Model of Treatment. Independence Press; 1st edition.

Chapter 28. Relapse Prevention Planning
- Beattie, M. (1986.) Codependent No More: How to Stop Controlling Others and Start Caring for Yourself. Hazelden; 2nd edition.
- Budney, A. (1998.) NIDA Therapy Manuals for Drug Abuse - Manual 2 (NIH Publication Number

98-4309.) U.S. Department of Health and Human Services, National Institutes of Health.
- Daley, D.M. (1999.) NIDA Therapy Manuals for Drug Abuse - Manual 4 (NIH Publication Number 99-4380.) U.S. Department of Health and Human Services, National Institutes of Health.
- Girion, G.A. (2011, September 17.) Drug deaths now outnumber traffic fatalities. LA Times.
- Gorski, T.M. (1986.) Staying Sober: A Guide for Relapse Prevention- Based Upon the CENAPS Model of Treatment. Independence Press; 1st edition.
- Hunt, W.A., Barnett W. & Branch, L.G. (1971). Relapse Rates In Addiction Programs. Journal of Clinical Psychology. 27:455-456.
- Perkinson, R.R. (2011.) Chemical Dependency Counseling: A Practical Guide. SAGE Publications, Inc; Fourth edition.

Chapter 29. Bonus 1: Eating Your Way to Recovery from Substance Abuse
- Brand-Miller, J., Colagiuri, S., Wolever, T., & Foster-Powell, K. (1999) The Glucose Revolution. Marlowe & Company.
- Caballero, Benjamin. Hopkins Insider: Protein: Too Much - Or Not Enough? Unpublished paper available for download at www.intelihealth.com.
- Eades, M, & Eades, M.D. (1998) Protein Power. Bantam Books.
- Hart, Archibald. (1995) Adrenaline and Stress. Word Publishing.
- Hellmich, Nanci. Diets, Scales, Fat-loss Books; It all can make you turn your back on dieting. USA Today, January 3, 2000, cover.
- Jibrin, Janis. Don't Have a Cow; Eat meat to lose weight. Men's Health, 1999, December: 78-81.
- Kendall, Pat. Zoning In On The Zone. Unpublished paper available for download at www.colostate.edu.
- Mandelbaum-Schmid, Judith. Carb Your Appetite? Walking, 2000, Jan/Feb: 36-40.
- Sears, Barry, & Lawren, W. (1995) Enter The Zone. HarperCollins.
- Sears, Barry. (1999) Enter The Anti-Aging Zone. HarperCollins.
- Steward, H.L., Andrews, S., Bethea, M., & Balart, L. (1998) Sugar Busters! Cut Sugar To Trim Fat. Ballantine Publishing Group.
- Weil, Andrew. Ask Dr. Weil; What's Up with The Zone? Unpublished paper available for download at www.drweil.com.

Chapter 30. Bonus 2: Finding Your Dream Job
- Love, Pat & Carlson, Jon. Loneliness and Addiction: Five Questions to Strengthen Recovery

I. Quiz: Do I Have a Substance Use Disorder?
- American Psychiatric Association. (2013.) Diagnostic and Statistical Manual of Mental Disorders, 5th Edition, Text Revision (DSM-5.) American Psychiatric Association; 5th edition.

IV. Key Statistics on Alcohol and Drug Use
- Center for Behavioral Health Statistics and Quality. (2016). *Key substance use and mental health indicators in the United States: Results from the 2015 National Survey on Drug Use and Health* (HHS Publication No. SMA 16-4984, NSDUH Series H-51).
- Girion, G.A. (2011, September 17.) Drug deaths now outnumber traffic fatalities in US. LA Times.
- National Alliance on Mental Illness (NAMI) www.NAMI.org.
- U.S. Department of Health and Human Services (HHS), Office of the Surgeon General, *Facing Addiction in America: The Surgeon General's Report on Alcohol, Drugs, and Health*. Washington, DC: HHS, November 2016.

VI. For Family and Loved Ones Part 1 of 5: Signs and Symptoms of Substance Use Disorder
- American Psychiatric Association. (2013.) Diagnostic and Statistical Manual of Mental Disorders, 5th Edition, Text Revision (DSM-5.) American Psychiatric Association; 5th edition.
- Anonymous, A. (2002.) The Big Book of Alcoholics Anonymous, 4th Edition. A.A. World Services.
- Anonymous, A. (2002.) Twelve Steps and Twelve Traditions. A.A. World Services.
- Butler Center For Research (October 2012.) Drug Abuse, Dopamine, and the Brain's Reward System, Hazelden Research Update.
- Center for Behavioral Health Statistics and Quality. (2016). *Key substance use and mental health indicators in the United States: Results from the 2015 National Survey on Drug Use and Health* (HHS Publication No. SMA 16-4984, NSDUH Series H-51).
- Cocaine Anoymous World Services. (1993.) Hope, Faith & Courage: Stories from the Fellowship of Cocaine Anonymous. Cocaine Anoymous World Services.
- Gorski, T.M. (1986.) Staying Sober: A Guide for Relapse Prevention- Based Upon the CENAPS Model of Treatment. Independence Press; 1st edition.
- Johnson, V.E. (1986.) Intervention: How to Help Someone Who Doesn't Want Help. Hazelden.
- National Institute on Alcohol Abuse and Alcoholism: Alcohol Facts and Statistics, March 2015
- National Alliance on Mental Illness (NAMI) www.NAMI.org.
- Perkinson, R.R. (2011.) Chemical Dependency Counseling: A Practical Guide. SAGE Publications, Inc; Fourth edition.
- Twerski, A.J. (1997.) Addictive Thinking: Understanding Self Deception. Hazelden; Second edition.

VII. For Family and Loved Ones Part 2 of 5: Codependency and Enabling
- Beattie, M. (1986.) Codependent No More: How to Stop Controlling Others and Start Caring for Yourself. Hazelden; 2nd edition.
- Bramness, J.G., Gundersen, Ø.H., Guterstam, J., Rognli, E.B., Konstenius, M., Løberg, E.M., Medhus, S., Tanum, L., Franck, J. Amphetamine-induced psychosis--a separate diagnostic entity or primary psychosis triggered in the vulnerable? BMC Psychiatry, 2012. 12(1), 221.
- Center for Behavioral Health Statistics and Quality. (2016). *Key substance use and mental health indicators in the United States: Results from the 2015 National Survey on Drug Use and Health* (HHS Publication No. SMA 16-4984, NSDUH Series H-51).
- Zvolensky, M.J., Lewinsohn, P., Bernstein, A., Schmidt, N.B., Buckner, J.D., Seeley, J. & Bonn-Miller, M.O. (2008.) Prospective Associations Between Cannabis Use, Abuse, and Dependence and Panic Attack and Disorder. Journal of Psychiatric Research, 42(12), 1017-1023

VIII. For Family and Loved Ones Part 3 of 5: Implementing Boundaries
- Center for Behavioral Health Statistics and Quality. (2016). *Key substance use and mental health indicators in the United States: Results from the 2015 National Survey on Drug Use and Health* (HHS Publication No. SMA 16-4984, NSDUH Series H-51).
- Drug Enforcement Administration: The Dangers and Consequences of Marijuana Abuse, 2014.
- National Institute on Alcohol Abuse and Alcoholism: Alcohol Facts and Statistics, March 2015

IX. For Family and Loved Ones Part 4 of 5: Intervention
- Johnson, V.E. (1986.) Intervention: How to Help Someone Who Doesn't Want Help. Hazelden.

XIV. Notes

AT HOME RECOVERY HANDBOOK

"I can't believe I relapsed. What happens now...?"

Reboot Your Recovery. Join the Author For Seven Days of One-on-One Counseling and More.

Before Keith Angelin was a licensed substance abuse therapist, interventionist and author of the book **AT HOME RECOVERY HANDBOOK: Recover From Alcohol and Drug Addiction in 28-days At Home!**, he was "hopelessly" addicted to drugs and alcohol. Addiction dominated his life for a decade. It brought to an end a prosperous career in the health and nutrition industry. Once, he was president of a multi-million dollar company and enjoyed a business relationship with one of the most iconic actors in Hollywood. Then, he was dead.

Says Mr. Angelin. "I was blindsided. I was very, very good at the job of being an addict. I went from having everything, to having absolutely nothing. Penniless... divorced... I lost the house to foreclosure, then squatted in my own empty home without electricity or water. I was defibrillated at the hospital ER on three different occasions. I tried rehab twice, and I watched a best friend die horribly from alcoholism. Yet, I still could not stop. How does that happen to an intelligent person?!"

With an "unsolicited" intervention from local law enforcement, he finally hit "bottom". He recounts how his pride was "crushed" that day: "Putting my hands in the air and saying I'm done... I'm exhausted... I surrender... lifted the blinders from my eyes". According to Angelin: "I was forty-eight years old. Nobody gave me a chance in hell to recover."

Yet, he recovered, and did it without the help of a fancy rehab. Along the way, he became an expert on addiction and recovery. Since then he has devoted his life to sharing the miracle with others through counseling. Recently he introduced a completely new way to experience one-on-one counseling for substance use disorder. It is called **Reboot**:

- **REINVIGORATE.** Break the relapse cycle. Reboot your recovery with a high intensity, highly personal counseling experience like no other.

- **REDEDICATE.** Seven days pampered in the paradise of Southern California. All-inclusive package means you pay for everything upfront so you can focus 100% on recovery. *(May be eligible for partial insurance reimbursement.)*

- **REEDUCATE.** Benefit from the same tools and education as top-notch treatment centers.

- **REACTIVATE.** Rediscover you purpose for living. Boost self-worth and motivation.

- **RECREATE.** Exciting activities immerse the senses in sober fun. Daily private boxing instruction on the beach.

Commit to one week that's all about you.

**(949) 269-8034 • InterventionRx.com
InterventionRxNow@gmail.com**

1-Bedroom Suite in a Luxury Waterfront Hotel

WHAT'S INCLUDED

Your all-inclusive package includes everything but airfare to/from San Diego airport:

- Seven days and nights at a luxurious 5-star resort located on the ocean and harbor.
- An ocean view suite with bedroom, living room, dining room, kitchen and fireplace.
- Refrigerator stocked with healthy snacks and beverages.
- All transportation beginning at the airport.
- Cost of daily, one-on-one counseling and supervision.
- Cost of private cardio boxing lessons.
- Cost of all activities.
- Copies of AT HOME RECOVERY HANDBOOK, AA or NA book, 12 & 12 and The Four Agreements.
- Fitbit®, Bluetooth headphones and Ipod® with music and meditation.
- Commemorative framed photos.

FREQUENTLY ASKED QUESTIONS

1. **Is Reboot different from an inpatient and outpatient rehab?** Yes. Reboot is a unique, high intensity, highly personal counseling experience that combines individual counseling with exciting activities and exercise.
2. **Who can attend?** Anyone over 18-years of age. Active duty military receive a 10% discount, complete confidentiality and opportunity to avoid self-disclosure and possible discharge.
3. **Is Reboot covered by insurance?** You may be eligible for partial reimbursement depending on your insurance plan. Once you receive a paid invoice, you can submit it to your insurance company as per their procedure.
4. **Does the cost include airfare or transportation to/from San Diego?** No. You make your own arrangements.
5. **When is payment due?** Payment is due when you confirm your attendance. Pay by cash, check or credit card. Checks are payable to **Counseling, Intervention & Assessment Services.**
6. **How far in advance do I need to confirm my attendance?** On average, usually no less than one month.
7. **Am I "guarded" 24-hours a day?** Absolutely not. You will be personally supervised from 8:00AM to 10:00PM every day, and exhausted in the evenings. The resort does not serve alcohol, nor is it in walking distance to anyplace that serves or sells alcohol. Further, your counselor is a short two-minutes away and is available around the clock should you have an issue.
8. **Will I be tested for alcohol and drugs**? Yes. In order to gauge your progress you will be administered a breathalyzer and UA test on the first and last days you are here.
9. **Can I still attend if I test positive for drugs upon arrival?** Of course. What you did before now is past history.
10. **Is there a dress code?** None whatsoever. Expect to be physically and mentally exhausted. Dress comfortably.
11. **What do I pack?** Remember you will be cardio boxing every day, so pack 7-days worth of workout shirts and gym shorts. You also need 7-days worth of the following: jeans and/or casual shorts, casual shirts, socks, underwear, sneakers, casual footwear, sleep clothes and picture ID. Pack a hairbrush, toothbrush, razor and deodorant. Check the weather in San Diego beforehand.
12. **How much money should I bring?** You may want to bring money for souvenirs, in case you forgot something or for an emergency. Otherwise, you do not need any money.
13. **Are computers and cell phones allowed?** Yes. Unlike rehab, you are staying in a hotel and are free to bring anything you like with the exception of drugs and alcohol. Realize, however, you will have minimal free time.
14. **Do I need boxing gloves?** No. All equipment is provided.
15. **What if I am completely out of shape?** No worries. Our cardio boxing personal trainer is expert at motivation and working with you exactly where you are at so you enjoy the experience. Regardless of your condition when you arrive, it will be much improved when you leave!
16. **Can I bring someone with me?** No.

 (949) 269-8034 | www.InterventionRx.com | InterventionRxNow@gmail.com

www.ingramcontent.com/pod-product-compliance
Lightning Source LLC
Chambersburg PA
CBHW080728230426
43665CB00020B/2662